Discipline Without Anger

A Parent's Guide to Teaching Children Responsible Behavior

("But Doctor, what do I do when . . .?")

Jerry Adams, Ph. D.

AuthorHouse™
1663 Liberty Drive, Suite 200
Bloomington, IN 47403
www.authorhouse.com
Phone: 1-800-839-8640

First published by AuthorHouse 8/15/2008

ISBN: 978-1-4343-7537-7 (sc)

Library of Congress Control Number: 2008903770

Printed in the United States of America
Bloomington, Indiana

This book is printed on acid-free paper.

With gratitude to Mom and Dad, who first taught me discipline,

This book is dedicated to children everywhere...

*And to the parents who love, nurture,
and guide them to become responsible
and caring members of society.*

Making the decision to have a child is momentous. It is to decide forever to have your heart go walking around outside your body.

~Elizabeth Stone

Table of Contents

Preface

If I had my child to raise all over again,
I'd build self-esteem first, and the house later.
I'd finger-paint more, and point the finger less.
I would do less correcting and more connecting.
I'd take my eyes off my watch, and watch with my eyes.
I'd take more hikes and fly more kites.
I'd stop playing serious, and seriously play.
I would run through more fields and gaze at more stars.
I'd do more hugging and less tugging.

~Diane Loomans,
"If I Had My Child To Raise Over Again"

Why another book about discipline for children?

There are, after all, already many useful books about how to discipline children. Two related experiences motivated me to write another book designed to help parents meet their goals..

Every time I give a talk as a child psychologist, whatever the topic, parents stay after to ask for guidance about all sorts of situations with their kids. The typical problem described is too difficult to resolve quickly. Indeed, one mother, who told me she "must have 20 books on parenting," was there asking for a quick fix for some troubling issue with her kids. Clearly a comprehensive approach to parenting is needed.

Second, over many years of clinical practice with families, I developed and refined a class to assist parents in providing effective discipline for their children. The goal was to help parents guide their kids to take suitable levels of responsibility for their own behavior. In addition to offering a list of suggested reading, I provided detailed and extensive handouts to support the approach I recommended. However, numerous parents reported needing more help and suggested that I "should write a book" to encompass the entire subject matter in one place.

Discipline Without Anger: A Parenting Guide ("But Doctor, What do I do When . . .?") was written to fulfill this request. It is designed to provide you, the parent, with an overall strategy for parenting and is structured so that you can consult it on an ongoing basis, as your needs and circumstances change.

I based my class presentations on confirmed research and I am grateful to those researchers for their ingenuity and perseverance in determining how behavior is learned and how it is changed, the building blocks of all of society.

In addition, over the years hundreds of parents attended my classes, and virtually every class helped clarify what is and is not acceptable to parents and what does and does not work in the real world. It was my goal each time to assure that everything I learned was incorporated into the next class I facilitated. I am grateful to these parents and to their children whose responses guided many refinements, for all that they taught me and for their dedication to the next generation.

It then became my goal to assure that *Discipline Without Anger* includes the best of that accumulated experience and understanding. This is a book intended for actual parents (and all those in parenting roles), parents with multitudes of demands on their time, with diverse life styles, with kids of all ages, with behavior challenges of many types, and with varying levels of interest and cooperation from their kids.

In preparing this book, I enjoyed and appreciated the interest and support of too many friends and colleagues to identify. A few, though, deserves special mention. My older brother Lee, a retired college English teacher, provided invaluable feedback on several drafts and his ongoing support was central to the final result. Friends and fellow family therapists Joel Oxman, Ph. D., and Jane Garland, L.C.S.W., read and commented on a revised draft. Lucy Jo Palladino, Ph.D., provided guidance and encouragement about the publishing process. Charlotte Thompson, M.D., also gave me invaluable insight into publishing and provided welcome support and direction. My good friend, Charles Styles, provided insight from the point of view of a parent, grandparent, former teacher, and former school district hearing officer. Jan Wright undertook a developmental editing of an earlier draft. Another good friend, Clover Press Publisher, Geraldine Kennedy provided encouragement and valuable tips about the cover design

Finally and most importantly, my wife Julie provided ongoing support and encouragement through all of many drafts and through times of discouragement, doubt, and uncertainty about this project; without her support this book would never have been completed. Our sons served as involuntary recipients of parenting in the style presented here – and our grandchildren are happy beneficiaries in the next generation.

All of these fine people, I thank from the bottom of my heart, and each deserves the gratitude of any reader who finds these pages to be useful.

One brief style note: Below the title of each chapter is a box highlighting a specific question from a parent, illustrating how varied are the issues dealt with in this book. Below each question is a page number indicating where in the book that specific concern is addressed. Be aware, however, that these responses can only be fully understood and appreciated within the context of the entire approach described here.

Section One

HOW KIDS LEARN
RESPONSIBLE BEHAVIOR

There are only two lasting bequests we can give our children. One of these is roots; the other wings.

~Hodding Carter, Jr.

Chapter One

"But Doctor, what do I do when . . . my son comes home from his dad's house all wound up, and then when I try to discipline him he tells me I'm mean and that he wants to go live with his dad?"

Page 229

INTRODUCTION AND OVERVIEW

*"Thank you, Dr. Adams, for your nice talk. It was interesting, honestly! But what we **really** need to know is what should we do when . . ."*

- *" . . . Moesha fights with her sister."*

- *" . . . Pedro promises to do his homework after he plays with his friends, but he never does."*

- *" . . . Elian sneaks into the baby's room and pinches her."*

- *" . . . Brie gets upset every time a friends uses her toys."*

- *" . . . Melanie sasses me when I tell her to clean her room."*

It seems never to fail; whenever I have been asked to talk to a group of parents, no matter the advertised topic, I have been confronted afterwards with a barrage of questions, almost always on the order of *"But what do I do when . . .?"*

These are always unsettling interchanges. After all, shouldn't psychologists know *what to do "when . . .?"* Well, maybe, but can anyone provide a truly effective one-minute solution to a problem that has been developing over a long time?

There are, of course, some easy responses:

- Allow Moesha to be with her sister only with supervision.

- Arrange for Pedro to complete his homework *before* he plays with his friends.

- Allow Elian in the baby's room only with supervision.

- Remove Brie from her friends any time she gets upset when they use her toys.

3

- Refuse to engage in bickering with Melanie, ever.

Such solutions are like the physician whose patient complains, *"It hurts when I do this!"* and who advises *"Don't do that anymore."* If such simple solutions really helped, parents would not ask *"What do I do when . . .?"* They would resolve things on their own and would not need a parenting class.

While there may be lots of easy ways to deal with children's misbehavior, none is likely to be effective with truly difficult problems and none provides an overall approach for dealing with the many challenges of everyday life with children.

When parents (or other parenting figures, including grand-parents, foster parents, and other guardians) ask "What do I do when . . .?" they are reflecting three compelling facts of life:

- That doing a really good job of raising kids is as difficult as anything parents will ever do,

- That raising children is parents' most important task, and

- That there is little agreement about how best to go about the business of child-rearing.

How true these statements are was clearly shown in a parent survey (discussed in more detail below) which revealed that:

- Most parents relied on some combination of verbal reprimands, restrictions of activities, and spanking in response to inappropriate behavior,

- Over two-thirds of the parents realized that their approaches did not really work,

- Most of the remaining third found that their "successes" did not lead to lasting changes in behavior, and

- Few parents recognized that positive responses to their kids' appropriate behavior actually has a major role in discipline.

These survey findings provide a discouraging picture of parents working hard to guide their children while relying almost exclusively on punishment which they, themselves, reported doesn't produce lasting changes in behavior.

4

Fortunately, well focused efforts to provide children with appropriate discipline can produce much more constructive results. My work with parenting classes showed that children respond to parental guidance almost from birth, as part of a natural developmental sequence, discussed at length below. By being aware of the process, parents can build an effective and loving overall approach to parenting, a positive approach that does not depend upon negative reactions from parents.

In fact, in keeping with what parents report from their own experience, a major operating principle of this book is that "discipline" and "punishment" are **not** the same thing. This principle is based on a great deal of evidence indicating that:

- Punishment is largely ineffective in changing behavior,

- When it does seem to work, the effects don't last very long,

- Punishment is least effective with kids most in need of help in controlling their own behavior,

- Often punishment distracts parents from their original expectations, so that their kids may serve their penalty and avoid their responsibilities,

- Punishment causes unnecessary and counter-productive anger and frustration in parent-child relationships, and

- Surprisingly often, punishment actually works against the intended goal by rewarding children with attention and a sense of control during inappropriate behavior, making them more, rather than less, likely to misbehave again.

Since punishment is generally ineffective, the central challenge for parents is to understand what **does** contribute to constructive outcomes in child-rearing, and then to apply that understanding in day-to-day interactions with their children. This book is intended to provide parents with the required understanding, along with a detailed and practical guide for establishing a home program for teaching children discipline.

It is important that we have a shared way of understanding what we mean by discipline. Throughout this book:

Discipline **is defined as the process through which children learn to take responsibility for their own behavior.**

In keeping with this definition, the focus throughout is not so much on what we do **to** kids, but rather on **what happens inside kids** and therefore on what influences maturation in children's own capacities to manage their own behavior.

This book, then, refocuses issues raised by all those "what-do- we-do-when" questions. Since we know that punishment after the fact is ineffective, our challenge is to determine **how to help children behave appropriately in the first place** and how to assure this becomes their pattern. That means we must focus on how to guide our children to behave responsibly as well as how to make it good for them to continue such behavior. This is in contrast to the typical focus on how to manage misbehavior after the fact (though we will also deal with those less frequent times when children still misbehave).

Rather than attempting to provide a bunch of Band-aids for a variety of parental concerns, my intention is to provide an overall approach, a coherent and well-planned strategy for you, the parent, to achieve discipline in your children without becoming unduly frustrated and resorting to anger. By the time you have read through this book you will:

- Understand how children learn to take responsibility for their own behavior,

- Recognize how your actions – intentionally or otherwise – influence your children's learning,

- Know how to build and maintain a simple home program tailored to meet your specific needs, to foster the development of responsible behavior in your child,

- Understand how to use your home program to influence your children even in settings where you cannot be there, such as at school or sports activities,

- Be prepared to stop unacceptable behavior as it arises, at home and away, in a manner that does not undermine the other aspects of your program,

- Understand how to measure your progress and how to make adjustments required by changing challenges so that your program remains effective over the long run, and

- Know how to incorporate all of this into your family life with a minimum of effort and a maximum of benefit.

To address these goals in a coherent and clear manner, this book is laid out with specific sections to support each aspect:

This Section   Provides an introduction and presents the principles that are known to support constructive parenting.

Section Two   Shows you how to put these principles into practice in your own home to assure your kids take responsibility for themselves.

Section Three   Provides a guide to reducing inappropriate behavior, both at home and away, in a constructive, loving, and effective manner.

Section Four   Describes how to monitor and maintain your progress over time.

Section Five   Provides some concluding remarks and a number of illustrative examples.

To highlight challenges you might confront, questions from actual parents are included throughout, along with my discussion to illustrate how the approach can be adapted to a wide variety of situations. You will find that the principles are maintained in every situation because they are based on what is known about behavior and behavior change. At the same time, you will see that the specific applications of the principles can be adjusted broadly to fit individual family needs.

The principles discussed in this Section form the basis for the approach and are discussed in detail so that you can fully understand how to effectively apply them in your everyday interactions with your children.

However, while understanding the principles is essential, few, if any, parents can live the principles day by day without some support. Because of that, the home program detailed in Section Two provides a structure to support use of the principles in daily interactions with children. Without the structure of the program, it is very difficult to maintain the necessary consistency, especially for people who are overly busy and stressed by the demands of their daily lives.

In keeping with this, my intention has been to make the discussion of the principles stand on its own for anyone who may be interested in the concepts but not the structure of the program. Even without the home program, though, these principles will be most effective when used with the material about eliminating unwanted behavior in Section Three.

However, my sincere hope is that you will undertake a structured home program from the beginning. I have worked with hundreds of families who successfully used the home program in their homes, and all found the structure helped them stick with the basic principles. On the other hand, those who skipped a structured home program reported only temporary successes in adhering to the principles.

On a more personal note, my wife and I applied a structured program in our own home with our two sons throughout their childhood and well into adolescence, and it would be difficult for us to imagine attempting child rearing without the benefit of the integrated approach. (If you are interested in more details about how I came to the approach presented here, please visit my web-page, http://disciplinewithoutanger.com/. It includes anecdotes from the early life of our sons, demonstrating clearly the learning process even before six months of age.)

Intended Audience for this Book

So far I have mostly addressed you, the reader, as "parent," and I will continue to do so for convenience and efficiency. However, if you play a significant role in guiding children, whatever your specific status or title, the principles and practices described in this book apply equally well to you and your situation. Thus, if you are committed to helping children learn to take responsibility for their own behavior, you will likely find this approach applies to your needs. Among those who can expect to benefit from this approach, in addition to those in traditional two-parent families, are:

- Single fathers and single mothers
- Grandparents
- Foster parents
- Step parents
- Couples of whatever gender
- Child care workers
- Teachers
- Any other sort of guardian involved in child-rearing

Similarly, this approach applies to children of all sorts, whether developing normally or challenged by any of a wide variety of special needs. Among the illustrative vignettes presented in Section Five, for example, is a question by parents of a child with Attention Deficit Disorder, a behavioral pattern very well addressed by these principles. In fact, these guidelines are designed to fit a program to the specific needs of the individual child. Of course the speed with which goals are met will vary according to the child's capacity to learn and to carry out the expected behaviors, all discussed in detail below.

Just as I elected to refer to "parents" rather than to "traditional and other parenting figures," I also have chosen to assume comments apply to "parent or parents" whenever I use either term. Similarly, I have assumed that use of "child" or "children" can appropriately be read as either, depending upon your circumstance, unless the specific context of their use indicates otherwise. And finally, "you" is meant to refer to either one or two parents, again depending upon your circumstances. I hope you will not assume a comment does not apply to you if you happen to differ in number or situation in some way from the specific wording of a comment.

You will find a considerable amount of repetition as you read through these pages. One reason for repetition is that some points deserve additional emphasis. The other reason is that it seems likely that you (or other readers) may, even a considerable time after reading the whole book, refer back to particular sections to refresh your memory. I wanted to assure that each section will largely stand on its own and provide a clear understanding without undue rereading of other sections.

*Life affords no greater responsibility,
no greater privilege, than the raising
of the next generation.*

~C. Everett Koop

Chapter Two

"But Doctor, what do we do when . . . our child responds to every thing we tell her to do by whining and saying, 'You help me'?"

Page 216

HOW PARENTS ENHANCE THEIR CHILDREN'S DEVELOPMENT

"Children are to be seen and not heard." "Spare the rod and spoil the child." Such slogans have guided parenting across the ages and were thought by many to contain a great deal of wisdom and truth. Hidden from view was an ugly by-product of these views of children and how to deal with them: children from all social settings are being mistreated, emotionally and physically, by the people upon whom they depended for everything, their parents.

Our society first confronted this betrayal of the most fundamental trust only after a long struggle against laws that treated children as property. It took the American Society for Prevention of Cruelty to Animals to extend animal protective laws to children, based on the recognition that children are, after all, biologically members of the animal kingdom.

In part in reaction to so much acceptance of harsh approaches to discipline, some parents in recent decades moved to the other extreme. They allowed their children great freedom and expected little from them. In fact, I have seen an advertisement for professional training on how to deal with the "over-indulged child syndrome," indicating concern that a good many kids have had too few limits set on their behavior.

Ironically, both the get-tough and over-indulgent approaches to raising children fail in what is most basic to effective parenting. Evidence is overwhelming that children do not fare well when they are raised harshly and without consideration of their developmental levels and emotional needs. At the same time, it is clear that children who are never taught that their behavior has consequences also do poorly.

Somehow, we as a society seem to have concluded that each of us must choose one extreme or the other. Indeed, even a great many people who claim that they use research-based approaches manage to align themselves with one extreme or the other. For instance, many schools say that they use positive reinforcement principles but then rely on "consequences," typically listing mostly failure behaviors and the

11

negative consequences – punishments – applied to each infraction.

Fortunately, a much more constructive and effective middle ground exists which:

- Respects the specific needs, attributes, and developmental levels of children,

- Accepts that it takes time and patience for children to learn what is appropriate and to comply with adult expectations,

- Acknowledges that adults are responsible to guide children to age-appropriate levels of responsibility for their own behavior, and

- Recognizes that demonstrating to children that responsible behavior leads to beneficial consequences prepares them to function as effective members of society.

Said differently, this approach lays a solid foundation for learning how the real world actually works:

- People who are productive can expect benefit from their efforts: *You do your part and you get a payoff,*

- People who cooperate with or help others are likely to receive thanks and praise: *You take the needs of others seriously and you get noticed and appreciated,* and

- Generally no one gets paid *in anticipation* that they may someday do something productive: *You don't benefit from making promises; you perform first and then benefit.*

To be fully effective in guiding children, you must understand that kids, as is true for adults, strive to meet their own needs in whatever ways they can. That is, children do what they sense is most likely to get them what they need. A boy whining incessantly for a toy in a store almost certainly has reason to suppose, based on his own past experience, that whining will produce the toy, at least some of the time.

Recognizing this pattern does not mean that parents must accept whatever their kids do. Rather, understanding what drives kids helps us realize that we cannot force children to cease unacceptable behavior. Instead, we must show them they can best meet their needs by doing what we consider appropriate so that they no longer have reason to misbehave.

We must recognize that guiding children to better self-control is not a battle between us adults, who have the answers, and our children, who refuse to accept our wisdom as readily as we'd prefer. Rather, such learning is a process; after all, if kids came into the world knowing how to do everything right, they wouldn't need parents and teachers. Mistakes or failing to fulfill a responsibility can best be viewed, not as a crime, but rather as an indication of need to learn more or better.

When we adults are honest with ourselves, we realize that we sometimes fail to meet our own standards. Just as we must forgive ourselves for those human inconsistencies, we must be prepared to understand and to forgive our children for theirs. Put the other way around, we must recognize that teaching responsible behavior to children requires responsible behavior on our own part. It also requires the patience necessary to provide the time, effort, and focus central to true learning. Or, said slightly differently still, teaching discipline requires that we maintain a modicum of discipline for ourselves, both with respect to understanding what we must do and with respect to doing it consistently.

Recognizing how preachy the foregoing sounds, I want to hasten to make another crucial point:

> **Any approach that suggests to you that you must
> be perfect in your work with your children is unlikely
> to be helpful to you or anyone else.**

This is clearly not such an approach! While it does require a reasonable level of commitment and discipline, it is based on realistic responses from actual people working with actual children.

The approach presented in this book has assisted a great many parents in guiding their kids. As far as I can tell, not one of those parents was a saint. Not one did things perfectly. Those who succeeded did so by working day by day to be more effective, finding ways to succeed when things bogged down and recovering from any slips into less constructive reactions. And most expected the same thing from their kids: doing better tomorrow when things didn't go perfectly today.

A Preview of Coming Attractions

So far I have attempted to set the stage for what follows. Just below is a bit more detailed preview of the remaining sections to provide a sense of what to expect as you read on. Throughout, in order to give the concepts more vibrancy, I have included anecdotes, some as questions and responses, illustrating actual concerns and experiences of families working with this approach. To maintain privacy of the families involved, each of these examples has been altered enough to hide actual identities while maintaining what is useful in each.

The rest of Section One provides a rationale for parenting based on the conviction that children deserve loving guidance as they move from infancy, with its relative lack of responsibility; through middle-childhood, with growing expectations of cooperation; to adolescence, with ever-increasing demands and responsibilities. I have attempted to make this a self-contained presentation from which you can consider adjustments in your approach to your children, whether or not you choose to use the structured program described later.

Section Two expands on the first by providing clear guidelines for building, implementing, and maintaining a structured home program for providing the guidance needed by children. It also includes details on how to extend your influence beyond your home to situations such as school when you are not there. In part, this section is included because it is clear that applying the principles from Section One is very difficult without the structure of the program, and I hope that you will consider adopting the detailed guidelines presented here.

Section Three recognizes that even the best program cannot assure that children never stray from expectations. It provides very specific guidelines for dealing with unacceptable behavior yet is completely compatible with both the principles from Section One and the structured program in Section Two. This feature is particularly important in that it is specifically designed to avoid undermining the home program with less carefully considered responses to inappropriate behavior. Included are detailed guidelines for eliminating unacceptable behavior away from home.

Section Four describes how to monitor your progress and to manage the structured home program over time, including how to adapt it to changes of various kinds. It also provides specific troubleshooting guidelines for assuring you are on track and for reviving a program showing declining effectiveness.

Section Five ties the discussion together, providing a summary, some conclusions, and a variety of illustrations taken from concerns of actual parents.

It should be stressed again that the principles discussed here constitute the core of the approach. The home program is designed and intended to provide a structure for application of the principles to support interactions with children. Keeping such interactions constructive can otherwise be difficult to maintain over time without that structure, especially for people who are overly busy and stressed by the demands of their daily lives.

To reiterate: Section One was written to stand on its own for anyone who may be interested in the concepts but not the structure of the program. This material can best be used along with the approach offered in Section Three; however, I hope you will give the home program some serious consideration. Most families with whom I have worked found that they were far more successful when they used the entire approach and were able to relieve difficult challenges or conflicts within the home.

If you want your children to improve,
let them overhear the nice things
you say about them to others.

~Haim Ginott

Chapter Three

"But Doctor, what do I do when . . . my 11-year-old son moves as slowly as he can, no matter how loudly we yell or how often we get after him to hurry up?" Page 92

THE GOAL OF THIS BOOK

The goal of this book is to provide you with an effective and efficient mode of parenting. Specifically, my personal goal is:

> **To help you help your children take appropriate levels of responsibility for their own behavior.**

Thus, my goal is not "to help you better control your children," for two reasons: first, we might help you control your child but leave the child misbehaving away from you. Second, our main job as parents is to teach our children to be responsible for <u>their own</u> behavior in keeping with their ages and abilities.

We teach two-year-old children to use the toilet instead of your favorite house plants or your slippers. We teach kindergartners to wait while other children take their turns doing things. And, we certainly had better teach teenagers to be responsible for managing 3000 pounds of steel and glass at high speeds before we turn them loose as drivers on the freeway.

Each of these is just a step in preparing our younger citizens to become responsible, contributing members of our society.

Please note that I am referring to children taking responsibility in the broadest sense of the term. Yes, this includes things like chores and homework but it also includes responsibility for how children relate to others, both their peers and adults, and for how they manage their own emotions. This is about learning to take control of their own lives and in the process to feel good about themselves as people. Of course such learning does not happen over night but rather as an ongoing process which most of us continue throughout our lives.

An important developmental process impacts our efforts to help our children become responsible individuals. Children typically get strong

17

positive reactions from others when they behave responsibly. If they receive enough such affirmations, kids come to feel competent and to act competently.

Among the many advantages of that development is that kids who feel competent are more willing to try new things. Trying new things in turn leads to new skills, which, if guided properly, yield still more responsible behavior, which then elicits more positive feedback. This cycle, that feeds on success, represents a crucial support for children developing a pattern of success and maturation.

Said a bit differently, this pattern of responding to success with further effort and further success is the stuff from which strong self-esteem is built. A lot has been written about the importance of telling kids how great they are, sometimes even in contexts where kids recognize they haven't done so well. However, the evidence is pretty clear: the instances in which kids observe and experience themselves doing things successfully are what really matters. Praise from others can support that process, but kids must believe it is real for it to matter. In fact, exaggerated flattery can backfire: kids may conclude that they must be pretty pathetic for people to have to pretend they are doing okay when they know they are not.

Now think about what happens to the kids who do not feel confident in their own skills. Almost any experienced teacher can tell of kids who fight doing school work, often actively breaking other classroom rules at the same time. Such kids often are found to work hard at avoiding any attempt to do things they "know" they cannot do even if they are severely hassled because of it. It has been said that kids would rather be thought of as "bad" than as "stupid." The idea is that kids can imagine getting over being "bad" but don't think it possible to get over being "stupid." Therefore these struggles are aimed at hiding their feeling of failing in school at whatever cost.

Since a lack of well-founded self-esteem is so very detrimental, more should be said about it; rather surprising twin observations will set the stage:

> • **The child who fails most in life may, in fact, turn out to be the child who succeeds the most, and**
>
> • **The child who fails least in life may, in fact, turn out to be the child who succeeds very little.**

Since many parents with whom I have shared these observations react with disbelief, I will elaborate:

Consider two kids, Austin and Timothy, both going to their first soccer practice at age six with no soccer experience.

Austin is a boy who has had little experience with doing well at much of anything. When the coach asks him to kick the ball around, Austin takes a tentative kick at the ball, almost trips, and shies away. Failure number one. Urged to try again, he makes a still more half-hearted try. Failure number two. And Austin may make few or no additional tries, in the end perhaps giving up on the sport entirely. In the process, he limits his attempts to no more than a few. Of most importance, while he has thereby limited his failures to a very few, he also almost entirely eliminated any chance at success. Attempts, few; successes, none! With enough similar experiences in a variety of settings, Austin is likely to see himself as a failure overall. This is the stuff upon which poor self-esteem is built, and it carries with it the makings of a self-fulfilling expectation that there is no point in trying since it only leads to failure.

Timothy, on the other hand, while also having no experience with soccer, has done well at a variety of things in his life. Asked to kick the ball around, he does so with some gusto. In his haste, he whiffs the ball, stumbles, and falls down. He may even complain a bit. Failure number one. But he jumps up and takes another kick at the ball. This time it goes a few inches, off the side of his foot. Another kid snickers. Failure number two. Again Timothy attacks the ball, but this time his foot goes over the top. He slips over the ball and is down in a heap. Failure number three. Timothy's face shows his frustration and his effort as he approaches the ball a bit more carefully. This time he stops before the ball and his kick barely moves it. Failure number four. This may go on for some time longer, through a number of additional failures, far more than Austin allowed himself. But in the end Timothy kicks the ball a few feet, more or less in the direction he intends. Success number one! He may go on to a good many more failures, but the successes start to mount as well. The crucial feature of this tale is the first success. Timothy's readiness to try long enough to achieve that magic moment sets him up for the many additional tries and successes that will shape his entire life and will help him persevere through whatever new activity he confronts in the future. And that is the stuff from which solid self-esteem is constructed. The result is likely to be a positive, self-fulfilling expectation that if he tries hard and long enough, he will succeed.

The point here is that our kids desperately need us adults – especially their parents – to assure that they have real successes from which they can build more successes and with them rich and meaningful lives. This does not happen through parents always doing things <u>for</u> kids (a rather direct way of telling kids we don't believe in them) but rather by parents supporting <u>kids doing things for themselves</u>.

This book details an overall approach through which parents can provide the kinds of experiences that assure children will succeed. Said differently, it provides a way to support children as they learn to take responsibility for their own behavior.

What You Will Learn from this Book

In order to fulfill our goal of helping children take increasingly adequate levels of responsibility for their own lives, I will pursue several specific objectives as we work our way through this book. My intent is for you to have a clear enough grasp of this material that you will be able to think through challenges in parenting as they arise and that you will have a clear basis for making whatever modifications become necessary in your approach over time.

If you follow the approach presented here to the end of this book, you will be able to:

- Understand some select and directly relevant basic principles of human behavior and understand what produces changes in behavior. While this is **not** a text on child development, I will review and discuss a few central principles that contribute to our overall goal.

- Understand the basics of an approach to teaching children to be responsible for their own behavior.

- Understand the components of a carefully designed program of behavior change for use in your own home.

- Develop a list of "target" behaviors which define changes you want your child to master. You will learn how to decide what behaviors you most want to change, how to convey this to the child, and how to adjust your efforts over time.

- Design an effective program specifically for your home to accomplish the changes you want to make.

- Extend your program and your influence into situations outside the home, even when you are not there.

- Take action in a way that fits with all the principles discussed here and that works both at home and away from home, when your child misbehaves.

- Clearly determine how successful you are with the program to be sure you meet your goals for your child.

- Adjust your program as needed, based on your judgment of your child's progress or on changes in your child's responses to the program.

- Identify anything that might interfere with success of your program and make any changes that are needed.

This list, which may sound ambitious to you, is based on work with dozens of groups of parents. Over the years, I had the pleasure of seeing them master the concepts and the practices presented here. The present book reflects the shared efforts and experience of a great many families.

Never fear spoiling children by making them too happy. Happiness is the atmosphere in which all good affections grow.

~Thomas Bray

Chapter Four

WAYS CHILDREN LEARN

Children learn in many ways, not all of them directly discussed in this book. However, considering other ways that kids learn helps make the rest clearer. Here are a few of those ways:

Direct Instruction

Probably the most natural and common way to teach children is by directly telling them things, including what to do and how to do it. When your child was an infant, you began naming objects and probably said things like "Wave bye-bye to Daddy" while demonstrating. This pattern has continued throughout your contacts with your child, and someday may even include your ideas about how to raise your grandchildren. (Of course, those of us who have successfully used the principles and practices presented here will have raised our children to be responsible adults. In turn, they are likely to use a similar approach in their own parenting. Isn't that a satisfying notion?)

Correcting Errors

Telling kids what they have done wrong is a variation on direct instruction. It is also a natural and common part of all our lives. I mention it separately here, though, to stress that too much focus on mistakes can be damaging to a child's growth and development. I will discuss reasons for this in detail as we continue through this book. For now it is enough to keep in mind that being told how wrong we are all of the time eventually undermines how well we do all sorts of things. This is true whether we are children often scolded by our parents or adults often criticized by our supervisors.

Modeling

We often see adults laugh heartily while watching children play grownup, matching our dress and actions in keeping with how they see us. Unfortunately, though, we often fail to notice when our kids mimic some of our behaviors that we really don't like. The old admonition to "Do what

I say, not what I do!" sounds good but carries little impact. Almost always children respond instead to the more powerful rule that "Actions speak louder than words." As an example, I often have had parents in my office complain that their teenager has taken up smoking, only to learn that the parents themselves smoke in the house. Without commenting on the difficulties that many people experience when they try to give up smoking, it is still likely that the teen is reacting to the behavior modeled at home.

In a related but somewhat different manner, parents sometimes encourage behaviors they really don't like by such actions as dressing the child in a shirt with "Little Devil" or some such across the front. Adults and children laughing at this little joke probably don't realize that they are directly reinforcing "devilish" behavior in the child who is basking in the glow of the laughter. Imagine how a child reacts to his parent's wearing a tee-shirt emblazoned with "I'm with Stupid" and an arrow pointing to the other parent. Surely the child will conclude from this "joke" that calling people such a name is cute and funny, not wrong – and may find respect for the "stupid" parent slipping as well.

The point here is that we parents constantly model behavior for our kids, whether or not we notice, and the more we are aware of and choose to model the behaviors that we prefer, the more our children are likely to behave appropriately.

Consequences of Behavior

In the last few decades, a lot has been written about the impact on kids from the "consequences" of how they behave. In the 1960's many people allowed kids to experience the **"natural consequences"** of their behavior, just as happens daily in the "real world." Unfortunately this whole idea led some adults to take a hands-off approach and "let children learn from their own mistakes." In some situations this may make sense, but carried to extremes, it can lead to real problems. As a clear, if rather grim example, imagine deciding your child should learn not to run into a busy street by experiencing the natural consequence of doing so.

Recognizing such shortcomings, some child-rearing specialists recommended an alternative which they referred to as **"logical consequences."** This approach relied on matching consequences to specific behaviors. It required adults to guide kids by showing them how their behavior caused problems and choosing consequences to fit the problem. For example, a child hits a baseball through the window, leaving broken glass all over the floor and no barrier to rain, birds, and insects. The logical consequence would depend upon the child's age.

A five-year-old might be expected to hold the dust pan for the parent sweeping up the glass while a 16-year-old might be expected to buy and replace the glass, with supervision. Here the issue is not whether the child did something wrong but rather that the window was broken and those involved are responsible to make repairs. Blame is neither necessary nor constructive. While this approach has much to commend it, one major drawback is that it typically involves waiting for a mistake to happen so that the child can learn from it.

In response to this limitation, a more proactive approach was needed. It is available in what might be called **"planned consequences."** The idea behind this concept is the basis for the program presented in this book. The term itself is not widely used, and, in fact, I will not use it again in this book. It is included here to clarify how it fits with other ways that children learn. Specifically, the notion is that:

- To develop responsible behavior, children need and benefit from adult help,

- Waiting for failures to occur is not a very useful way to teach kids to be responsible for themselves, and

- Adult help can best be provided in a thoughtful, planned, proactive fashion that emphasizes the benefits of success.

I will be going into considerable detail about the profound implications of these simple ideas.

What's a good investment?
Go home from work early
and spend the afternoon
throwing a ball around
with your son.

~Ben Stein on CNN

Chapter Five

"But Doctor, what do we do when . . . our kid constantly complains about how unfair we are for making him do so many chores since none of his friends have to do any?"

Page 97

HOW DISCIPLINE LEADS TO RESPONSIBLE BEHAVIOR

To reach our goal of teaching children to take more complete responsibility for their own behavior, we must understand how responsibility is learned. After all, babies do not come into this world capable of taking responsibility for their own behavior. Everyone seems to recognize that *discipline* is central to this process. Therefore it is essential that we start with a clear understanding of what discipline is and what it is not.

The term *discipline* is used in a variety of ways, most commonly as a synonym for punishment. In fact, this notion appears to be institutionalized in society:

> In 2004 the British House of Lords upheld the right of parents to spank their children though no adult is allowed to hit another. A spokesman for Prime Minister Tony Blair was quoted as saying, "The government wants an outcome that maintains the balance between the parent's right to discipline, and protecting the child. That is why we don't want to criminalize parents. That is why we are opposed to outright bans. The government wants to send a signal that parents do have a right to discipline the child."

Clearly this debate reflected the conviction that to discipline is to punish – physically. Since this widely-held view is very different from my own, we need to establish a clear and shared way of talking about discipline here.

The entire discussion in this book is based on this definition:

> *Discipline is the process through which children learn to take responsibility for their own behavior.*

27

The emphasis here is not on what we do <u>to</u> children but rather on what happens <u>inside</u> them. The focus is on increasing the ability of children to control and manage their own behavior, exactly the goal I identified for this book from the beginning. That means that a full understanding of the concept of discipline is essential to our efforts to meet our goal.

What Parents Say About How They Discipline Their Children

Parents in a clinic where I worked routinely completed a questionnaire about their families. One question asked, "How do you discipline your child?" and another asked, "Does your approach get the desired results?" To better understand the answers, I analyzed the responses to 100 consecutive questionnaires. The results were very revealing.

To the first question, "How do you discipline your child?," most parents reported that they used one or some combination of the following three approaches:

Verbal approaches

Verbal approaches to discipline reported by the parents ranged from cozy talks to lecturing, nagging, and out-and-out yelling. Probably everyone uses verbal reprimands in some form. The issue is whether talking with kids is effective or not.

Some years ago I was asked to talk about discipline to a group of mothers of two-year-olds. I didn't realize that the mothers would arrive with their little tykes in tow, and quite a few brought babies as well. Picture the scene: about 15 mothers with strollers, diaper bags, toys, and 15 or more active, curious two-year-olds in constant motion.

From the beginning my attempts to talk to the mothers were drowned out by the hubbub, and I mostly observed. The tykes did what tykes do best: explored and tested. The mothers chatted and occasionally chided the kids when something went awry: "Ernest, stop that," "Salim, put down the chair," "Skye, don't pull the baby's hair." Most of these pleas went unheard or ignored. The typical mother repeated the instruction more loudly, increasing the noise level and decreasing the chance that any child would comply. Only mothers who took action had any impact on their kids. Some attempted to guide their kids while most simply swatted little behinds. The latter produced whoops of pain and indignation (generally justified, since the kids were unlikely to have any clear idea why they were swatted), typically followed by return to the fray when the tears had dried. Sometimes talking is doomed to failure.

Restrictive approaches

Restrictions reported by our parents ranged from a few minutes in the corner to no television for a while to "grounding" for weeks. The severity of restrictions varied both in how long they lasted and in how narrow the limits on the individual's freedom. For instance, a child may be restricted to a bedroom or simply required to stay home for the specified time.

Taking away privileges appears to be a very common approach to discipline. In fact, limiting privileges underlies the discipline in many schools, vaguely labeled "consequences." Based upon reports of many parents and direct observations in numerous schools, such consequences almost always boil down to some sort of punishment for inappropriate behavior.

There is a subtle but powerful difference between removing privileges and providing privilege only when a child has completed assigned responsibilities. I will discuss this distinction in considerable detail later. For now note that when a parent takes away a favorite toy or television time, the child is likely to see this loss as "mean old dad or mom taking my stuff." Things are subtlely but powerfully different when a child understands that privileges depend on responsible behavior. On some level the child is likely to recognize that the restrictions in choices are also based on the child's own prior choices, for example, that the privilege of playing with friends comes only after chores have been completed responsibly.

Physical approaches

As the name implies, the parents reported using corporal punishments that ranged from a slap on the hand to a swat on the behind, with some acknowledging pretty severe spankings.

Parents differ widely as to whether they employ spanking as a form of discipline, and controversy continues to rage about whether it is constructive or abusive. (My own views will become clear as I discuss the likely impact in later sections.)

Commonalities among these approaches

These three approaches – verbal, restrictive, and physical (and combinations of them) – accounted for about 95 percent of what parents reported to be their methods of discipline.

As was noted, the harshness of each approach can vary markedly. But the three approaches also have a couple of key elements in common:

- All are applied only <u>after</u> a child has done something inappropriate (it would be very weird to spank a kid before doing something wrong!) and

- All can accurately be considered <u>punishment</u> in that each represents a negative response to inappropriate behavior – perhaps not surprising, considering how often people use the words "discipline" and "punishment" as synonyms.

The point here is that when asked how they disciplined their children the vast majority of parents reported relying solely on one or more of several common forms of punishment.

Reported impact of these approaches

Our parents were also asked, "Does your approach get the desired results?" Given the widespread use of it, this question really amounted to asking: "Does punishment get the desired results?" A count of the answers revealed these results:

- About 70 percent answered "no" indicating that they generally did **not** get the results hoped for and

- Of the 30 percent answering "yes" to this question, nearly all acknowledged that the changes they observed in response to punishment were only momentary and therefore their children did **not** show lasting benefits.

Of great importance about these results, very few of the parents felt that their attempts to teach responsible behavior through punishment were successful over the long run. This was true whether they used verbal, restrictive, or physical approaches. In fact, many parents said that they had never considered discipline as related to responsible behavior. Instead they thought of discipline as what they did when their kids misbehaved. I hope this discussion will encourage a broader view of the role and the benefits of discipline.

Things We Know, in General, About Punishment

So, parents report that they rely almost totally upon punishment for discipline and that they rarely get the results they hoped for. In the light of this, it is important fully to understand punishment and what is known about it. In this regard, it is helpful to summarize several things that are pretty well established regarding the effectiveness of punishment in changing children's behavior:

- **Punishment is best at teaching what <u>not</u> to do.**

  If a child is pulling the cat's tail and you yell loudly enough or spank hard enough, the child will likely stop, at least for the moment. On the other hand, as parents often find to their chagrin, if a child is really resistant to doing homework, there may be no amount of yelling or nagging or spanking or grounding that will produce any serious effort whatsoever. I have heard of parents becoming virtual prisoners in their own kitchens after insisting their child stay at the table until at least a few math problems are done. Punishment is typically ineffective in teaching kids to do their homework. The same also applies to other behaviors which kids can avoid by stalling and resisting instead of complying.

- **Even the limited effects from teaching what not to do through punishment tend not to last very long.**

  Research supports the reports of our 100 parents that even when a child stops a behavior following punishment there isn't much likelihood that the child has learned not to do the same thing later. That is, the parents have not achieved the goal of helping the child internalize responsible behavior.

  This observation should not be surprising. We have prisons full of people showing the same pattern. Bureau of Criminal Justice statistics show over two-thirds of prison inmates are re-arrested within three years of release, and who knows how many of the other third simply are not caught for their repeated crimes?

- **Kids who are most in need of help to change their behavior are generally the least likely to benefit.**

  Probably everyone has known a little girl who almost always does what is expected of her and who, when chided for even a minor misbehavior, will – perhaps with tears in her eyes – snap back into line and may never show the same behavior again.

  And, unfortunately, probably everyone has also known a little boy – all too true to the stereotype – who repeatedly breaks a family rule and who continues the pattern no matter how harshly punished. Indeed, some may actually challenge parents to punish them more, perhaps smirking as they do so. This can lead to a vicious cycle of misbehavior and increasingly harsh punishment as parents react to what appears to be complete disrespect and a direct challenge to their authority. When such kids trust a therapist enough, they may admit that such swats hurt like the dickens and that they were surely not smiling on the inside; they just were not about to let parents know how they felt. As a result, for such kids even punishment used more often or more severely is unlikely to be of any benefit whatsoever and, as we shall see in the next paragraphs, may even have a sizable detrimental effect.

- **All too often punishment serves to distract parents from their original expectations so that their kids may serve their penalty and avoid their responsibilities.**

When parents give in to misbehavior by punishing, there is a very strong likelihood that in the process they will lose track of the original expectation. Often that will mean that the child never does complete whatever responsibility was being avoided in the first place. In fact, I have known children who admitted preferring a slap to doing some detested task. It is important for parents to maintain their focus on the task at hand, realizing that side-tracking to punish may be self-defeating.

- **Punishment causes unnecessary and counter-productive anger and frustration in parent-child relationships.**

It is rare for parents to punish because they really want to; rather, they do so out of frustration with their lack of success with other forms of discipline. Similarly, children react to punishment with hurt and frustration, as well as anxiety about disruption in parental love and support. It this joint distress is allowed to become a family pattern, it may lead to resentment and anger that can come to taint all parent-child interactions.

- **In an unexpected way, being punished may actually increase the very behaviors giving rise to the punishment.**

Frequently I have had a parent come into my office and say something like:

> "Joshua pinched his little sister hard enough to leave a red mark. I got so mad I spanked him until I felt bad myself. But, the next day he went back and did the same thing again! I sometimes wonder if something is wrong with the kid. I just know he knows better!"

Now, if you think about it, the ideas that "something is wrong" with the child and that "I just know he knows better" are contradictory. Experience tells us, though, that the parent is almost always correct and that the child really does "know better." I have actually seen kids, out of view of their parents, mouthing, word for word, what the parents were saying they had told the kids at home. It is not that they don't know. And it is not that there is "something wrong." I have worked with individuals with even severe disturbance, and I have never seen anyone disturbed enough not to avoid pain.

But if we accept this view, then we are left with the question: why would the kid do the same thing that just led to severe punishment? The answer, it seems clear, is that **there is something positive in it for the child, something gained, that is more important than avoiding the pain or inconvenience of the punishment.**

In this example, a child caught up in such intense conflict with a parent may be enraged but dare not attack the parent directly. The child is too small and inept to duke it out with mom or dad. But on some level the child may be aware of the pain inflicted on the parent and get some satisfaction out of knowing that.

It is widely known that child abuse is a serious problem in our society. I was always struck, though, working in this field, by how really rare it is to come across parents who actually somehow get pleasure from abusing their children. Most parents who mistreat their kids do so because of their frustration and because they don't know what else to do. Typically they were abused as children themselves, and all they know how to do is react aggressively.

Think about what that means. When parents end up so frustrated with their kids that they verge on abuse, **the children are controlling the adults**, rather than the other way around. Parents get into this situation not because they carefully plan it out but because they don't know what else to do. In that situation children may have a real sense of control or at least recognize the attention they receive. So, parents do things which they hope will stop behaviors they don't like, and instead they end up reinforcing the very things they want their children not to do. The same can be true for parents who are not at all abusive to their kids.

Though parents typically don't notice it, the pain and inconvenience of punishment almost always are mixed with other factors which actually may work against their intended goal. These include the attention that the child receives from the parent who is doing the punishing.

I worked with a family who spent a lot of their time dealing with their then ten-year-old son's serious and chronic childhood illness. They had to make frequent and unpredictable trips to clinics and hospitals to care for the boy. In the middle of one session dealing with family time and effort, the five-year-old brother suddenly, asked, "Daddy, do you remember when I was little and always pitched fits at you?" The father nodded and said he remembered all too well. The boy then asked, "Do you know why I did that?" When told the dad did not know, this little boy stated, "I did it because then you would spank me. That way I knew I was part of the family." In this simple fashion, which brought tears to the eyes of the rest of us there, this little boy demonstrated how far children may go to meet their needs to be noticed and feel important.

Further, in any given interaction between parents and children, including those involving punishment, there may be other ways in which children's needs are met. This means that inappropriate behavior is reinforced even though that reinforcing such behavior is exactly the opposite of the parents' best intentions. There probably are many circumstances in which this can occur, and typically the impact is subtle and difficult to identify. Just as one example, a child who is caught up in intense sibling rivalry might well accept being punished along with the sibling to gain satisfaction from hurting the sibling who is seen as unfairly favored by the parent.

As already indicated, even children with no great need of increased attention may get satisfaction from feeling in control during punitive interactions with parents. Because this struggle about who is in control can sneak into family life unnoticed and can be so difficult to deal with, it is discussed next, even though this represents a bit of a side-track from the general flow of our discussion.

Chapter Six

"But Doctor, what do I do when . . . my kids get wild and won't listen so I get fed up and yell at them and end up feeling like a terrible mother?"

Page 219

HOW CONTROL STRUGGLES
INTERFERE WITH DISCIPLINE

Over years of working with families struggling with children's misbehavior, I have observed frequent and intense battles of will between parents and their kids. All sides often seem locked in combat that no one can either win or escape. Because this pattern is so common, though the intensity varies widely, here are some thoughts about the power struggles. What follows is based on my work with children in individual psychotherapy as well as observing family interactions in joint sessions. It represents my best attempt to put into words a subtle, unspoken, yet powerful pattern of interactions that tends to occur without clear overt markers.

Childhood Apprehensions and the
Development of Control Struggles

To set the stage, there are some basic observations upon which this understanding is based, all of which you are likely to think are reasonable:

First observation

The world is a scary place for anyone who is paying attention. Every newscast and every newspaper is filled with reports of burglaries, rapes, murders, wars, auto collisions, tornadoes, earthquakes, and the like. Clearly children are exposed to a great many frightening things, including many we adults may not even be aware of.

An eight-year-old boy was on an extended hospital stay while being treated for a bone infection. Despite weeks in traction with a pin in his knee and with an IV tube in his arm to administer medication, he had been consistently delightful and cooperative with staff. However, on the eve of having the pin removed so he could go home, he became unruly and belligerent. Even his favorite nurse him could not calm him. The staff asked me to consult.

Screams and curses room guided me to this small boy's room. He

35

was in a rage, screaming complaints that revealed intense terror. With help he expressed fear that his leg would fall off when the pin was removed, just as he'd seen in his sister's doll. Once he was reassured that his leg had healed and he no longer needed the pin or traction, he relaxed, resuming his previous sweet style.

Fear of the unknown can be most distressing, and often adults are unaware of what is unknown – or imagined – by children.

Second observation

Adults deal with the many threats in the world in various ways to manage their fears and anxieties. One common strategy for adults is telling themselves such things as:

"Those shootings are in that bad neighborhood on the other side of town," or
"That hurricane was in far away New Orleans," or
"The terrorists will be caught and we'll be safe in our area."

For most adults, these efforts usually manage their concerns, though circumstances can overwhelm even the best defenses.

Third observation

Children, on the other hand, are less able to use such mature approaches to managing their fears. For example, they are less able to rationalize their concerns, instead taking many things as very personal threats. Children tend to be very concrete and not to understand time and distance that may serve to comfort adults. Further, many children are, at best, inconsistently capable of separating fiction from reality. They may vividly remember frightening television programs long after viewing, troubling their sleep even for several nights. Further, they tend to mix things that they don't understand with what they do, often compounding their concerns.

During another consultation on a pediatrics ward, I met with a boy who had a tumor behind his left eyeball. To learn what he understood, I asked him what "tumor" means, and he told me he had a "tissue" behind his eye, a seemingly accurate and mature notion. Pursued just a bit more, however, I learned that the child imagined he had some sort of gunky, nasty, facial tissue wadded up and jammed into his head, somehow growing there. While the actual tumor was indeed a serious threat, it seemed clear that what the boy imagined was more troubling to him than a more accurate picture might have been.

Fourth observation

To handle their fears, children look to the adults in their lives for protection and a sense of security, and, of course, parents are the first adults most kids turn to, followed by others such as other older relatives, teachers, neighbors, and so on.

Toddlers in a new situation can be observed venturing a bit away from their mothers' knees, only to rush back for reassurance when they get too far, a bolder child does something scary, or someone makes too loud a noise. As kids grow older, they use the same approach in different ways, for example wanting to sleep with the parents, or asking for scholastically unneeded help with homework.

Fifth observation

Children feel less safety and security if they sense that their parents lack the strength or power necessary to take care of all the potential threats in the environment. This is particularly likely to occur if a child feels in control of the parents. A frightened child who feels in control of parents will conclude that the parents cannot be very strong.

Because the experience of being in control can have such a profound impact on a child and on family interactions, it is important for parents to have a clear understanding of the implications. First it is necessary to grasp the ways in which a child may come to feel in control of adults.

In this regard, it is generally accurate and useful to understand that **children are in control of adults whenever:**

- Adults wear down and "give up" in the face of their children's persistence; for instance after hours of repeated, "Please, Dad, can I, please, please, please?", the father finally reacts angrily with, "Oh, okay! But just this one time!" – perhaps for the hundredth time.

- Adults change decisions they think are appropriate if they can't justify them to the child's satisfaction, for instance when "all the other kids get to go" and Mom can't think of a good, compelling response to that.

- Adults, against their better judgment, strike out at the child (physically or verbally) in frustration. Sometimes they rationalize these reactions even though they would not accept similar reactions from their children. Whenever parents becomes angry enough at children to respond in ways that violate their own standards, it seems reasonable to conclude that the parents are not really in control of their emotions or of the situation.

37

- Adults react to child provocation by doing something not otherwise likely, in any other situation that might arise.

The Way the Process Works

With these observations in mind, let us discuss how the struggle for control between kids and parents plays itself out. Whenever a child is in control of important adults (or perceives it to be that way, which amounts to the same thing), the child will experience a sequence of reactions:

- The first reaction will likely be a brief but intense sense of satisfaction. This experience of having "won" powerfully reinforces whatever behavior is occurring at the time, however inappropriate. Sometimes kids are seen as smirking, which tends to enrage parents. This anger may be a reaction to feeling that if the child "won," then the parents "lost." No one likes to "lose," but losing to one's own child in this way may make parents feel incapable of protecting the family. This could account for the intensity of the parents' reaction in such circumstances.

- Almost immediately after that first surge of satisfaction, the child is likely to recognize a scary dilemma, raising an unexpressed but troubling question on the order of:

    "Gosh, if I am in control of Mom and Dad, who the heck is taking care of all the scary stuff out there?"

Imagine being a child facing the dilemma in that situation. If your parents relinquished control to you, then you must be stronger than they are. All this scary stuff is going on and you don't have anybody to take care of it. Now you've got to be strong enough yourself to deal with all the frightening things in the world.

So what are you going to do? The most likely thing is that you are going to try to convince yourself that you are able to handle all those scary things on your own. But how are you going to achieve this?

You are most likely to do what you know best how to do: whine more, fuss more, poke at your parents' soft spots, and keep up this pattern until they give in one more time. That will demonstrate anew how strong you are... maybe that will mean you are strong enough.

But this approach to reducing fears about being in control and to feeling less threatened can never really work. No matter how often the child manages to "succeed" in such a struggle, it remains clear the child is still incapable of handling all the threats in the world.

I conclude that one of the cardinal features of maturity is the capacity to accept that *none of us is strong enough to handle everything and that we must and do depend upon others to survive*.

In our world we cannot have milk without depending upon – and trusting – perhaps a dozen people between us and the cow, all of whom have to do the right thing for the milk to be okay. Yet, because generally we are able to trust others, we buy milk and rarely think about the many points at which it could be contaminated.

But a child who feels in control of adults does not dare to feel trust for anyone or anything, a burden of almost unimaginable magnitude. Given the extent of children's dependence on adults for protection, the intensity of this quandary can hardly be overstated.

Therefore, in response to this dilemma, the child struggles to feel strong enough to handle everything that might come along. This is accomplished by testing the adults' and the child's own resources, that is, by pushing the limits of inappropriate behavior. It must be stressed, however, that no child will consciously think this all through; it remains outside conscious awareness, rather than a conscious decision of how to react.

- The most common response from parents, when their children test the limits, is increased frustration followed by doing more of whatever they did earlier in the sequence (e.g., giving in, wearing down, or striking out). Unfortunately, because of the intense feelings involved, any such responses are not likely to be well thought out, and they are likely to be expressed harshly enough to give the child still more evidence of being stuck in "control."

- That feeling is likely to lead the child to renewed worries about being in control, continuing the entire process.

- All of this results in a vicious cycle that reflects the common experience of families caught in such patterns:

  - The more the child remains in control,
  - → The more anxious the child becomes,
  - → The greater the need to challenge the limits with unacceptable behavior,
  - → The more likely adults will become frustrated and react angrily and ineffectively,
  - → The more the child's sense of being in control is confirmed,
  - → The more likely the entire process will be perpetuated.

Possible Resolutions to the Dilemma

On the one hand, then, we have a child who tries the parent's patience, who brazenly challenges every rule, and who tempts the parent to react harshly, thereby leaving the child in control. On the other hand, that tiresome, frustrating child is, in fact, frightened and struggling to allay fears by acting as if able to control whatever scary things come along.

Caught in this dilemma and with no understanding of what is happening, the child cannot fix things. Therefore, adults must overcome their frustration and find a loving way to respond, in order to calm the child's fears and eliminate the struggle.

The fundamental basis for addressing the dilemma is that **the parent must resume control**!

What isn't so clear is how to accomplish this, but this analysis provides some very clear direction. To repeat the point, **the key is understanding that the child is reacting out of fear and apprehension** even though the behavior may appear challenging, disrespectful, and even mean.

Ironically and sadly, when a parent feels least nurturing is precisely the time when a child caught in a control struggle most desperately needs comforting. Specifically, a child caught in this dilemma needs concrete reassurance that adults will manage all threats from the environment. This means demonstrating strength that is not threatening to the already terrified child, the strength to keep the family safe.

Parents in our classes volunteered a couple possible ways to deal with this challenge:

• Some parents asserted that, "If the little so-and-so needs to see strength, I'll show him strength!," typically said with fist aggressively slamming into hand. As reasonable as that seems at first, we must ask whether a threatening stance is likely to provide the reassurance so deeply needed by a frightened, if challenging, child.

  As I have discussed above, except when angry, parents almost never want to strike the children they brought into this world to love and cherish. Even the majority of parents who have been harsh to the point of abuse typically report they lash out because they don't know what else to do, not because they truly want to hurt their children. That is, parents almost never react punitively based on their own reasoned reaction, but rather they react to – and therefore remain controlled by – their child's reactions.

- Other parents suggested that "If Tyler would just quit testing me all the time, he'd see I am here to take care of him and his needs." This, too, seems like a perfectly reasonable idea until we look closer at it.

First, this assertion suggests that Tyler delegate authority to the parent, and it is clear that a person delegating responsibility remains in charge. (As President Truman put it, "The buck stops here.")

Second, for Tyler to back off so that his parents can exhibit their strengths, he would have to trust that his parents can handle things. In these circumstances, trust is completely beyond the capacity of the child. In large measure this is the reason the pattern occurs in the first place.

So if reacting harshly or waiting for the child to relinquish control is not the solution, what is? Well, in keeping with the underlying dynamics that generate and maintain this troubling pattern, what is required here is for parents to:

- Establish clear boundaries between what the child can and cannot control (that is, set appropriate limits) and

- Consistently and effectively enforce those boundaries. "No" must mean "no," both when it is said and when it is challenged.

The idea is to show the child that the boundaries are there, they are firm, and they provide protection and not just limits.

You and three-year-old Paul live in a house with nothing but a few feet of grass and the sidewalk between your front door and a very busy street. Paul wants to explore out the front door but you know that you must set clear and firm limits. You recognize that confining Paul to the house would assure safety but would also severely limit his opportunities to learn about and deal with the larger world and thereby gradually to become more independent. To avoid stifling his growth, you might install a fence to keep Paul safe while also giving him greater freedom. It is true that Paul could fall and hurt himself in a fenced yard so that you would not have protected him against all mishaps. But the fence would balance freedom to expand horizons with safety from any major injury. This concrete example illustrates the role parents must play in establishing limits suitable to their child's needs in all areas.

Therefore the message is that children need their parents to establish clear boundaries:

- Within which they can go about the business of learning about the world and

- Beyond which they cannot venture. Period.

I recognize that most parents already accept these as ideals and typically have tried valiantly to achieve them. I also recognize that it is not easy when a child consistently challenges the limits parents set. Therefore, we must discuss how these principles can be effectively applied in a family where such dynamics have been operating.

Fortunately, once we have a clear understanding of the dynamics operating in such situations, it is possible – and not as difficult as parents often fear it will be – to establish a parenting style and approach that will make sure children do adhere to limits set by parents. And, it is clear that when that happens, even children with long histories of challenging behavior are relieved from the anxiety that drove them earlier. Thereafter they can find renewed joy in their families.

I will be discussing these matters in several ways as I go along. In fact, establishing such a parenting style is central to this entire approach. For the moment, just keep in mind the importance of *avoiding power struggles* and of *setting and enforcing suitable limits* on your child's behavior.

Chapter Seven

"But Doctor, what do I do when . . . my child's father, who lives in an apartment across town, won't agree with anything I say about discipline?"
Page 228

DISCIPLINE AND RESPONSIBILITY REVISITED

This concludes our diversion to discuss situations in which struggles over control have dominated family life. I started this "side track" in the context of discussing the limitations of punishment as a tool for instilling responsible behavior in children. To summarize the points made thus far:

● Punishment is best at teaching what <u>not</u> to do.

● Even then, the effects of punishment tend not to be lasting.

● Punishment is more likely to be effective with children who least need outside help to become responsible.

● Punishment causes unnecessary and counter-productive anger and frustration in parent-child relationships.

● To make things worse, punishment often works against the intended goal through providing attention, a sense of control, and/or other benefits, thereby inadvertently reinforcing the very behaviors parents want to eliminate.

All of this is consistent with what parents report when asked how they discipline their kids and how well their approaches work for them.

The conclusion:

> *In general punishment is ineffective
> in teaching responsible behavior.*

After a statement that some people may find extraordinary, I hasten to add that I recognize that you, as was true for me, may well have been raised by parents who on occasion relied on negative comments, restrictions of one sort or another, and even spanking as methods of discipline. Since those of us with that experience became responsible adults – enough so, in fact, to be investing our time and effort here on how best to raise responsible children – you may well wonder how I can claim that those things don't work.

Based on all the indicators that punishment is ineffective as a tool of discipline, the answer appears to be that as children we learned to be responsible not <u>because</u> of the spankings and other punishment we received, but **in spite** of them. Almost certainly there were enough other ways in which we were taught to behave responsibly that we largely learned through those methods, not because we were punished for our errors.

That is, our parents, even though they likely did not realize it, employed other, more effective tools to teach us, from which we learned how to behave appropriately. We will discuss such tools a great deal as we continue.

Thus, given the conclusion that punishment – reported as encompassing most of what parents do for discipline – is just not very effective, we are confronted with the challenge to identify methods that **will** get the desired results. The rest of this book is devoted to just that purpose.

Chapter Eight

"But Doctor, what do we do when . . . our 11-year-old daughter says she has cleaned up her room but we think it is still way too messy?" Page 87

HOW CONSTRUCTIVE DISCIPLINE RISES ABOVE PUNISHMENT

We have learned that most parents report that they rely on punishment to discipline their children and that punishment is generally ineffective. This, then, poses a critical question for parents everywhere: What is an effective way to help children take appropriate responsibility for their own behavior?

The answer to that question involves a strategy for discipline with two equally important components, each discussed below.

Reducing Advantages of Inappropriate Behavior

The first half of our strategy, based on the above conclusions about punishment, requires *reducing the advantages to children of their inappropriate behavior.* That means not reacting to misbehavior so that children do not benefit from it.

Many alert parents immediately recognize, quite accurately, that this statement boils down to this:

> **To the extent possible, <u>ignore</u> behaviors you consider inappropriate.**

Your are not alone if you read that with apprehension or disbelief. Often parents' instincts tell them that if they dared to follow this guide, their kids would go wild. The reassuring thing is that those instincts are almost certainly correct; it is quite true that if parents <u>only</u> do this part, it will likely make things worse, even much worse, at least for a time.

An educational specialist was asked to observe in class a boy whose behavior distressed his teacher and his parents. He was described as a "class clown," constantly doing "cute" things that in the classroom caused problems, partly because other kids watched him and giggled at his antics. Between the referral and the consultant's arrival, the

45

teacher had decided that the child was behaving this way for attention from his classmates, and she decided to deal with that fact directly.

When the consultant arrived, she observed a surprising scene. The teacher was in front of the class with all of her pupils, except one, paying close attention to her. The little clown, on the other hand, was out of control, running around the room, crawling under desks, and making weird sounds. I never did learn what sort of magic the teacher used to keep the kids attending to her in the face of this behavior. But, not surprisingly, despite this success with the rest of the class, the class clown had the teacher quite distraught, and she was giving serious consideration to burning whatever book had suggested this approach.

At the risk of sounding like the Monday-morning quarterback, I must say that it was predictable that what happened would happen. It is likely that the teacher was exactly right in the notion that the child was being reinforced by the attention that he received from his classmates. However, her solution of simply removing the attention failed to consider a crucial aspect: a child working so hard for attention must have a strong need for it.

> If the child had been behaving in such fashion because of a desperate thirst, surely the teacher would not have withheld water while expecting a reduction in struggles to get the water.

Similarly, withholding attention from the class clown served directly to increase his need. In response, the child did what we should expect, in order to meet those needs: he intensified the behavior that had met his needs previously, namely his clowning.

In theory, what the teacher attempted *was* a possible solution to the problem. It is well known from research that if reinforcement of a behavior is discontinued, then eventually the behavior can be expected to "extinguish," that is, no longer occur. However, in a classroom full of active children, it would be impossible to assure that the child <u>never</u> was reinforced again. Even <u>occasional</u> attention, such as one child giggling, would be enough to keep the behavior going. As a result, attempting to extinguish the behavior would just frustrate the teacher and would impose a heavy burden on classmates expected to ignore the clown. Further, this approach would be very hard on the boy himself. He would have to live through a long unsuccessful struggle to meet his need for attention and to feel important to others, all the while being criticized for his misbehavior.

Fortunately it is not necessary to put any of the players through such a difficult sequence. What is needed, instead, is to understand that, while the teacher's approach had merit, it failed to provide the child with a workable alternative way to meet his needs. That is, she did not provide the child a way to gain attention without clowning around during class. Understanding how to deal with the missing part then becomes key and is covered here next.

As this example illustrates, it is important to recognize that ignoring inappropriate behavior, the first component of our strategy, is only one part of a successful overall approach to teaching children to be responsible for their own behavior.

The other part makes use of a tool not often mentioned by parents. It is seldom thought of as an aid to discipline and therefore is not used very effectively. It is a tool that many parents may use, but because they don't think about it as related to discipline, they are unlikely to get the fullest benefit from it. For now I will leave you to wonder about this magic tool, and come back to it from another angle.

Providing Advantages for Responsible Behavior

Developmental Factors

Let's back up a bit – well, quite a bit. Picture your child as a baby just a few days old. Several times every day your baby gets hungry, and, as babies do, cries. When you pop some milk in the baby's mouth, the crying stops, replaced by sucking. This very clear change in behavior, based on a natural, instinctual reaction, can be referred to – for lack of a better term – as **a response to "material" reinforcement**. While this is so natural that hardly anyone pays much attention to it, it is the very important first stage of a lifelong pattern of responding to "stuff," continuing later as responses to such things as cookies and, later yet, to pay checks.

Now picture the same baby, three or four months later. The baby gets hungry and cries, just as before. But typically by this time, when the baby spies mom hustling in, the crying stops, at least for a time, even before any food is provided. Often the crying is replaced by sucking motions, maybe accompanied by cooing and gooing and smiling and flailing of arms and legs. Now this may not last long, particularly if the baby is very hungry, unless food is provided. Nonetheless, this initial response, one not seen in the newborn, is the beginning of another important, lifelong pattern, **a response to social reinforcement**. Almost always at first the response is seen in reaction to mothers, but typically it generalizes, carried over, pretty quickly to others who are close at hand: fathers, siblings, grandparents. What is so fascinating about this development is that within a very few weeks after birth you were seeing a change in your child's behavior from innate and instinctual to learned. This provides solid evidence of the capacity of even such little ones to learn and equally solid evidence that parents have a significant and direct impact on the child's behavior. How exciting is that?

As we have seen, babies come into the world instinctually responsive to material reinforcement, and by a few weeks of age, they have learned to respond to social reinforcement. Those are two critical steps along the way to the third and final level, when the child **responds to internal reinforcement**. Interestingly, this can also be seen as the **goal** of parenting, the stage in which the child has learned to take responsibility for his own behavior. Said differently still, the child's responses become based on experience with the same or similar situations and with the previously received reinforcement.

It is more difficult early in life to identify a clear example of this third level. However, a couple illustrations may be useful in clarifying the idea.

Imagine a child about a year old who has not yet walked but who has pulled up and is standing while gripping a coffee table. The child spies a bright red shiny ball on the sofa just a couple steps away for a walking child but out of reach while the child just hangs on. In the normal course of things, the child would drop to all fours and crawl toward the object, likely losing track of it in the process and never reaching it. But the first time the child lets loose of the coffee table and takes those couple steps to reach the sofa and the ball, two wonderful things happen. First, the child reaches the ball, immediately achieving the *material reinforcement.* And second, if anyone is watching, suddenly the air is filled with squeals of delight, the ooh's and aah's of parents who are pleased with the child's first steps, and with calls to grandparents. This second part represents intense *social reinforcement*. And, with each new success, typically each time followed by material and social reinforcement, the child's proficiency in walking grows.

Now clearly there is a physiological maturational aspect of this process as well, but central to when and how well the child moves through the learning process is the payoff that accompanies the behavior. The impact is so powerful that a few weeks later the child will be motoring around so smoothly and confidently that it might be difficult to remember exactly how clumsy and tentative those first waddling attempts really were.

Another example has proven helpful to parents in our classes, this one admittedly a little weird to talk about. In addition, I can't even cite any proof that what I will describe is true. However, most parents seem able to relate to the ideas and to recognize the pattern in a way that clarifies what internalized reinforcement really is about.

Imagine a toddler who is well toilet-trained by two and a half or three years old. Then imagine asking the child, at age five or six, to wet his or her pants. (No, I haven't ever actually done this!) Chances are you couldn't get so much as a drop, even if you asked a bunch of such kids. The reason is that, by five or six, children who are well toilet trained by age three have so fully internalized their behavior that it is as if they are reinforcing themselves for using the toilet properly.

This odd example can be extended to the adult world:

I attended a conference with perhaps a thousand people crammed into a large meeting room. We all had breakfast before settling into the room, where each chair was arranged behind a narrow table containing tumblers and ice water. The room was stuffy and warm, the meeting long, and a lot of water was consumed. Within an hour or so a lot of people were squirming in their seats. The lucky few seated near aisles slipped out, gained some relief, and returned, but the vast majority sat in growing discomfort.

The remarkable thing is that probably no one in the room thought. "Gee, this is uncomfortable. I'm just gonna let it go!" (No, I didn't do a survey to prove this one either.) That is, hundreds of adults sat in considerable distress and likely not one considered that simple solution. This is the end result of the process described above, the internalization of reinforcement for relieving one's bladder only in certain places at the right times after receiving material and social reinforcement for just that restraint during toddler-hood.

The "Other Tool"

Earlier I referred to another "tool" that our parents likely used with us and that contributed to our learning to be responsible citizens, whether or not we were punished as well. Understanding that tool can help us understand how our parents accomplished what they did, probably without ever recognizing that what they were doing influenced our behavior so heavily.

It is likely that most of our parents, much of the time, responded positively – that is, made it good for us – when we did the appropriate things as we were growing up.

Typically an observer who reacts with delight to a one-year-old child who has just taken a first step fails to think about it as a teaching moment. In similar fashion, our parents likely demonstrated their pleasure at many of our constructive behaviors without thinking of it as "discipline." Fortunately, the benefit still applied, even without conscious recognition of what a valuable thing they were doing for us.

I have already discussed some of the potential negative effects of punishing children, even when parents intend it to teach more appropriate behavior. What is so very reassuring about understanding the natural developmental sequence of learning that occurs through material, social, and then internalized reinforcement of behavior is that parents impact their children in very positive ways, sometimes without even thinking about it.

More reassuring still: by **consciously thinking** about the processes involved and by arranging responses to children accordingly, parents have a great deal of power to teach their children to behave as the parents consider appropriate. In the process children learn to internalize those patterns of behavior so that they become their own. That is the basis for our approach:

> *Consistently responding to appropriate behaviors while consistently withholding response to inappropriate behaviors produces lasting, internal maturation in our children's behavior.*

With this groundwork laid, let us go on to define clearly the specific fundamental principle underlying these notions.

Chapter Nine

"But Doctor, what do I do when . . . I try to talk to a friend on the phone and both my kids start breaking rules so that I have to stop to deal with them?"

PRACTICE MAKES PERFECT . . . DOESN'T IT?!?

We all have grown up with the adage that "practice makes perfect" and usually accept it without question. As you strive to guide your children to responsible behavior, however, it is useful to think further about this notion. As will become clear in what follows, a more accurate statement would be that "practice makes permanent." Whether it is perfect depends entirely upon your point of view.

After so many pages devoted to developing background ideas, it seems a bit odd to announce that pretty much everything said so far is summarized neatly and powerfully in one simple statement, but that is, in fact, the case. The **Principle of Positive Reinforcement** – probably the most widely demonstrated and fully accepted principle in all of psychology and related disciplines – states that:

> **"Any** behavior which <u>occurs</u> and is followed by <u>reinforcement</u> is <u>more likely</u> to occur again."

I learned this principle early in graduate school and could quote it and many studies on which it was based. However, only when I began working with families using this approach did I fully appreciate the implications. That recognition has prompted me to emphasize the richness of this principle in hopes that you will have a more satisfying experience. As simple as the principle appears to be, to understand it fully there are several aspects that must be kept firmly in mind, reflected in the underlined words in the quotation.

First, note that the principle refers to <u>any</u> behavior, regardless of whether the behavior is appropriate and desirable or just the opposite. That is, the principle is neutral with respect to the type of behavior so that literally any behavior is covered.

You are talking to a friend on the telephone, fully engrossed in an enjoyable conversation so that you don't notice your little girl is across the room drawing crayon pictures on the wall. However, she is watching you, equally unaware that your responses have nothing to do with her and, hearing your laughter at your friend's comments, is reinforced for what is going on at the time.

Here, behavior that isn't even noticed by the parent is reinforced directly by the parent's unrelated reactions. But a similar impact can occur when you are aware, sometimes to your own dismay.

One day I discussed concerns about their son with parents while he explored my office, typical behavior for kids in a new setting. At one point the father made a particularly funny comment, at which all three adults laughed broadly, just as our attention was abruptly drawn by the sound of ripping paper. We all turned to the sound, still with smiles on our faces, to find the boy tearing a page from one of my favorite books. Despite ourselves, at that moment we directly, though absolutely unintentionally, reinforced the behavior of tearing pages out of books.

Actually, I have already anticipated the notion that "any" behavior can be affected by reinforcement in the earlier discussion of the frequent negative impacts of punishment. There I noted that punishment may reinforce a child's inappropriate behavior by giving a sense of control, attention, or other subtle benefit. Here we can clearly see that enough practice makes "permanent," but not necessarily "perfect!"

Since any (and all) behavior is subject to the principle, it is critical that parents avoid inadvertently reinforcing behaviors they consider inappropriate for their children. As it was expressed in Chapter Eight, **to the extent possible, <u>ignore</u> behavior you would like to eliminate.**

I will be discussing this issue and its application to child-rearing at length as I go along and in special detail in Chapter Thirteen.

Second, the behavior must actually <u>occur</u> for the principle to mean anything. To use a silly example, if you want to teach your child to fly around the room by flapping arms, the principle indicates that if it happens once and the child is reinforced, it will be more likely to occur again. Of course you can't get that to happen in the first place; thus it is irrelevant.

What is relevant, though, is the discouragement many parents feel about this point. Based on their experience that they can never get their children to do what they want, they are left wondering how this whole idea can help.

I won't attempt to address fully that issue right here, but please be assured it will be a central part of our discussion later on. For now it is enough to know that we have very effective tactics to help you achieve your goals. You will learn how to get your kids to do what you want them to do, and when that happens, you can rely on the principle of positive reinforcement to assure that the likelihood of their doing it more of the time will increase.

Third, what follows a child's behavior must be <u>reinforcing</u> from the <u>child's</u> viewpoint in order for a behavior to become more likely. For example, we might assume that offering a child a trip to Disneyland (to pull out one of the biggest rewards first) for some appropriate behavior would assure maximum compliance. However, it matters not a whit that all the adults in the world are sure that a particular thing will be rewarding to a child if the child isn't interested, and there are, for whatever reasons, children who are not interested in the Magic Kingdom.

The point here is that the selection of rewards is of great importance in the application of the Principle of Positive Reinforcement. In later pages you will find a detailed discussion of how best to handle this aspect.

Fourth, it is important to recognize that the principle refers to an <u>increased likelihood</u> of a behavior occurring again, once it is reinforced. That greater likelihood, however, does not mean that the behavior <u>will</u> occur again. Of course everyone knows this because if it weren't true, no one would need to make much effort to have any child behave properly all the time. But it is important to approach the rest of our discussion fully aware of this implication:

Changing behavior requires a sustained effort over some period of time to assure the behavior will continue to occur.

Thus, it is critically important to understand the "likelihood" notion. It can be helpful to consider the concept using a scale that depicts changes in the **likelihood** or probability that a behavior will occur, when the child receives additional reinforcement, like this:

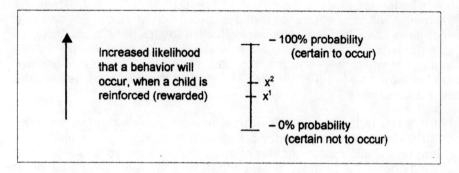

Probability of a behavior occurring increases with reinforcement

The line on the left indicates that the probability or likelihood that a behavior will occur increases with reinforcement. On the right, the scale ranges from certain <u>not</u> to occur (0 percent probability), to certain to occur (100 percent probability).

To illustrate the use of the scale in understanding the likelihood notion, suppose Johnny has taken the trash out a few times as instructed, but often he does not do it when and how he was told to. There is no good yardstick with which to measure – no certain way to determine – exactly where on the probability scale Johnny is with respect to taking the trash out. What is clear, though, is that he is somewhere above zero probability since he does it some of the time. And it is also clear that he is somewhere below 100 percent likelihood since he doesn't do it all the time. He does sometimes; he doesn't other times.

For convenience I have placed Johnny at "x^1" percent probability (the superscript "one" indicating it is where he started), as indicated on the scale, with no assumption about where on the scale his start actually lies. Now the principle of positive reinforcement tells us that if Johnny takes the trash out again sometime and that if he is reinforced – if he is given some reward he values – the probability will go up, by some amount, that he will do it again. This is indicated by "x^2" on the scale. Note that even though there is no way to know exactly how much change occurred, it is clear some did occur.

This change still does not mean he will ever do it again, but it does mean he is more likely to.

What is crucial to understand and is exciting to realize is that if his parents can arrange for Johnny to take the trash out enough times and reinforce him enough times, **it is virtually certain** that his behavior will reach the 100 percent likelihood of occurring. Said differently, the behavior will become internally reinforced, our goal.

Many times parents have told me that they "tried" a reward program of some sort – "chip system," "point system," "red card-green card system," or whatever – and "the program didn't work." When describing those experiences, parents typically told me that:

- They tried the approach for a time,
- The child seemed to do better,
- They relaxed and came to take the change for granted,
- They gradually lessened the frequency and certainty of the rewards, and
- The behavior reverted to whatever it had been previously – and sometimes even got worse.

What our simple probability chart illustrates is that we can expect exactly that sort of result for any parent who uses the approach but stops too soon. That is, increasing the probability that a child will do a certain thing as directed is important, but **the reinforcement must be continued until the child is operating on the basis of internalized reinforcement**. Otherwise the old behavior is likely to reappear once outside reinforcement is stopped.

As indicated earlier, there is no clear yardstick to tell us where on the scale a particular child is at any given moment for a particular behavior. Unfortunately it is also true that there is no gauge to tell us how many more steps – how many more reinforced times – it will take for a child to internalize reinforcement of a behavior. This is inconvenient, but in practice it turns out not to be a big deal. In Chapter Twenty-Two I will discuss effective steps for determining when a child no longer needs to be rewarded to carry out a specific behavior.

*In the final analysis it is not what you
do for your children but what you have
taught them to do for themselves that will
make them successful human beings.*

~Ann Landers

Chapter Ten

"But Doctor, what do we do when . . . our seven-year-old daughter stays in her room all the time because she is too shy to make friends and play with other kids?"

Page 90

REDUCING INAPPROPRIATE OR UNDESIRABLE BEHAVIORS

The Bad News

The Principle of Positive Reinforcement indicates that **any** behavior that has been reinforced enough times will become internalized. This may explain why many behaviors parents dislike in their kids keep occurring despite their efforts to stop them. The parents may very well have been inadvertently reinforcing that behavior over a period of time.

Parents who dislike whining often are seen giving in to their child because they really hate listening to the whining. By doing this they teach the child, over time, that whining works, no matter how often they have heard it condemned. The old adage that "actions speak louder than words" comes to mind here. What the parents do is stronger than what they say, and when the child meets important needs while whining, that is the lesson learned and upon which future behavior will be based.

Note that this dysfunctional interchange works both ways. When parents finally get fed up and give in to the whining, the resulting peace and quiet provide instant, strong reinforcement for the parents' response of giving in. As a result, the likelihood of giving in the next time also goes up. This powerful reality and the subtle nature of how it works explain how it is that parents tend to repeat their part in a pattern they deplore.

Consider the concept of "spoiling" children. Typically that word refers to children who fuss and whine to get their way from harried and discouraged parents. The negative label is almost always a criticism of the children, and other people choose not to be around them. Viewed in the light of this discussion, though, it seems more accurate to recognize that such children meet their needs using methods that pay off. These children have been reinforced enough times to have internalized behaviors that from outside seem inappropriate. From the child's perspective, the behavior "works" even though their unintentional rewards are accompanied by a good deal of pain and sadness from the negative reactions to their behavior. It seems neither accurate nor fair, then, to refer to the child caught in this

57

pattern as "spoiled." It seems even less so if you consider that the parents – the adults – participate in the pattern by meeting their needs in an equally undisciplined, if understandable, manner.

The observation that children may behave inappropriately due to inadvertent reinforcement highlights a significant problem. Once a behavior is truly internalized, it is very difficult to dislodge. In fact, psychologists, if they are fully candid, might acknowledge that we really don't know any consistently effective way directly to eliminate inappropriate behaviors that are fully established.

That is the bad news.

The Good News

The good news, on the other hand, is that through careful application of the Principle of Positive Reinforcement, it is possible to overcome this potential roadblock. We can do so by selectively focusing on behaviors which parents consider appropriate alternatives to those they consider inappropriate.

The effective way to approach undesirable behaviors that occur often, then, is to start by remembering the first component of our overall strategy: **to the extent possible, ignore behavior you would like to get rid of.** If this aspect is not faithfully followed, then even very careful attention to the rest is much less likely to be fully effective. And, as I have discussed earlier, if all that a parent does is ignore the inappropriate behavior, things are likely to become very difficult. The moral of the story is to incorporate and utilize both parts in an overall program carefully:

- The first component is to reduce advantages to kids of their inappropriate behavior so as not to provide them with a payoff for behavior parents consider inappropriate.

- The second component, then, requires identifying new behaviors to replace those to be eliminated and making it good for the child to do those things.

(I know I've already said that, but it is so crucial it bears frequent repeating.)

The ongoing challenge is to incorporate both aspects appropriately:

> *To reduce or eliminate an established inappropriate behavior,*
> *you must replace it with an alternative behavior that is both*:
>
> 1. **Desirable** *and*
>
> 2. **Directly incompatible with the undesirable behavior,** *a*
>   *behavior which,* when it is occurring, will prevent the other
>   behavior from occurring.

Efforts to deal with a boy struggling with adjustment at school provide
a very clear illustration of this concept. The teacher described him as
very disruptive. Sometimes, in his darting about, he even was mean
to the point of pulling the hair of a girl in the back of the classroom.

The teacher had tried the usual steps to correct the situation. She
kept the boy in at recess. She lectured him about staying at his desk
and paying attention. She had him write numerous times that he
would not misbehave. She sent him to the principal's office. She
called his parents to intervene. She moved his desk right next to hers
in the front of the room (of little benefit since he was rarely at his
desk). None of these steps helped, and the problem seemed to
increase.

Finally the teacher called in a school psychologist who unobtrusively
observed the child for a while and then took the child aside to talk with
him. When he left, the boy was sitting at his desk right next to the
teacher's where he mostly stayed during class from then on.

What was the reason for the change? Well, the specifics of what
happened are less dramatic than the story might demand. The
psychologist drew up and taped to the child's desk a simple chart on
which the child was to mark every ten minutes that he stayed seated
at his desk. The teacher was enlisted to monitor the checkmarks and
to initial that the child was recording accurately. And the parents were
asked to provide a material reward of some sort for a certain number
of checkmarks. All that is fairly straightforward.

What is missing from that description and matters most here is the
psychologist's reasoning process. What he asked himself was:

> "What is it that the teacher wants the child **to do** which is also
> **directly incompatible** with the behavior she wants him **not to
> do**?"

Clearly she wanted him **not** to run around the room causing problems, and particularly not to pull the hair on the girl sitting in the back of the room. What she **did want** was for him to sit at his desk, and clearly he could not run around the room and pull the hair of the girl in the back of the room while sitting at his desk. The behavioral program focused on the child sitting at his desk, for which he earned positive attention from teacher and parents, as well as a material reward from his parents. At the same time, it indirectly but effectively stopped him from wandering around and stopped his aggressive behavior elsewhere in the classroom.

I must point out that this simple but elegant solution has limitations. There is no guarantee that this boy will pay attention or even that he will stay quiet while sitting at his desk, though clearly the odds improved with his sitting within arm's length of the teacher, who also was serving as part of the reinforcement chain. A complete resolution of this situation likely would require considerable more effort and planning. Nonetheless, eliminating a major part of the problem was a great start – as the girl whose hair was no longer pulled would likely attest – and clearly demonstrated that the child was amenable to change with appropriately targeted reinforcement.

To summarize, success in reducing the boy's inappropriate behavior of running around the classroom and pulling his classmate's hair was achieved by actively reinforcing him for sitting at his desk where he could not perform the other behaviors. Pulling hair in the back of the room is **directly incompatible** with the desirable behavior of sitting at his desk in the front of the classroom.

Thus, direct attempts to get rid of inappropriate but already internalized behavior are not likely to be successful; thus any efforts in that direction are likely to be futile. However, directly reinforcing appropriate behaviors that also specifically prevent inappropriate behaviors provides a way to replace those inappropriate ones.

Taken together, the good news completely outweighs the bad.

Chapter Eleven

"But Doctor, what do we do when . . . we have to remind our 12-year-old son to take the trash out whenever he is supposed to?"

Page 97

PUTTING IT ALL TOGETHER: SUMMARY OF THE BASIC RATIONALE

Our stated goal is to help children learn to take adequate responsibility for their own behavior – appropriate to their levels of maturation – so that as they move from infancy toward adulthood they become more and more capable of handling the increased freedom and choice allowed them.

It is clear both from parents directly and from other research that the most commonly used tools of discipline – verbal reprimands, restrictions, and spanking – generally fail to change children's behavior over the long run. Further, it is clear that punishment is generally best at teaching what not to do, as compared to teaching what to do, and that even then any benefits tend not to last. Further still, it is clear that punishment often backfires by inadvertently providing children with gratification from attention and perhaps a sense of control or other more subtle benefits for their less appropriate behavior.

Based on these notions, our strategy involves two equally important components:

- First, parents must <u>reduce</u> the advantages to children of their inappropriate behaviors; put simply, they must, to the extent possible, **ignore inappropriate behavior**.

- Second, they must strive to **help children meet their important needs by a positive response to appropriate behaviors**.

And they will accomplish all this by:

- Consciously using the natural developmental progression over which parents have considerable control, **selectively providing material and social reinforcement for behaviors they choose to increase,** and

- Continuing to **selectively reinforce the appropriate behaviors long**

enough to assure their children have internalized reinforcement of their own appropriate behaviors.

In this discussion we have considered the nature and implications of the principle of positive reinforcement, that **any behavior that occurs and is followed by a reward is more likely to occur again.** And we have recognized and stressed that with sufficient reinforcement a behavior becomes internalized, no longer dependent upon external reward.

We also have noted that the principle applies equally to desirable and undesirable behaviors, the latter of which may be unintentionally reinforced to the point that direct efforts to eliminate them are unlikely to be effective. In response, we have considered an approach that focuses on increasing appropriate behaviors that are directly incompatible with those considered inappropriate as a way to replace, and thereby eliminate, the latter.

This provides the basis for the next section, which focuses on how these concepts can be systematically incorporated into a structured program for use in your home, providing you with a powerful way to enhance your children's capacities for responsible behavior.

Section Two

DEVELOPING A HOME PROGRAM

It is better to bind your children to you by a feeling of respect and by gentleness, than by fear.

~Terence

Chapter Twelve

"But Doctor, what do I do when . . . my two boys are bickering, and when I try to stop it, they blame each other and they each complain that I am unfair for talking to both of them?" Page 167

OVERVIEW OF THIS SECTION

So far I have discussed the principles underlying how kids learn to take responsibility for their own behavior. I have tried to be complete enough to provide any readers who do not read on with at least a better understanding of how they influence their kids' behavior and constructive ways to respond to them.

It is very difficult consistently to avoid reinforcing inappropriate behavior while rewarding appropriate behavior day after day. To help with this problem, this section provides support for applying those principles everyday in your home.

Now we turn to the practical applications of these principles: the steps and important details to keep in mind while developing a program you can use in your own home with your own children, taking into account your busy schedules. To give you a clear idea about where this discussion is going, here is a quick overview of the pieces that make up the program, each of which will be discussed separately in detail below:

First, you will learn how to think through and how to develop a detailed statement of behaviors you expect from your kids.

Second, you will learn to set up a system for providing your children with suitable benefits for fulfilling your expectations.

Third, you will learn to develop a set of procedures designed to keep the **focus on your children's more mature, growth-enhancing, desirable behaviors** to assure that:

- You and each child are clear about your expectations,

- You follow through accordingly, and

- You are consistent in your follow-through.

More specifically, to develop a home program for your children, you will

65

go through these steps:

- Writing down your expectations for each child in a set of positive statements, using the format:

  "(Your child's name) is successful when . . ."

- Setting up a way to provide suitable rewards by assigning appropriate "credits" (sometimes referred to as "tokens," "points," or "stars") for successful completion of tasks, for example:

  "Taking the trash out of every room in the house on time – 10 credits,"

  and by providing suitable choices of "material" rewards for which the credits can be exchanged, for example:

  "Playing catch with Mom for 15 minutes – 50 credits."

- Developing suitable **operating procedures**, which:

  - Are easy to understand and easy to carry out,

  - Use simple but clear charts for recording outcomes,

  - Set up times each day for review of progress,

  - Retain and monitor records to guide modification over time, and

  - Support follow-through with socially reinforcing successes when they occur.

Remember that this is just an overview of the process. I will go through each component carefully in detail. The goal is to assure that you gain mastery of each aspect so that you can both develop a program that is just right for you and your family and modify it as circumstances warrant.

Chapter Thirteen

"But Doctor, what do we do when . . . my wife says I am too hard on the kids and I think she is way too soft and doesn't expect enough from any of them?"

Page 220

STEP 1: SPECIFYING YOUR EXPECTATIONS TO YOUR CHILD

As noted, three steps are required to develop an effective home program. The first to specify exactly what you expect.

In order for your child to learn to behave responsibly, you must be very clear about your expectations. "Well," you say, "surely our child already knows since we have stated what we expect often enough!" I have no doubt that you have, but it is often the case that children are in fact confused. At different times parents may say things differently, or they may sometimes insist on compliance while other times they let things slide. Also sometimes kids really just don't understand, or they forget, or over time they confuse one set of rules with another. It is important to remove all such confusion to assure consistent follow-through and compliance. Both require very clear statements about your expectations.

There are two aspects of the task of specifying your expectations:

- The first (A) involves thinking through the areas on which you would like to focus your efforts.

- The second (B) involves carefully stating the expectations in terms that will assure kids comply and continue to mature.

These will be discussed in order.

A. Identifying Behaviors of Concern

To clarify your own expectations, start by considering what about your child's behavior concerns or bothers you. You likely will find that your child's tiresome or frustrating behaviors come to mind right away. Examples might be that the child whines for what is wanted, or pulls the cat's tail when it appears you aren't looking, or fails to complete assigned homework even while saying it is done.

Next, think whether you have noticed any behaviors that don't seem to work well for your child or that may interfere with the child's own comfort or happiness. Since this means trying to see the world as the child does, this may require a bit more thought and even conscious observations over a few days to be sure you tune in to such things. Examples could include a child with no friends who is excessively demanding or selfish with peers and a child who spends most of the time alone due to reluctance to go out to play with neighbor kids.

Consider what help your child might need to succeed, even if the area doesn't obviously interfere with the child's happiness. Examples here include a child with difficulty concentrating on homework so that it takes too much of the child's time, or one spending too much time watching television instead of playing actively and improving health and fitness.

It also could be useful to explain the program briefly and then ask your child for suggestions for things to include.

> Parents asked their eight-year-old daughter to suggest things she wanted help with. After a few minutes of thought, she asked if the program could help her make friends. The parents were astonished because they thought she had many friends, but they recognized her serious wish to feel better in this area. They found a way to build into the program an item focused on her concerns. The girl did very well on the program, perhaps in part because of her own motivation to have more friends.

To make this process easy and straightforward, use the worksheet called "Identifying Target Behaviors" which appears in Appendix 1. The top portion appears on the next page for reference during this discussion.

You will notice that the worksheet lists the typical portions of the day. In the sample here, you can see the portion dealing with "before school." Under each part of the day, I have listed some of the associated tasks, which in our sample includes items such as "getting up" and "getting dressed." Parents often have identified problems related to these tasks. The space to the right is provided to allow you to write in details about your concerns for your child. In the sample you can see a few behaviors that parents might wish to help their child change.

This form is meant only as a guide to your thinking. Not all parts will apply to you and your child. Feel free to add or ignore tasks. For example, for the first task, "Getting up," if your child typically stays in bed until you've yelled half a dozen times and you finally have to resort to dynamite, or the child gets up but has one shoe and the opposite sock on, you might indicate that on the form. On the other hand, if your child

Identifying Target Behaviors

Child's name _____ *Johnny* _____   *Date* ____ *July 9, 2005*

ISSUES IN CHILD'S BEHAVIOR	ISSUES IN CHILD'S BEHAVIOR
– Before school –	
Getting up	*Have to call him five or six times to get him up*
Getting dressed	
Cleaning up (hair, teeth, etc.)	
Eating breakfast	
Getting off to school	*Never has his backpack ready, so is always late*
Other (specify_Television____)	*Often is distracted by watching cartoons*

Sample of identified target behaviors for beginning of a child's day

handles the start of the day fine, just skip over that part and go on until you identify an area of some concern.

For each issue you think of, write a brief description next to the specific task, including when it occurs. For example, for "After school: coming home," one parent wrote "Often misses bus." Another wrote, "Forgets his lunch at least twice a week." Be sure to include each behavior as many places as it applies. One parent wrote, "Teases Bridget," including it before and after school. Use more paper as needed to be sure you have covered all your concerns.

When you look at the worksheet in the appendix, please note that in the introduction you are urged to be as thorough as you can be in this process. This is not so that you will suddenly become overly critical of your child. Rather, the idea here is to be sure that you identify all the possible candidates for items to include in your program so that you don't miss any. During review of their programs, parents frequently report things going well, except that what really bothered them wasn't on the list. Therefore they were dissatisfied with the whole thing. Let's be as sure as possible that you don't have the same experience.

Once you have completed going through the worksheet, there is a simple test (noted on the form as well) to determine if you have thought of everything that you might want to include in your home program. Simply ask yourself this:

> ***"If my child changes all of the things I've written down, will there still be significant problems?"***

69

If in response you find something leaping to mind (for example, "Oliver pulls the cat's tail whenever he doesn't get his way") which doesn't fit the precise format of the worksheet, then find somewhere to add this new issue to the list – even if it is just on the back of the page. Then ask yourself the test question again, repeating the cycle until you think of no more concerns. When you find yourself saying "Hallelujah!" (that is, "if we could change everything on the list, then there would be no more problems"), you can feel confident you have completed the list well. This should not be construed as a promise that you **will** fix every concern you might have identified, but rather as assurance that you now can focus your efforts to address those things that matter most to you.

At this point you deserve to feel pleased that you have done a complete job. You can feel confident that the next steps will be easier and more effective.

B. Defining Your Expectations for you Child

Now that you have a pretty complete list of behaviors of concern, the next step is to select the specific ones you will start working on. Simply go through your form item by item and select those that you consider to be most pressing or which you think will produce the most important benefits to the family. In doing this, pay attention to the rule of thumb in the box below.

> Plan on <u>a maximum of one item per year of your child's age</u>, with an upper limit of ten or so since more than ten seems to be too difficult to keep track of.

This means that for a five-year-old, five items is a good upper limit while for a twelve year old about ten would be enough to challenge most parents' organizational skills.

I should note that many authorities stress starting much more slowly than this, either focusing on only one item or perhaps on one behavior to increase and one to decrease. My experience questions this conservative notion, for two reasons:

First, parents who are very concerned about their kids' behavior often get discouraged when limited to too few items and may give up entirely, and

Second, Most children and their parents do fine with the number of items suggested by the rule of thumb, as long as they follow the guidelines provided here; thus there is no reason to risk such discouragement.

Once you are clear about which behaviors you will focus on, you are ready to define exactly what you mean for your child to do in each area. Our approach here is based on what directly influences behavior change in children. It is designed to make sure your child succeeds from the beginning. Therefore you should carefully define your target behaviors. What follows are the details to consider carefully as you develop your target behavior statements.

Assuring a Constructive Format

It turns out that even the way you word your statements has a substantial impact on progress in the program. In order to focus your efforts most effectively, start by developing a series of success statements using this format:

"(Your child's name) is successful when . . ."

But how do you write success statements to be sure that they are effective? The idea here is to focus on what you want the child to do, taking care to be absolutely clear. Both elements are discussed in detail below.

Characteristics of Well-worded Success Statements

Here are the three characteristics of well-worded, effective success statements, based on experience with the program. Each is discussed in turn below.

1. Expectations must be realistically reachable.

Assure that your expectations take into account such factors as your child's age, ability, and past successes.

A number of people have come into my office for consultation and said something like, "Dwayne and Latisha fight all the time." Well, experience has taught me that I'd better learn more about such a concern by asking what "all the time" means. In one family that might mean once or twice a week while in another it might be a hundred times a day. For the sake of this discussion, let's suppose Dwayne and Latisha hassle each other twenty times a day on the average. An item about this for Dwayne's program might say:

"Dwayne is successful when he doesn't fight with Latisha."

However, for most families, expecting children <u>never</u> to fight, as this wording implies, would not be realistic. An alternative could be:

"Dwayne is successful when he doesn't fight with Latisha for an hour"

This may be quite realistic for another child but perhaps still asking too much of Dwayne, who had bickered with Latisha twenty times a day – meaning typically well more than once each waking hour. The time frame may, in fact, have to be reduced to just a few minutes for one success at the beginning.

As discouraging as that might seem to busy parents, if they don't make the effort, chances are that they will continue to be dragged into the conflict many times a day to stop hassles with no improvement (and possible worsening because of their attention). However, if they start small enough to assure that the child can be successful in this program, they can work toward longer and longer periods without fighting.

Fortunately, parents' instincts tend to be very reliable with respect to their kids. If you ask yourself how long your child can be expected to do a certain thing, chances are you'll be pretty close with your answer – if you make a point to be realistic rather than wishful.

If, in our example, Dwayne's parents had first decided on an hour, they would need then to ask themselves if they could imagine the kids getting along for that long. If they find themselves thinking "No way," then they will need to adjust the expectations downward until they can say, "Yeah, we probably could do that."

This is solid guidance, but you probably recognized that this could be a very demanding thing to manage. Keeping track of every half hour, for example, could be pretty tedious and burdensome. There are ways with a simple timing device to reduce the burden, however, as this example demonstrates:

Imagine that you are busily working on your income taxes while your two kids are playing a board game across the room. In keeping with your program, you have told them that they are each successful for every half hour they play together nicely. You begin your work while trying to remember to reinforce the kids at a half hour if they have done okay. You know that if they don't, the hassles will catch your attention so you needn't worry about that side. As you get deeper into the paperwork, your mind only occasionally comes back to the kids, and you worry (and feel the stress) about remembering to notice the

72

time. Gradually the demands of the forms fill your attention entirely. A half hour comes and goes, as does 40 minutes, and you don't notice.

Finally at 45 minutes the kids begin to hassle, with one grabbing the other's "man" and refusing to put it back on the board, resulting in lots of shouting. The noise catches your attention, and you look at the clock. You realize that you goofed and then that you are in a dilemma. What do you do now? The kids earned their credits and your praise, but if you provide them right then, you will be reinforcing hassling with each other. That realization is likely to be accompanied by recognition that you failed to do your part, about which you feel guilty. Now, none of us likes that awful feeling; to avoid it, you concentrate on the kids' hassles and start telling yourself things like, "Darn it! Those kids are old enough to be able to get along! It's their fault we have to mess around with this dumb program, after all!" As a result your guilt turns to anger, and you lash out. Soon you decide the whole idea is a waste and not worth your time and effort and you at least consider dropping the program.

Fortunately, some simple preparation and the use of a timing device can avoid this discouraging scenario. A simple kitchen timer or an inexpensive wristwatch with a timer on it can be set to alert you when the set time has elapsed. You set it, get on with your business, and respond only when the timer alerts you.

In this example, when the timer goes off, you would go to the kids, praise their good play together, comment on the credits they had earned, reset the timer, and go back to what you were doing.

Both in this example and in general, the whole interchange when the timer rings is likely to take no more than a minute or so, freeing the parent to engage fully in other activities. The general point here is to find ways to minimize intrusions from the program and its demands. While this may seem to be a little thing, I have seen it make the difference between parents giving up and parents continuing a very effective program.

This illustration points to another solid **rule of thumb**:

It is important to set the goals for your child <u>as high as you can</u> (that is, don't greatly under-challenge kids), but <u>as low as you must</u> in order for the child to be successful <u>no less than about a third of the time</u>.

While this is a useful standard, in fact if you underestimate your child and success comes easily most of the time, you may find you are so pleased with the results that you won't mind that you are reinforcing more than might have been required. On the other hand, if you set the standards too high, you can take comfort in knowing that there will be plenty of opportunity to refine your expectations to assure success.

Time factors. One further consideration: most items in your program should include a time frame for success in order to assure there is no confusion about your expectations. An example of an item without clarity regarding time might be:

"Emma is successful when she has her homework done on time."

The vagueness in this statement would allow Emma to work on her assignment until midnight or even to leave for school with it incomplete with the intention of finishing it between classes. While this might be acceptable for some parents, probably most would find themselves quite uneasy with either alternative. This raises the likelihood that the parents would end up fussing at Emma to get her work done, risking, in the process, reinforcing procrastination by providing attention.

In order to avoid this, specifying an exact time is important. An improved statement for this example might be:

"Emma is successful when she has her homework completed for all classes by 8:00 p.m."

Note that this modification includes an element that requires comment. The time indicated does not say when Emma should *start* her work, but rather specifies a ***deadline for completion***. There are two reasons for stressing this distinction:

• **First**, knowing when something must be ***done*** allows the child to plan how to manage time and parental expectations.

  Consider an item requiring that Joshua have the lawn mowed by noon Saturday. Joshua knows as the weekend approaches that he must have the lawn mowed before he can engage in any planned afternoon activities. If he has things in mind to do Saturday morning, he might elect to mow Friday afternoon, since doing so would meet the deadline as well as let him keep his plans. Knowing what choices he has allows Joshua an appropriate level of control over his own life, providing a key experience for learning responsible behavior. Of course if the parents do not want the lawn mowed on Fridays, that aspect should be part of the statement of the item (e.g., "Joshua is successful when he mows the lawn Saturday morning and is done by noon.").

- **Second**, alternatives to specifying a deadline for a behavior are either to leave it up to the child (read that as "never") or to state when the behavior should start. Anyone who has told a reluctant child to "get started on your homework" is likely to have the experience of hours later sending the child to bed with the homework still undone. This approach invites stalling and procrastination in children inclined to push the limits. One reason for this is that it sets up a power struggle between parent and child, and typically children can "win" such struggles since it is relatively easy to "start" and still *not* actually to do things.

You will likely recognize that as important as specifying deadlines for successful completion of items is, adding a time factor can also add extra work for you in monitoring your child's behavior. However, some advanced thought and planning, taking into account your child's age, can minimize this extra effort.

For older kids, those capable of telling time, the timing process itself is typically fairly easy. It is a matter of clearly specifying the time frame for success and then noting whether the child has met the standards on time. A sample item might be:

"Joshua is successful when he has the lawn mowed by noon on Saturday."

For younger kids who can't tell time by a clock, it is important to choose a realistically short time frame and then to use a timing devise that will help the child keep track. A simple kitchen timer, for example, will serve this purpose. A suitable sample item might be:

"Samantha is successful when she has all her toys put away from the family room by the time the timer rings."

There are several things to consider here. At first, little ones are likely to ignore the timer, and it will be tempting for the parent to "remind" the child, maybe even repeatedly. While this is pretty natural, it provides the child attention for failing to do the task and keeps the responsibility on the parent, rather than teaching it to the child. Instead, show the child the timer the first time you use it and let the child see it run for the specified length of time before applying it to a behavior. Then reset it for the task at hand. Many young children see beating the clock as a game. Their successes provide an opportunity for rewarding them with both praise and credits, such as a token.

Be aware that some kids quickly learn that they can reset the timer and therefore think that they don't have to worry about time. The ideal way to avoid this fudging is to use a timer that can't be manipulated by a child. However, from a practical point of view, most of us won't have such a device. The easy alternative is to make it clear that the timer is there to help the child keep track of the time while you are using a clock or watch for the same purpose. Show the child how the two timers work the same. The first time or two, you will need to be sure that you actually watch the clock or, even better, that you set a separate timer of your own. The timer on a kitchen range or on some wrist watches will work just fine. The idea here is to make it clear from the outset that the clock is an objective monitor so the child's energy goes into completing the task, not into finding ways to manipulate things.

There is one other important aspect of defining time expectations for younger kids. When setting the criteria for success, it is important to consider about how long you think a task would typically take for your child, then set the time limit a bit longer than that – but not a lot longer. For instance, if your four-year-old girl is to pick up the toys from the family area, and you think it would take her four or five minutes to do it if she stuck to it, you might set the standard at eight minutes. If you are more generous, say setting it at 20 minutes, the child would be likely to lose track of the task long before that, and thus be less, rather than more, likely to succeed. Allowing a little extra time, on the other hand, might well increase the likelihood of success within quite appropriate limits.

All this is by way of assuring that your expectations are defined so that they are **realistically reachable** by the child and so that the conditions are supportive of success in meeting them.

2. Goal statements should be worded positively.

I have already discussed at length the importance of focusing on behaviors you do want, including those selected because they are incompatible with behaviors you don't want. This idea is so important that it warrants restatement as one of the prime characteristics of well-written success statements. Be aware also that it is very easy to allow negatives to slip into these statements and to be aware of ways to avoid this pattern.

An earlier example considered the item *"Dwayne is successful when he doesn't fight with Latisha."* That wording seemed to demand perfection and therefore was asking too much. To make the statement more realistic, the item was amended to read, *"Dwayne is successful when he doesn't fight with Latisha for an hour."*

While this change does respond to the need to be realistically reachable, it fails to focus on the desired behavior, instead addressing what is *not* wanted. Fortunately, it is pretty simple to fix this, perhaps with a statement like *"Dwayne is successful when he <u>gets along with Latisha for an hour,"</u>* intended to be both realistically reachable <u>and</u> positive

Remember: Focusing on a behavior that you wish to eliminate is likely to work against your intended goal by providing attention and perhaps a sense of control (that is, positive reinforcement) for continuing the very behavior you wish to be rid of. Think about the example presented earlier about the boy's pulling the hair of a classmate and the success achieved once the focus was on his sitting at his desk, after all the failures that came with the focus on stopping the hair pulling.

3. The criteria of success should be very clear

The goal in writing target behaviors should be that you will know and your child will know exactly what is expected. One benefit is showing your child there is nothing to be gained from haggling with you about whether or not your expectation has been met.

A mother told me that she and her son had developed a pattern of daily two-hour or more arguments about her son taking the trash out. At first I supposed she exaggerated; would anyone argue two hours about a two-minute task? She convinced me that it indeed did happen that way. At a certain time each day she would tell him to take the trash out, and he would say, "In a minute, Mom." A bit later she would tell him more sharply to "take the trash out." He would say something like, "But Mom, I'm in the middle of my favorite TV program." Still later she'd yell at him to get it out, and the conflict would continue to escalate.

This led me to wonder why anyone would waste 120 precious minutes to avoid a few minutes of work. All I could conclude was that after the first few minutes, the issue moved from getting the trash out to determining who was the boss or who was in charge. That is, the argument was not about the trash at all but really about who had what control.

It was sad to realize that nobody could win in this situation. If the mother gave up so her son didn't take the trash out, he saved a bit of effort. However by then he had wasted time when he could have been enjoying life, and he likely felt bad about the conflict with his mother. On the other hand, even if the boy finally took the trash out, the mother didn't really win. She could have done it easier herself, and she also was left feeling upset, like a poor mother, and overall miserable. How much better to return the focus to the simple behavior of taking the trash out and to the benefits to both mother and son when it is done!

Elements necessary to assure each item is clearly stated include **who, what, how much, by when, and how will you measure success**? (I might note that the same elements are included in many constructive human interactions, such as when skilled managers give assignments to their staffs.)

The idea here is to maintain focus and energy on the successful behaviors and in the process to eliminate bickering and badgering about whether the child was successful. Here is an example of an item with clear criteria:

"Alejandro is successful when he has the trash out of every room in the house by five o'clock on Tuesdays."

> **Who?** *"Alejandro . . . "*
> **What?** *". . . has the trash out . . . "*
> **How much?** *". . . from every room in the house . . . "*
> **By when?** *". . . by five o'clock on Tuesdays."*
> **How can we tell if the task is successfully completed?** By checking the trash cans and the clock.

In order for this – and pretty much any other approach to parenting – to succeed, it is essential that you mean exactly what you say. Thus, if the criteria include being done "by 5:00" and the child gets done at 5:10, I urge you <u>not</u> to accept that the task has been successfully completed. This is based on the certainty that if ten minutes late is okay today, the next night it is likely to be 20 minutes, and then 30, and so on. No matter how easy-going a parent is there is likely to come the time when the delays lead to frustration and an argument. At that point the child may, ever so innocently, ask, "Why the big deal?" since being late had been okay before. And the child would have a point: how can he or she know what you really expect if the expectations are fluid? The important thing here is to avoid teaching the child that it pays to fudge, badger, or negotiate, and you can readily accomplish this by meaning what you say – **this time and every time** – and by acting accordingly.

When You Cannot Meet All Three Characteristics

Unfortunately, it is not always possible to fulfill all three criteria of realistically reachable, positive, and clearly stated standards of behavior. Because of that, I would like to stress that

- It is <u>critical</u> that the goals be realistically reachable,

- It is <u>extremely important</u> that they be put in positive terms, and

- It is <u>very important</u> that the criteria of success be clear.

In the real world, however, it sometimes occurs that items cannot be both positive and absolutely clear.

> For example, as I pointed out previously, *"Dwayne is successful when he gets along with his sister"* is not likely to be a very realistic item. Adding the phrase *"for a half hour"* may make it more realistic; however, twelve reasonable people could have a dozen different notions about what it means to *"get along with"* his sister. Unfortunately, nearly any effort to define that phrase tightly is likely to rely on such notions as "doesn't hit," "doesn't tease," or "doesn't argue." In fact, I have challenged hundreds of parents in my classes to come up with a better way to define such an item and have yet to hear a good alternative. I am sure you will notice that each of these attempts to clarify focuses on exactly what the parent does <u>not</u> want the child to do.

Consistent with these concepts and based on the experience of a great many parents, I can offer this important guideline:

> When the criteria for success cannot be both positive and absolutely clear, **being positive is more important**.

Now, this is a clear-enough idea, but it leaves a potential flaw in the system. A bit ago I stressed the importance of setting things up to avoid arguing with kids about whether they have met your expectations. Having realistically reachable goals that are positive goes a long way toward this end, but vagueness in a statement can leave room for just such disagreements:

> *"I did too get along with him, but he was on my side of the car and he was making faces."*

I urge you <u>never to respond to or participate in haggling by your children</u>. Because this notion, as attractive as it is to most parents, is easier to say than to accomplish, some clear guidelines are needed to help you avoid such interactions. What follows is offered to assist you in avoiding this quagmire.

Some Guidelines for Dealing with this Dilemma

Getting ready for a positive interaction with your child

Often it isn't so easy to avoid haggling when kids push the limits. That means it is important to be ready to respond in a positive and constructive way that doesn't suck you back into haggling. It is true that sometimes you can't be both positive and define clear-cut criteria of success. We already have mentioned an example: *"Dwayne is successful when he gets along with his sister for an hour,"* since " . . . *gets along with . . ."* is not as clear as we would like.) The following guidelines should be kept clearly in mind for times such as these:

- First, remember that **you are the parent; therefore you decide success**, as fairly as you can. This is not a power play. You simply have a great deal more life experience to draw on in setting standards than your child does. This stance also avoids the potentially serious side-effects that can appear when children are in control of the adults in their lives – as discussed Chapter Six.

- Second, get comfortable with the notion that **you don't have to be perfect** in your judgments. Too often parents feel they must avoid ever being unfair to their children at almost any cost. Just as often, children learn that with enough fussing they are likely to be able to convince their parents that they are unfair and thus get them to give in. This is particularly likely to be a problem when parents can't put into words exactly why they feel their child's request should not be allowed. I think far more children have suffered from parents' unwillingness to make a firm decision than from being denied some special privilege, however dramatically they might complain at the time.

- Third, understand that **being decisive and meaning what you say is not the same as being cavalier about your child's feelings**. To show respect for your child as a person, it is important to <u>inform</u> your child as to <u>why</u> you made your decision, providing the opportunity to understand and to learn. For some kids this will end the discussion. For many others, however, this is likely to result in complaints or begging, requiring the next guideline.

- Fourth, **be prepared to respond constructively to continuing challenges** to your decision. As a general guideline, I suggest that you explain your decisions to your child a second time <u>only</u> if you genuinely feel you can improve on your first explanation; therefore it should be in the form of clarifying what you first said. This leads to a very solid and constructive **rule of thumb**:

> *Do not explain yourself to your child more than twice unless you have a very clear reason to think that after the next explanation your child will understand and accept your decision.*

Anytime that you find yourself continuing to respond to your child's fussing after a second attempt to explain your decision, there is a very good chance that you have moved from providing <u>information</u> to offering <u>justification</u> to your child. Accepting that you just justify yourself to your child amounts to agreeing that your decision counts <u>only</u> if you can convince your child that you are correct. That would surely put the child firmly in control. And when was the last time one of your repeated "explanations" to your fussing child led to a comment like, "Gee, Mom, now that you explain it like that I see why I shouldn't be able to stay up until 2:00 a.m. Golly you are smart! I should have realized!"?

- Fifth, since you know and I know that this very reasoned approach will not put off a great many children, you must **be ready for more fussing**. Here the idea is to respond as calmly as possible to convey this important message:

  "Well, Dwayne, I'm sorry if you don't understand, but I've explained the best I know how, and <u>that's just the way it is</u>."

While there may be many ways to say the same thing, this wording is actually very effective and avoids giving the child reason to think that there is still room for discussion. I recommend that you stick to this way of saying it, at least early in your experience with this approach.

In keeping with this, I urge you to avoid what some may see as very similar statements, such as *"Because I said so!"* or *"Because I'm the parent, that's why!"* Both of these reactions put the focus on you rather than on the decision, and so they amount to a challenge to engage in a battle for power. This is the opposite of our goal. To make sure the distinction is very clear, I suggest that you read the statement I have suggested aloud, along with *"Because I said so!"* and *"Because I'm the parent, that's why!"* and notice how different they sound.

Assuring a constructive interaction

Once you have conveyed the above to your child, avoid any further discussion. If the child fusses further, as many will, there are several ways you can terminate the interaction:

- **Leave the room yourself.** This is self-explanatory and may be quite effective in stopping a heated interchange between parent and child, as long as it is used with reason.

    A mother told me that she had been instructed by a previous therapist to lock herself in the bathroom whenever her son became too unruly and demanding. While I can imagine instances in which this might be required for safety, I'd hate to think of this as an ongoing solution. For a parent to deal with a child's challenging behavior by making herself a prisoner in her own bathroom hardly seems like the way to teach the child responsible behavior. It would clearly communicate to the child that he was in control, something to be avoided for all the reasons I have discussed previously.

    Of course, many children will follow their parents anywhere they go in order to continue such interactions; thus one of these other alternatives may be needed;

- **Remove the child from where you are.** Sending or taking a child to an area away from you can also be effective, if this can be managed constructively. However, sometimes it isn't possible to remove a really upset child. I will discuss in Chapter Eighteen how to accomplish this effectively with children who challenge the parent, a more complex process than can be included here;

- **"Turn off" to the child until the fussing stops.** In instances when neither moving away from the child nor removing the child from you is practical, there is another deceptively simple but often powerful way to disengage from the child. It involves carefully controlling your response to the child even in the face of persistent fussing.

    A woman with two very young kids and a baby told me her kids seemed constantly to be clamoring at her knees. This happened each day, particularly about the time she was busy cooking dinner before the father was due home. She felt she could not remove the kids from her nor could she leave them in the kitchen. In my own attempt to be helpful in this difficult situation, I hit upon the suggestion that inside her head she "turn herself off" to the kids.

Stop for a moment as you read this and notice all that is going on in your immediate environment. What do you hear? What do you smell? What does it feel like to sit as you are? How much had you noticed these things before? To pay attention to your reading, you had to ignore everything except this page, e.g., television sights and sounds, barking dogs, honking horns, and fussing children.

The point to this mother was that she did not need to attend to all the fussing going on while she was cooking. In fact, there is a rather gimmicky technique some parents find helps with "tuning out." To use it, as you tune out, imagine "turning yourself on to *robot*." That is, **imagine yourself a robot with all your own characteristics but, as a robot, without emotions.** With no emotions, you need not react to your child's fussing, so you are not tempted to fuss back or to otherwise pay attention to what your child is doing to get a reaction. As a robot, you can go about whatever you have to do without interacting with the child.

An additional note: little kids, in particular, took at faces to see how parents are reacting. I have had kids run completely around me, while I turned around in place, in order to check my reactions. This can be pretty comical, considering how quickly I can turn and how far that is for a little tyke to run. Given that observation, you can be more effective in turning off to your child by turning your face away. And when you can't turn away, you can keep your face blank. Note, though, that this is not about rejecting your child, but, rather, it is about ending an interaction which otherwise would reinforce inappropriate behavior.

"Turning off" to the child, to be effective, must be continued long enough for the child to recognize that there is nothing to gain by persisting and that, in fact, it is better just to go on to more interesting things. If the child continues to fuss and finally gets you to react, that reaction will reinforce the persistence, and you can expect your child to fuss even longer the next time.

The idea of all these approaches is to make it clear by your actions – which indeed do speak louder than words – that the discussion and the interaction are over.

Thus, consistent with our overall approach, all of this is about assuring that you do not reinforce inappropriate behavior. But it is also important to include the second component of our overall strategy, the final step that will complete this interaction successfully. A few minutes after things have calmed down, it's important to go to your child and reestablish contact. However tempted you may be to do so, this is not a time to lecture about cooperation or to otherwise comment on the previous interaction. Rather it is a time to show the child that your love and concern remain strong even though you did not give in to the haggling. The contact at this point should simply be warm and demonstrate that the previous hassles are over. A comment about something the child is doing, a pat on the head, or any simple warm gesture likely will be enough.

Keep clearly in mind that the goal of all this is to teach the child that it is in the child's best interests to put energy into successfully completing the task assigned, rather than attempting to manipulate you. In the process it also teaches the child how good it can feel to complete tasks responsibly, while reducing the fear of being too much in control of adults, the concern I have discussed several times in other contexts.

One additional note: it is crucial that you **use this approach only if you are confident that you will be able to persist** and stick with your decision to withhold responding to the child. If the child succeeds in wearing you down and can keep the haggling going, the lesson learned is likely to be that if a little fussing is not enough, then more might work. That's the stuff that major family conflict is made of.

To summarize, well-constructed target behaviors use the format *"(Your child's name) is successful when. . ."* and include **realistically reachable expectations** which are **put in positive terms** with **the criteria of success clearly defined**.

Sample Sets of Target Behavior Lists

Target behavior items for a sample home program suitable for a nine-year-old boy appear in the Figure on the next page.

There are several things to point out about the list:

1. The list includes nine items for this nine-year-old boy consistent with the rule of thumb of no more than one item per year of age.

2. However, you'll also note that Item 4 consists of three parts, all related to school. It is reasonable to consider this as one item for counting purposes since it does not add more things for the parents to keep track of. All items deal with the school card (discussed in detail below), which folds right into the rest of the program.Also note that, in order to make expectations very specific, Item 7 requires that trash is to be taken out on only three days of the week.

3. Item 5 specifies that staying friendly with Billy will be counted in 30-minute intervals, which means that the exact number of successes

```
┌─────────────────────────────────────────────────────────────┐
│                                                               │
│              Johnny Jones - nine years old                    │
│                                                               │
│  Johnny is successful when:                        Credits    │
│                                                               │
│   1. he is up, dressed, and done with breakfast by 7:30   10  │
│                                                               │
│   2. he is home from the bus by 2:45                      10  │
│                                                               │
│   3. he has his school clothes changed by 3:00             5  │
│                                                               │
│   4. he succeeds at school (see card completed by teacher):   │
│        a. he cooperates with teacher during reading period  5 │
│        b. he is friendly on the playground during recess    5 │
│        c. he turns in his math on time, at least 75 % correct 20│
│                                                               │
│   5. he stays friendly with Billy (per 30-minute interval)  5 │
│                                                               │
│   6. he plays outside with other kids (per 30-minute interval) 5│
│                                                               │
│   7. he has the trash out of every room in the house by 5:30  │
│         (Monday, Wednesday, and Friday)                     5 │
│                                                               │
│   8. he eats the dinner prepared for him within 20 minutes 15 │
│                                                               │
│   9. he is in bed and quiet:  by 8:30                      10  │
│                               by 9:00                       5 │
│                                                               │
└─────────────────────────────────────────────────────────────┘
```

Sample set of target behaviors for child of reading age

possible varies from day to day. Some days the kids' schedules may have them hardly cross paths, while other days, especially weekends, they may be together for many hours and so could earn lots more credits. That will be important to consider in determining the number of credits to be traded for specific rewards, discussed below.

4. Finally, Item 9 introduces another wrinkle: these parents really preferred Johnny to be in bed at 8:30 but know that he often really likes to stay up until 9:00, for example to complete a TV program. Because their preference isn't too strong, they elected simply to make it better for Johnny to get to bed earlier by providing more points for doing so. Of course if they really wanted him in bed at 8:30 each night, they would not include this variation, included here simply to

show how versatile the program can be. I will discuss other aspects of "Johnny's" program later.

Because target behaviors for children younger than reading age tend to look somewhat different, though generally the same in overall structure, I have included a sample listing for a five-year-old girl in the box below.

Sally Smith - five years old

Sally is successful when: Tokens

1. she is completely dressed by the time the timer rings (15 minutes)   1

2. she plays quietly in the family room while the baby sleeps
   (per 30-minute interval)   1

3. she stays at the table and eats all the food from her plate
   by the time the timer rings - 20 minutes (per meal)   1

4. she has all the toys put away in the family room
   before the timer rings (10 minutes)   1

5. she cheerfully does an extra task assigned by Mommy or Daddy   2

Sample set of target behaviors for pre-reading age child

One obvious difference in this listing is that it refers to "tokens" instead of "credits" the child can earn, recognizing that younger kids do better with something more concrete. Another difference is evident in that only one or two tokens are offered since younger kids tend not to comprehend bigger numbers. A couple other items merit comment:

- Item 3 indicates, in parentheses, that Sally can earn a token for each meal. As with Johnny's school items, this behavior is counted as only one item even though it likely occurs at least three times during the day. This can be done because it is not particularly more challenging to the child and it does not add much to the parents' tasks of monitoring the program.

- Item 5 represents a departure from all the other illustrations in that it does not, in itself, identify a specific behavior. It is included here to show another way in which the program can be tweaked to meet specific parents' needs. In this case, it actually amounts to a kind of bonus – or miscellaneous – category that might be written by parents with a child who in many aspects of the day tends to be whiney or otherwise uncooperative. It allows each parent to specify instances in which the child can succeed by doing in a cheerful manner what is assigned to her.

It must be stressed that such an item places considerable demand on the parents. Each time they give the child a special assignment they must <u>clearly</u> present <u>realistic expectations</u> in <u>positive</u> terms, all that while also maintaining their usual monitoring. As a result, such an addition to a program should be undertaken sparingly, and, even then, probably used rather infrequently during the course of a week.

Some Illustrative Examples

While I hope that what I have written so far has been clear and useful, I also know that some of the concepts and ideas will seem rather vague and that their full richness may not show. To flesh them out better, here are discussions of some questions from parents about writing target behaviors. They are presented here with just enough alterations to assure privacy for those involved.

Our 11-year-old daughter has a very messy room, and whenever we check it, she says it's clean but we think it is still too messy. What do we do about that?

This kind of disagreement shows up in many families and can be the cause of a great deal of conflict. Kids tend to see it as about their rights and freedoms, while parents see it as about their standards for their homes, as well as about what they want to teach their children. Your main challenge when building your home program is in tightening your definition of a "clean room." The key is to include whatever standards you use to determine when the room is cleaned up.

Since your daughter typically fails to meet your standards, make sure that each item is realistically reachable. Be sure to consider both her actual abilities and her history of actually doing such tasks. If she never does the job as you expect, then you may need to break it into parts and provide reinforcement for each part. Consider dividing your current item into separate items addressing things such as hanging up her clothes, putting away her toys, making her bed, vacuuming the floor, or whatever fits your situation. Each item should make it very clear how you'll judge her success. Each item also should have its own deadline to assure that it stays separate from the others. Smaller tasks are much more likely to be completed. Splitting items will require that you monitor the progress more closely to assure you provide praise and credits for each completed task.

When you have completed refining your items, you should be clear enough that there is no longer room for dispute about whether the room is messy or not. It will be clear from the items and the appearance of the room. That doesn't mean your daughter won't attempt to continue the haggling, however, because she likely was getting some satisfaction from it. Your job at this point will be to inform her of any incomplete items and what you see that makes you consider them undone and then to disengage so that you do not perpetuate the haggling.

We have our program working pretty well, but what is still bugging me is that I can't talk on the phone without both kids acting up. Any ideas about how to handle this?

Lots of mothers express this concern. Typically kids who act up this way have somehow learned that they can get mom to react if they do their thing during phone conversations. Some may actually feel envy for the attention mom gives to the other person on the phone. Whatever the cause, though, the approach to dealing with it can be pretty much the same. Start by defining a success behavior for each child, something like:

> *"Susie is successful when she stays quiet and calm for X minutes while Mom is on the phone."*

Note that "X" here just stands for the number of minutes you judge as realistic to expect your child to be able to comply. Once the item is added to the program, what remains is for you to provide your child the assigned credits for each X minutes that she is successful. If a phone call goes on longer than X minutes, excuse yourself briefly, go to your child, praise her behavior, and provide her with earned credits, or at least tell her they will be put on the chart. Of course this may be inconvenient in the beginning, but over time it will teach your child to tolerate longer periods while you are on the phone.

One other point: many conversations may end in less than the specified number of minutes, technically not allowing the child to succeed fully. I suggest that you treat any such time as a success if your child is aware you are on the phone and it lasts more than a minute. That way the child may have lots of successes to build on, and she won't feel cheated that the conversation stopped too early for her to benefit after trying to remain quiet.

Our two sons, seven-year-old Austin and nine-year-old Hunter, constantly pick at each other. It's hard to figure out how to write an item that will stop it. We doubt the program can help with something that has been going on for years. Any ideas?

88

Concern about kids bickering is among the most common I hear from parents. I initially had misgivings about how to deal with this in a positive way. It is hard to define what you want without listing all the things kids should not do, It turns out, though, that many parents report success in this area. As discussed at length elsewhere, the item may be as simple as:

"Hunter is successful when he gets along with Austin for X minutes."

A similar item would be included in Austin's chart. The biggest challenge may be defining how many minutes would be reasonable to start with, but your instincts are likely to be good at deciding what is realistically reachable for each child. The rest of the job is one of assuring that you monitor success and provide the specified praise and credits for each success.

At first I was unclear about why so many parents reported good outcomes with this approach since *"gets along with"* isn't very clear – something I discussed at some length in Chapter Thirteen. Over time I came to see that it might work so well because there appear to be three circumstances under which kids will succeed, and only one in which they will not:

- If Hunter really wants to succeed, even if Austin is in a mood not to care, chances are any bickering will fizzle since it really does take two to tangle.

- Similarly, if Austin wants to succeed, even if Hunter doesn't care, any fussing will likely stop because Austin won't participate.

- And, of course, if both want to succeed, things will go fine.

Therefore, only if both boys happen at the same time to have no concern about earning their credits will bickering between them continue. Three out of four represents pretty good odds.

Keep in mind that when the bickering goes beyond what is acceptable to you, it is a good time for you to intervene in the manner discussed in detail in Section Three. In doing so, though, it is important to separate the kids enough that they can't keep the hassles going by taunting each other.

You should know that even kids who fight all the time typically like being together; thus separating them often provides extra incentive for them to calm themselves. If you make it clear that being together is a privilege achieved only through behaving appropriately toward each other, many kids will change their styles, though maybe only after testing the limits a few times.

We have an eleven-year-old and a six-year-old. The older one is always picking on the younger one. Then she gets upset when we punish her and says her sister is pestering her all the time. How can we deal with this problem?

Much of what I said in the previous question applies here, though the sizable age difference may make it less likely that the older girl actually does want to be around the younger, at least frequently. A girl her age really does need time with her age-mates, away from her sister who is so much younger and who has such different interests and skills.

Be sure you have included age-appropriate and realistically reachable target behaviors in the girls' charts to deal with the problem. Once that is done, take time to observe carefully what really goes on between the girls. When an older child picks on a younger one, often the younger has learned to retaliate against the older until getting a reaction. When the older reacts negatively, the younger screams and that brings parental help. Sometimes the younger can be seen snickering to the older out of parental view. That enrages the older child, who feels victimized by the younger child. That rage, in turn, makes the older child all the more resentful of the young one's pestering; therefore the next reaction can be triggered by even a little pestering. This sort of vicious cycle can take over family life with the parents increasingly annoyed at the older child, whose distress and need for positive attention grows and grows.

If there is any chance of such a pattern in your home, you will need to make changes to stop the cycle. One big part of that is to be sure each child is clear about what positive behaviors will win your attention and praise. The other part is to remove the kids from each other (discussed in Section Three) if they continue bickering after you have told them to stop – without your blaming one or the other. It also is important to act calmly and without emotion.

Our seven-year-old daughter is very shy and seems to have no self-esteem, especially at school. How can we help her feel better about herself?

There are two parts to this question, one about shyness and the other about self-esteem. Sometimes these two are linked, but not always, so I will discuss them separately.

As I have discussed elsewhere, generally self-esteem is directly connected to an individual's own experience of her capacity to deal effectively with the world around her. Because of that, the more successes your daughter has, the better she will feel about herself. Because that is true, the home program provides a very straightforward way for you to define age-appropriate responsibilities. Then when she is successful, you can provide honest praise and material benefits for her successes as evidence to her of her abilities. Over time – often not all that much time – a child with reasonable success is likely to begin seeing herself in a new, more positive light. Central to this is that the child can see that her parents are basing their praise on real behaviors, not just on their wish to be supportive (which many kids discount because "you have to say that").

For some kids who appear shy, seeing themselves succeed will increase their confidence, and they will interact more capably, and therefore they may no longer seem shy.

Still, shyness can be a very big burden for some kids, and it is important to recognize that some kids seem to be shy by nature. Some may never become outgoing no matter how much effort parents make to change that. Since some shy kids seem to be happy and to get along fine, it is a good idea to observe your child carefully over a period of time to see if her shyness itself is causing her unhappiness. Sometimes parents who were themselves shy suppose their kids are as sad about it as they remember being, and they may work extra hard to overcome something that may not be as big a deal for their children. In fact, the parents' extra effort in this regard could backfire because all the fussing about shyness could convince the child there really is something wrong. Watching and listening for evidence of how the child is doing may be a help in deciding how much attention to give to this issue – though it can be difficult to be sure even after careful observation.

Fortunately, one of the strengths of the home program approach is that parents don't have to know with certainty where kids stand on such things. When the program is designed carefully and with due respect for the child and the child's individual needs, it is possible to encourage without burdening the child. That is, the program can provide the invitation to manage a behavior in a different way and an incentive for doing so without unduly pushing the child.

With those ideas in mind, if you wish to increase your child's interactions with other kids, you can encourage it by including it in your program. Take care to assure that what you are asking is realistically reachable, that is, basing each step on what you have observed in your child's past behavior. An example of a first-step target behavior item for a child who appears to have few or no peer interactions might be:

"Amy is successful when she learns the name of one of her classmates."

For a child who seems to know her classmates and the neighbor kids but seems to spend all her time alone, an item might be something like:

"Destiny is successful when she plays with Monica for 15 minutes the next time she and her mother come to visit."

Later on, or maybe sooner for a child who seems to be ready, this sort of item may be appropriate:

"Briana is successful when she invites one of the neighbor kids over to play."

Of course the actual item must start where the child is and add a small challenge to encourage going a bit beyond her usual. You can decide on the basis of what you have seen the child do, as well as on your sense about what things she seems capable of doing even if she seems reluctant.

You likely noted that several times here I used the word "encourage." Because of the way these programs are structured, the child has the choice of whether to complete each task. Unlike more traditional reactions, in this approach we do not give the child a hard time for failing to complete the task. Rather, we attempt to make it good for the child to succeed. In the case of a shy child learning that it can be okay to interact with others, we can lay out the expectation, carefully defined, based on what seems realistic. The child, then, can elect to comply and thereby earn your praise and credits toward a tangible reward or not to comply with no negative consequence. Because of this, you need not be so concerned that you are pushing the child beyond her limits. Of course if the child never completes the item as defined, you will need to reconsider the level of expectation, lowering it to be more realistic or, perhaps, upping the number of credits the child can earn for succeeding. If after all of this you remain concerned, I'd suggest you discuss the situation with your child's physician or with a mental health professional.

My 11-year-old son moves as slowly as he can whenever we tell him to hurry up. We tell him over and over that he causes us to be late and also how much better his life would be if he'd move faster so that he has time to do other things he likes, but we aren't getting anywhere. Ideas?

You have described an almost classic example of a child controlling his parents by dawdling. It appears he get lots of attention and a sense of control by causing you to repeat "over and over" how he inconveniences you. While your reaction surely is understandable, it almost certainly is self-defeating because it reinforces the very behaviors you dislike.

The remedy is to go to the basics of the home program. Define success behaviors to address your concerns. In doing so, make sure that you include realistic but clearly defined deadlines for each part. Your description suggests that you will have to start by accepting a fairly low level of progress for each item, a fact that you may find discouraging. However, if you can assist your son in completing even one part of the sequence required to get you on your way at the time you need to, you can build on that to a second part, and so on. Then be sure to withhold reaction to his stalling behaviors. I hope you will find that some progress, however small, is more encouraging than it is to stay in a pattern that is likely otherwise to go on and on or even get worse. I also am concerned about the potential implications of the boy having this much control over adults, and I suggest you reread the discussion of control issues in Chapter Six.

Our kids, aged three and five, are very picky about what they eat, so I end up preparing different things for each of them. How can the program help me out of this bind?

Getting kids to eat what parents want them to is a problem that appears to be growing and may contribute to the alarming increases in childhood obesity. In my experience, it is not terribly difficult to modify eating habits in kids up to age 11 or 12. After that age, it becomes more difficult because by then many kids have convinced themselves that certain foods are so terrible that they resist even tasting them. This means you can expect greater success in overcoming hassles about food in younger kids; thus you are starting at a good time. Fortunately, many parents have reported good results with this approach.

The first step is to define the target behavior. A good starting point might be to include an item in your program, such as:

"Jordan is successful when he stays at the table and eats all the food on his plate within X minutes (or, for younger children, " . . . *by the time the timer rings)."*

Of course you should include specific details that fit your family's style. I suggest you set time limits based on the typical time it takes other family members to eat. While it is common to talk of the "meal hour," families rarely use that long. It is reasonable to expect your child to eat within the same time-frame that you all use unless you happen to be folks who really wolf down your food. If your child often dawdles over meals, it will be important to avoid letting this become a power struggle. Your goal should be to assure that your child learns to fit into the family's routine. Therefore, set your standard based on how your family functions overall and work to reinforce your child for meeting that standard.

Once you have the behavior expectation defined to suit you, the rest has to do with how you manage meal time. I will discuss each aspect separately.

- One aspect of the target behavior is *"stays at the table,"* which for some kids is no issue since they already do that part. However, if your child typically leaves the table and wanders back later to eat some more, I urge you to tell the child ahead of time exactly how things will work before you start using this item in the program.

The message should very clearly state that in your family you stay at the table during meals, and that when you leave the table, the meal is over for you. I'll come to the implications of that in a minute.

- Another aspect of the item is *"eats all the food on his plate,"* which may be easy for some kids. For many others, though, they are inclined to complain about what you serve, to the point that some mothers, as you describe, find themselves serving as short-order cooks in their own homes. That seems utterly unfair to the cook. But however willing you might be to follow that path, it cannot be in your child's best interest to be so picky and demanding. Among other things it can raise the specter of the child's feeling in control, with all the dark potential discussed above. Further, it is not good for a child to come to feel deserving of exactly whatever is wanted whenever it is wanted since that style will be impossible to maintain at school or in other interactions away from home.

In order to handle this with a child who is regularly used to having specially catered meals, I suggest you start by stressing to the child the new way things will work in your family. Next, carefully plan the first meals you will serve using the program. In order to assure the task of cleaning the plate is realistically reachable for your child, plan to combine some of his favorite food with small amounts of foods you want to serve but that has led to resistance in the past. For example:

Suppose your child likes only macaroni and cheese and hates vegetables, fruit, milk and other nutritious foods. For the first meal on the program, you might put a modest amount of macaroni and cheese on the child's plate, along with no more than two or three green beans and a slice of apple, and serve them with just a little glass of milk. The idea here is not only to make the first step relatively easy but also to assure that the child cannot satisfy hunger by eating only the favored food. Let him know that he can have more of what he wants if he succeeds with the first amount you provide, so that he need not go hungry.

Note that our target behavior stresses that the child is successful when he *"eats all the food on his plate."* Considering the extent of eating problems in our society, this requirement deserves further comment. The idea here is not to force kids to eat too much – or too little – to meet their health needs. Instead, our goal is to teach children to participate more naturally in family meals. Good eating habits depend upon learning to attend to our own body's needs so that we eat the right amounts of nutritious foods. If we grow up associating mealtime and eating with power struggles or the belief that we can only tolerate junk foods, we aren't likely to develop healthy ideas about food and its role in our lives. To assure you are helping your kids to a lifetime free of struggle about food, I encourage a matter-of-fact focus on eating to live and not on power struggles.

- The third component of the target behavior is to **assure the meal is eaten within the time limit**. To make this clear to the child, set the timer or point out on the clock how long he has to be done and then have the family continue with eating as usual. Stifle any urge to prod the child to hurry so you don't reinforce dawdling.

- Finally, make sure your child understands the way things will be working from now on.

  Remind your child that he must stay at the table for the entire meal and that leaving means the child's meal is over.

  Remind your child that success means a clean plate within the time limit and that, when done, the child may have more of anything you served. This does not mean the child can demand any other type of food.

If you serve dessert to your family, your child would be eligible for a share if the regular meal is completed and there is still time for sweets within the time limit you set. This, of course, would not be the case if the child left the table early or did not eat all the food on the plate within the time limit. This way of handling dessert makes it like the rest of the meal; anything other than the original food on the child's plate is available only if the first serving is completed. This avoids the risk of making dessert a direct reward for eating, a connection which may play a role in some childhood obesity.

Another point: to provide the child with the best chance of success, all family members should be expected to stay at the table and to eat all the food on their plates, and each should fill his plate accordingly. The one exception for most families would be the cook, who in many families has occasion during meals to jump up to get things. This special role should be explained in simple terms to the child with focus on how the cook benefits everyone by those efforts.

So far so good. If the child eats the food provided within the time limit, your job will be to provide reinforcement for the success by praising and by commenting on the credits earned for being successful. Avoid lectures about how the child should have learned this long ago. Additional comments to others at the table, if any, about how pleasant it is to have the child there and eating so well might add to the reinforcement value of the experience. And if the child requests more of food he likes, he will be further rewarded by the food itself.

This is the basic outline. At the next meal, use the same idea, but gradually add a bit more of the foods you would like the child to eat. Over a matter of a few days broaden the range of things you add to the point that eventually you serve the child the same food in the same way that other family members get theirs. Depending on the child, this could take a good while. Be patient and do not push too fast. Once the child gets used to eating what is presented in a reasonable time, you may notice that the choice of specific foods seems less and less important.

But what do you do if your child complains and leaves the table? The answer is already mostly defined for you: the meal for that child is over. Once the child is gone, remove the plate from the table and meet any complaints by calmly repeating that once the child left the table his meal was over. Likely the child will look greatly pained and complain of being hungry – maybe even starving – and you can respectfully repeat that food will be available at the next meal of the day. You are likely to hear a good deal of fussing, and it is very important that you not participate. Start by telling (not asking) the child to leave the room. If there is resistance and continued complaining, this is a good time to remove the child from the room in the manner discussed in detail in Section Three, coming up soon.

You may find yourself feeling very mean at this point and feeling sure that your child will suffer from hunger. You may be tempted to provide some snacks along the way to the next meal. If you do that, you will have become an "enabler" of the very behavior that you set out to eliminate, that of picky eating. While it may seem mean to withhold food, there are very few children in our part of the world who will suffer any real harm if they miss whatever part of a meal they don't eat in this situation. Exceptions may be appropriate for children with diabetes or acid reflux. For their parents, a discussion of the problem with the child's physician is in order. Pickiness about food for such kids can be serious enough to complicate things, but that also makes solving this problem all the more important. Almost any other child will survive if they don't eat a whole meal. Far better a day or two with a little hunger than ongoing battles about eating, potentially the seeds for all sorts of long-term difficulties.

Typically parents who follow these steps in a calm and non-punitive fashion find that their children rapidly learn that it is in their best interests to eat as their parents expect. Success leads to improved nutrition and family interactions. It also helps prepare kids for eating with people who may not serve macaroni and cheese for every meal. And with these experiences kids gain confidence for meeting the social world on equal terms.

Luis is getting the trash out on time now, but we are getting tired of always having to remind him that the deadline is almost there. How can we get him to do it on his own?

While it is understandable that you want to assist your son, if Luis is able to read and tell time, he has the basic skills to fulfill his own responsibilities. In fact, reminding him prior to the deadline for completing the task means that you are not allowing him the opportunity to succeed – or fail – on his own.

I suggest that you change your tactics. Start by telling Luis that you are no longer going to remind him and that he is responsible to get the trash out on his own and on time. Since he has had your reminders as a crutch in the past, he may not succeed the first time on his own. If that happens, go to him very soon after the deadline and tell him that since he missed the deadline, he no longer has a choice about when to do it. Then instruct him to *"take the trash out now."* If he protests, help him to his feet and guide him through the process, providing as much supervision as necessary to get the trash out. That will help him understand that it is his responsibility and therefore he may as well do it correctly and by the deadline so that he can earn his credits.

We get so tired of our kid telling us every day how unfair we are for making him do so many chores since none of his friends have to do any. What can we do to stop this?

Lots of kids complain about how mean their parents are for giving them so many chores while their friends get a free ride. Perhaps it is the friends who are mistreated, however, if they really have no chores. First, they are not getting the chance to contribute to their family's well-being, and second, they are not learning to see themselves as responsible people. Both of those omissions leave big holes in these children's preparation for taking a place in our society. My guess is that most parents, when they think about it, will agree with that sentiment.

So, how can you deal with a child who has a different idea of what you should expect of him and who is all too ready to say so? The start of a constructive response is to accept the child's feelings, which you can express something like:

> *"Well, Thomas, I can understand you may not like the idea of having chores to do. . ."*

Of course accepting the feeling is not the same as agreeing that your child should not have to do any chores and that you are an ogre for expecting him to. It is a good idea to say so by continuing the above remark:

> *". . . but in our family we work together to get things done. Each of us has things to do. We know you are able to do your part for our family and it is our job to help you get used to doing it. We understand that it is kind of hard for you to get yourself started on your chores. We have made our home program to help you. You will earn credits for finishing chores, and you can trade them for rewards."*

It might even be useful to acknowledge the rest of the complaint so that he doesn't suppose you missed his powerful logic, perhaps something like this:

> *"We are sorry if your friends' parents don't feel they should teach your friends to help their families. We think it is important for you to learn such responsibilities, just as we did when we were growing up. We will continue to teach you the things we think are important so you will grow up to be the responsible person we know you can be."*

After that, avoid further discussion so that you don't risk reinforcing complaining and stalling. You really don't have to listen to complaints after you have dealt with them. In fact, if the complaints continue, you could use the techniques described in Section Three to give the child time to regain his control.

Chapter Fourteen

"But Doctor, what do we do when . . . people tell us that we should reward our kids for things they are supposed to do anyway, and we both think that's just a fancy way to say we should bribe our kids?"

Page 215

STEP 2. MAKING IT GOOD FOR YOUR CHILD TO DO AS YOU EXPECT

So far I have discussed telling your child what you expect, which may not seem very different from what you have always done. However, I have highlighted the overriding importance of **clearly defining realistically reachable expectations based on what you do want your child to do.**

Your next challenge is to make it good – provide reinforcement -- for your child to comply with your expectations. Theoretically, you could follow your child around all day and every time something on your list is successfully completed you could pat the child, smile warmly, and provide some reward. In practice, however, this is not even possible since you can't be with them all day. Beyond this, it would not be good for your child always to be immediately reinforced. One of the important aspects of maturation is learning to delay gratification, a fact that neatly fits with the practical demands of any reinforcement program.

Since you can't reward kids instantly, how can you have an effective system that maintains the vital power of rewards? In addition to considering what will be effective with your child, you also should be sure that you consider your own time and other family resources. Our way to deal with both aspects is through a system of "credits," to which I have alluded several times already. You child can "earn" credits for successful completion of each task. For example, when Brittany has her room suitably cleaned by noon on Saturdays, she earns 10 credits. Over the course of the day, she can earn as many credits as are included on her target behavior list.

So far so good, but what child is eager to earn a bunch of "credits," whatever they are? Of course not many are interested – until they understand what "credits" are good for. To assure they are "good for" something meaningful, you must allow kids to trade their credits for opportunities or things that are important to them. This idea will be familiar since it is the same system that gets adults to go to their jobs. In their careers they engage in work, earn "credits" toward wages, and at the end of the pay period they receive paychecks which they can spend (just another word for "trade") for things they want.

The home program requires that you decide the relative importance of each target behavior, assign credit values for each behavior accordingly, and provide meaningful reward choices. Each of these three tasks is discussed below.

Decide the Relative Importance of Each Target Behavior

The first task is to determine the relative importance of each item on the target behavior list. That is, the parents need to decide what completion of a particular behavior is "worth." There are two different views to consider here:

The parent's perspective

Consider how important each item is from your perspective. For every parent, there are likely to be items on the target behavior list that are of considerable importance, and there may be others that are of interest but as compelling.

> For instance, for a family living in a high crime area, an item such as *"Aaron is successful when he is in the house within five minutes of being dropped off at the bus stop"* may be considered critical for the parents. For the same family an item such as *"Aaron is successful when he has all his toys picked up from the family room by 8:00 p.m."* may be desirable but not nearly so critical.

If your program includes items of varying importance, weigh how much each matters to you.

The child's perspective

Not surprisingly, the other consideration here is how much effort and commitment each item requires from the child. As with parents, some tasks may seem like a big deal while others may not, so also consider your child's reactions.

> For example, it may take only a few minutes to complete an item such as *"Nicolas is successful when he cleans the backyard of all dog waste by noon on Saturday."* However, he may find doing it to be so repugnant that he will need considerable reinforcement to get it done.

On the other hand, it might take a long time and significant effort to complete an item such as *"Nicolas is successful when he has the entire back yard mowed by noon on Saturday."* However, if he actually enjoys mowing but is slow to get started, he may not need so much support.

A program considering the child's views of each task, and reinforcing accordingly, will be a good deal more effective than one that treats all tasks as pretty much the same.

Assign Credit Values for Each Target Behavior

Once you have determined which items you care most about and which items make the biggest demands on your child, your next step is to weigh all such factors and to assign credits to each task. To some extent, this involves using your best instincts to determine what level of reinforcement it will take for your child to be successful on each item as well as for the program as a whole.

Here your child's skill levels matter. It is best to assign credits differently for children to ages six or seven, who can't yet read or do math well, from the way you assign credits for those who can.

For the older group

For children who can read adequately, plan on assigning about 100 points to cover all the tasks expected on a typical day. There is nothing magical about this number, but older kids seem to work harder for larger numbers of credits. The number 100 is easy to work with while larger numbers can become cumbersome and smaller ones may not have as much impact. Use your decisions about the relative importance of each item and assign credits accordingly with numbers ranging perhaps from five points for the easiest and/or least critical items to 20 or more for those that you consider really vital.

Once you are satisfied with the credits you have assigned to each item, add them up to see what a typical day could total. If it comes out at 85 or 120 or whatever, there is no reason to worry about it; the 100 is just a rough starting point. The total you have for your program simply provides a basis for determining how many credits you will require the child to trade for select rewards as discussed in detail below.

You may not be able to determine the exact number of credits your child can achieve on a given day because of variations in when the items apply. For instance, an item stressing kids getting along with each other for half an hour could be counted a few times on a week day and many more on a weekend. None of this will cause a big problem since the exact number of credits your child can earn does not matter a lot. You just need an overall sense of how many credits can be achieved and therefore what level of rewards you will need to provide.

For the younger group

Since younger children do not understand numbers so well, plan to assign one credit for most behaviors and give two only for behaviors that are especially important. Typically kids beyond three or so will understand that two is more than one; therefore any item worth two credits will catch the child's attention and provide extra incentive.

Since the word "credit" won't mean much to younger kids, it is helpful to provide something more concrete, a "token" of some sort. At our home we happened to have some old plastic poker chips which we found very easy to use and keep track of. We cut slots in the plastic snap-on lids of old coffee cans, making them into token banks which our sons could manage themselves. Other choices could be buttons or even small pieces of paper cut out just for this purpose. The only concern is to assure that the child does not have unearned access to a supply of whatever you use. Generally making use of coins such as pennies is not a very good idea. For young children, avoid small objects that could be a swallowed.

Keep track of tokens earned on a chart (discussed below) since little guys are prone to lose things and ought not to be penalized in the program for doing so.

Provide Meaningful Reward Choices

Now that you have assigned a credit value for each item, your next task is to make your child want to earn "credits" (or "tokens"). Imagine that each day at your work, you were rewarded with useless credits; chances are that you would not continue doing your best to earn those rewards. Like you, kids need real incentives to keep up their efforts.

It is simple to attach value to earned credits. Just develop a "catalog" of rewards your child can choose from by trading in credits. Here are some key steps in developing the catalog.

Consider what your child cares about

The most important step is to be sure that your child is interested in the reward choices offered. We parents might all agree that a trip to Disneyland would be a great choice (yes, Southern California and

102

Florida parents might actually include this on their lists). However, if the specific child has no interest in Disneyland, then it won't matter what parents think. Given this reality, how do you develop a suitable list? The simple first step is to explain to the child in general terms how the program will work, saying something like:

"We want things to work better in our family. From now on we will not get after you all the time to get things done. Instead, we will use a new program that lists what we expect you to do, as well as when and how. It also shows how many credits you can earn for each thing you do as assigned. And it lists rewards you can trade your credits for. The idea of this program is to help you take responsibility for these things on your own.

*"We have worked out the list of things you are to do and the list of credits you can earn for each thing. But we want to be sure the reward choices are ones that really interest you. What would you like us to **consider** putting on a list of rewards you can choose from?"*

Note that the phrase "to consider" is emphasized. This is so both you and your child understand that <u>you</u> will decide what actually ends up on the list. Your child is free to suggest any reward at all, but <u>you</u> will decide whether or not to include it.

In making the decision about whether to include possible items on your list, consider the discussion below.

Consider what you can afford

If any possible rewards cost money, agree to them only if you think they will fit comfortably within your family budget.

A father described his son to me as "out of control," and he was afraid the boy might end up in serious trouble. The parents developed a home program for this boy. They included as a reward choice renting a motor boat and fishing with dad. The boy did well and in due time earned enough credits for this reward. One Saturday they went off to the lake. Upon arrival, the father discovered the price of the boat and motor was much more than he expected and more than he thought it was worth. He suggested that they fish from shore and use the savings later for a deep-sea fishing trip. His son agreed and they fished from the bank.

The following Monday morning the father called to tell me what a stupid program I had set them up with. Later in the office he was still upset and repeated that fishing together "was supposed to make things better, not worse," He said that the day had ended unremarkably, but the next day the boy had become sassy and testy. By that evening, he seemed to the father much as he had before we began. And Monday morning the boy had refused to go to school.

In private the boy told me that he felt cheated when they didn't rent the boat as the reward list said. He agreed to fish from shore, but watching other kids zooming around the lake in boats, some of them even getting to steer, was just too disappointing, and he felt the contract was broken.

My point here is not that the father should agree to something that he didn't feel he could afford but rather that he should be prepared to provide whatever he agreed to. Similarly, it is important that you avoid agreeing to a reward even if you can afford it if you are likely to resent actually providing it.

Note that this program does not require parents to be rich. I have worked with people who had no money for extras like toys but who still had very effective programs. How this can be done will become clear as we go along.

I urge you to be realistic about what you agree to, no matter how generous you want to be or how desperately you want your child to do better. If you get to the point that the child has earned credits for a reward that you can't provide because you can't pay for it, you can expect the child to feel cheated. This would be much the same as you might feel on payday if your employer told you the company couldn't afford to pay you. So, choose things that fit your family finances with the full confidence that you will make the program work using your choices.

Consider your time limitations

Along with finances, time constraints may limit some reward choices; therefore agree only to rewards that you clearly will have time to provide. Even things from a store have to be purchased. If your schedule is so busy that you can't arrange shopping within the time limits defined in your reward list, your child will feel cheated. Not only is a child who feels cheated unlikely to be fun to live with, but also you will have undermined the effectiveness of a program that, handled properly, offers powerful support for your efforts to develop a responsible child.

Consider your family values

Along with resource limitations, consider whether a requested reward fits your value system. Sometimes parents are so concerned about correcting their child's difficult behavior that they may agree to things that they really don't want for their child. Be sure that any reward you agree to fits your standards. Then you will be able to reward your child's successes joyfully.

Worried parents agreed to their 12-year-old son's request to go to a particularly raunchy R-rated movie that "all my friends got to go." They may have supposed he never would do well enough to earn the required credits, but he did. By that time, he was behaving responsibly in so many areas that the parents were no longer frantic, and they could see things more clearly. That left them in a quandary. They wanted to honor the agreement with their child but could not accept their son's seeing the movie. Fortunately, negotiations during a family therapy session led to an agreement. The parents, in effect, bought out the boy's contract with a number of pretty grand substitute rewards.

The moral of the story: don't violate your own values!

Consider constraints on delivering rewards

Some rewards may not be so easy to deliver exactly when the child reaches enough credits to deserve them. It is important to plan ahead about such items by including a time frame or other limit directly in the listing of the reward choice. Then the child will know ahead of time that choosing a specific reward might involve some delay or other potential disappointment.

Natasha has earned enough credits to select Disneyland from her reward list. Unless told otherwise, she might well suppose the family will leave for the park the moment she earns enough credits – even at 8:00 o'clock on a school night. With such an expectation, waiting until morning might seem really unfair, and waiting to the weekend, or even waiting for weeks, might result in feeling downright cheated. To avoid this, the reward list should say something like: *"A trip to Disneyland within a month of achieving xxx credits."* A child unable not tolerate such a delay would never choose it. This is far better than setting the child up for disappointment rather than reinforcement.

Consider special time together

As stated earlier, do not agree to rewards unless are sure you have time to provide them. Be aware, though, that among the most potent rewards you can offer your child is special time with family, especially parents.

Parents whose kids have caused them a great deal of distress often doubt those kids would ever work for special time with them. That feeling is understandable, especially in families with frequent parent-child conflict. In each case, however, I urge all parents to consider adding at least a few items involving special time with family. Some simple sample rewards:

"A half hour playing catch with Mom," or
"15 minutes with Dad, reading a book selected by Josephine," or
"A family cookout at the park."

Most parents who follow through despite any misgivings find that their kids frequently choose such rewards. This is true even for kids who typically have refused to do things with mom or dad in the past. I think there may be two reasons for this:

- The program tends to change the emotional climate in the home so that warmer feelings come easier.

- Spending time with parents appears to feel significantly different for a child who clearly has earned the choice to do so. In a sense, the child is even able to command the interaction in that trading earned credits includes that right.

Keep in mind that the worst that can happen if you include some such reward choices is that your child will not select one, not a problem since having the choice is what matters.

Consider how to keep your child interested

When you build your reward list, it is important that your child always finds something on the list that is enticing. To assure success in this aspect, I suggest a **rule of thumb:**

Include at least five reward choices on your reinforcement list, ranging from some requiring only a rather small number of credits to some grander ones requiring a larger number of credits, to assure the child always has something of interest to work toward.

Consider a ten-year-old boy who loves baseball. He is on a reinforcement system, earning credits that he is saving for the baseball glove that he has been wanting for some time. It is September and playoffs are in the air, and he is eager to reach his goal. But, he hasn't quite earned enough credits for the glove when the World Series occurs and then is over. Suddenly interest in baseball is nearly gone.

If this boy's reward list were limited to the glove, he might well lose interest in the program. However, with several other enticing rewards to choose from, he may shift his focus to a fall sport such as football and not miss a beat in his progress toward becoming a more responsible child.

Among the five or more choices of rewards, it is important that you include items that can be attained with a day or so of modest successes. Other items should provide incentive for sustained effort. Choices for younger children should include some that can be selected fairly soon after the responsible behavior occurs. But even kids as old as 12 or 13 can be so dubious about the reward system that they also may need more immediate gratification for a time to keep interested. Some seem to need to trade in their credits daily for a time before they can consider working longer for a bigger reward. What matters is not how grand the reward or how long the child works for it, but rather that the child stays interested and continues to complete the expected behaviors. Remember that every time the behavior occurs and is reinforced, it is more likely to happen again and is on its way to becoming an internalized behavior.

Consider differences for younger kids

Children from three or so years of age to six or seven will understand the connection between their behavior and the rewards only if the reward comes soon after the behavior. That means that they will need evidence of benefits for their efforts almost immediately while older kids soon learn the association between behavior and reward, and hours or even days can pass between their acts and the associated rewards.

A simple and inexpensive "grab bag" works well as a reward with lots of younger kids. The parent select several small toys or other objects such as party favors from toy stores. One item is placed in each of several small paper bags and stored together in a larger bag or basket. When the child elects to trade in credits for a grab bag, then a big part of the reward is the chance to select a bag and to have the toy to use at will. What seems to make this work well is not the object itself but, rather, the surprise aspect.

Sample Sets of Reinforcement Lists

To illustrate how a reward list for a child in the older group might look, the box on the next page provides a sample designed for our mythical

```
Johnny Jones - nine years old

Johnny can trade his tokens for:                          Credits

1. Chance to choose special dessert for dinner              100

2. 25 cents (15 cents to spend and 10 cents to save)        200

3. Trip to the beach (on weekend)                           350

4. Family outing to get ice cream (within a week)           500

5. One night overnight at friend's house                   1000

6. New baseball glove                                      1500

7. Fishing trip to a local lake with Dad (within a month)  2000

8. New snorkel and fins                                    3000
```

Sample home program reward list for nine-year-old

nine-year-old Johnny Jones. The specific reward choices are of no importance, other than to show what some parents have included in their lists. What should be useful, though, is the overall structure – a set of several items and the "cost" in credits to earn each, with items ranging from easy to earn all the way to choices that would require a good deal of sustained effort.

Also note that several items include clauses that define further what the child can expect should he elect to trade credits for a certain item. For example, Item 7 states that the father has a month to deliver on the fishing trip; however, it would be best if he would plan ahead so that Johnny would have as little delay as possible to strengthen the **reward value** of the choice.

Your own reward list will likely look quite different but should still include the elements reflected in this sample.

To illustrate how a reward list for a **younger child** might look, the next box provides another sample, this one for a five-year-old girl. There is

```
┌─────────────────────────────────────────────────────────┐
│              Sally Smith - five years old               │
│                                                         │
│ Sally can trade her tokens for:              Tokens     │
│                                                         │
│ 1. one stick of sugar-free gum                  5       │
│                                                         │
│ 2. an ice cream cone                           10       │
│                                                         │
│ 3. playing a game with Mommy or Daddy (for 15 minutes)  20 │
│                                                         │
│ 4. a grab bag toy                              30       │
│                                                         │
│ 5. going out for ice cream                     50       │
│                                                         │
│ 6. a special toy approved by Mommy or Daddy    100      │
└─────────────────────────────────────────────────────────┘
```

Sample home program reward list for a five-year-old

little difference in the nature of this list from lists for older kids, other than the use of tokens instead of credits. The parents, of course, will determine the content, considering the specific interests of the child. Later, I will discuss a simple way to help a young child understand how the "cost" for each reward relates to the amount of tokens earned.

Some Illustrative Examples

For most families, arranging the reward side of a home program is pretty straightforward. However, there are a number of concerns that can arise that aren't so obvious. To assure you have support in thinking through any complications in your own family, I have included a number of real-life illustrative examples of issues focused primarily on the reward side.

We developed a program and started it, but our eight-year-old daughter just isn't interested enough in any rewards to make it work. What can we do?

A child who appears disinterested in any incentives that you can think of can present a real challenge to parents. Kids do vary widely in how interested they are in choices and opportunities, from those eager for anything new, to those who seem content with a few of the same old things. Your key will be to observe what your child's interests are and how she spends her time. Then think about what you might offer that fits with what you observed.

Generally each of us has a "price" that reflects what is important enough to get us to do things. As one painful example, people even go to war and put themselves in harm's way to protect what they hold dear. Therefore the challenge is in determining what those things are that we value most.

Imagine that you are chatting with colleagues during your coffee break when a recruiter comes to your group asking for people to work on a job for her company. All the workers building a skyscraper downtown have just quit to work overseas. The project is in a crucial stage and the company is offering top pay. Several of your group express interest. But when the recruiter mentions that the job is to rivet steel girders on the 30th story of the structure, interest wanes. The recruiter senses that and states that the pay will be $50 an hour with time-and-a-half for overtime. Some of the group groans at passing this up, but none is willing to take the job. Again the recruiter senses the mood and ups the offer to $100 an hour. Would you be willing to take on the job of riveting girders far above the ground? Is there any amount of pay that would entice you to do so? Clearly answers will vary from some people quite ready to take the job and others not willing to take the job at any level of pay.

I actually have presented this little fantasy to many parent classes and found that typically if the promised pay went high enough, there would be one or more parents who would be willing to accept the job. At the same time, it was also clear that there isn't enough pay in the world to get others to consider such a job. There are two points to be made from this.

- There are some things that we are unwilling to undertake no matter what the incentive is. To cement that point in, almost none of us willingly or intentionally seriously would endanger other human beings for any amount of incentive.

- Other than for extreme things that are too dangerous, too frightening, or too much in violation of our values, most of us will attempt most things if enough incentive is provided. For example, a girl who "can't wake up" mornings for school is offered a trip to Disneyland if she is ready to leave on time. You can pretty well bet that most such kids would be sitting in the car before the sun comes up.

Thus, the challenge is to determine what will be of enough interest that your child will exert effort to achieve it. Despite the expectations of many parents, most children will work especially hard for time with parents, particularly if they are allowed to specify the activities. Of course parents must set some limits on the choices, but even within those, most kids will find choices that interest them. If you are unsure what to offer and your daughter will not make any suggestions, you might try to include on your reward list something like this:

"Planning a Sunday outing for the family (within two weeks). You can plan for up to three hours for an activity that must take place within a 30-mile drive from home and it can't cost more than $20 for all of us to participate. Also, Mom and Dad must approve the plan at least a day ahead of time."

Of course you should insert your own standards. It appears that for kids who respond to this sort of item it is the idea of being allowed to make plans for the whole family that seems compelling, and I know of a number of families who found their kids eager to trade credits for such a choice.

If none of these ideas solves your concerns, I encourage you to keep looking for alternatives for a time. However, if you cannot hit upon something to interest your child, she could actually be depressed, and I encourage you to seek a professional assessment to find out if that could be the case. If so, she may require some other treatment before she is able to participate fully in your home program.

Our kids like going on outings with Mom or Dad, but we don't know how to handle it when one wants to trade credits for such a reward and the others either don't have the credits or don't want to use them that way.

This circumstance is rich in opportunities and choices, depending upon your family style, values, and such. Among your choices are these:

- Allow for kids to pool their credits in order to achieve a family outing. In this alternative, you let each child contribute credits so that the total adds up to whatever you have set as the required number. This can be very effective if all kids are interested in a particular reward, but it will be important to consider potential hassles. For example, does each child have to contribute an equal number of credits, or might one who wants it more or sooner be able to agree to a larger share? Also, might an older child try to influence a younger one unduly to use credits for something the older one wants more than the younger, and if so, how will you handle this? These questions should be answered ahead of time to avoid a new battleground, but if you can work them out, this can be a viable resolution.

- Specify on the reward list that this choice is available only if and when each child has earned enough credits and agrees to use them for that way. This can work, but it also can be a bit dicey. It could set up all sorts of conflicts or disappointments. The good side could be kids learning to negotiate and cooperate. The down side could be added family hassles as one child presses for the others to agree. Also, any child with no interest in the reward, would in effect, have veto power. That situation could cause enough resentment to make the item negative and not a reward at all.

- Treat each reward choice individually so that when a child earns and selects a reward, you provide it regardless of whether the other kids have a similar interest. This choice can work fine and may add the special aspect of time alone with one or both parents, but it also can mean added expense and time for the parents.

- Make it clear that if credits are traded in for a particular outing, the child is, in fact, electing to treat the whole family. This would mean including such a provision in your definition of the specific reward choice, something like this:

    "Hosting a family trip to Ben and Jerry's for ice cream (within a week)."

This alternative makes it clear to the child that choosing to use credits this way amounts to a decision to share. Clearly for some kids this represents a major negative, and they would never choose this alternative. However, some kids see such an item not as having to share, but as getting to, thus the use of the word "hosting." It appears that some kids like feeling they can treat everyone. Sometimes this leaves parents astonished because they had seen their child as too selfish to share. Perhaps being able to host gratified a sense of importance that the child otherwise did not feel.

Keep in mind that none of your children may ever select this choice. You should accept this as no bigger deal than any other reward that is never selected. That is, don't feel hurt if the child selects other rewards and not those involving time with family.

The main idea here is that you make sure that the reward choices you offer to your kids are ones you have the time and other resources to provide and then that you consider what will be the most rewarding way to handle these things for your own family. There is no right or wrong answer, except that whatever is acceptable to you and contributes to the kids' interests in meeting your expectation is right for you.

We follow your program idea, but wouldn't it be a lot easier just to give our son a certain amount of money for each thing on the list, rather than fooling around with credits?

There are advocates of teaching children through behavioral approaches who would agree with the thought behind your question. And I can see how it could be somewhat easier to manage some aspects of a home program by just providing money to your child for each success. However, I also can see a number of drawbacks.

Our society has become commercialized enough that the true values of many things often are badly distorted. Halloween, once a time for clever homemade costumes, now involves elaborate decorations and factory-made costumes. Weddings often seem to be measured by the costs. Even how loved the deceased was is sometimes judged by the cost of the casket. In such a world it seems a good idea to keep rewards for your children clearly focused on their effort and not the slippery meanings of the monetary world.

Further, because money is so universal, kids have access to it from a variety of sources, such as birthday gifts or even finding it. Adding such money to the results of their efforts in the program would tend to obscure their progress and likely would undermine the effectiveness of your efforts to teach how beneficial those efforts really are. If a child can find as much money in the sofa as can be earned by concerted effort over days through the program, it will be difficult to make the program attractive to the child.

Money also can be used in so many different ways that it could become quite difficult to associate the money earned by responsible behavior with what the money buys. In the process, the vital association between the effort and the material reward might well be confused or lost entirely.

I have discussed another issue several times already. Time with parents is a powerful incentive for children. You could define such a reward and assign a monetary cost to it, but it seems a bit crass to have a child trade 50 cents for 15 minutes of playing catch with mom or dad. Even if you are comfortable with that, the mingling of money from the program and other sources to achieve the reward could undermine the effectiveness of the program.   I recommend that you maintain the clear connection between your child's efforts and special time with you.

For all these reasons, I suggest you adopt a "credit-"based system which will preserve the integrity of the entire program. And I think you are likely to find rather quickly that doing so is quite simple and straightforward and will not be a burden at all.

This program sure is different from the way I was raised, but I'm

willing to give it a good try. What I can't accept, though, is the
money thing. I don't mind spending time with my kids when they do
well, but paying the kids to do things that they should do really
bothers me. What do you think?

This question addresses the issue discussed in the one just above, only from the opposite point of view. I said above that there are reasons not to include money as a choice of rewards. However, if you look at the sample program on page 101, you'll note that one of the reward choices is *"25 cents (15 cents to spend and 10 cents to save) – 100 credits."* I included this because parents sometimes ask how to incorporate monetary rewards into the overall program. This item was included to assure money would not be the only choice. I added the clause about saving part of it to limit further the monetary aspect.

My point here is that you can construct a very effective program without compromising your comfort about "the money thing." Many of the most powerful rewards relate to privileges, especially those which involve special time with family.

To be sure that I have addressed all of your concerns, I should make one more comment. You mentioned your discomfort with paying your children to "do things they should," and of course in some sense of the phrase, the entire program involves "paying" (with credits, not money) for things parents think their children "should" do. In part this approach is based on the observation that the way the wider world operates overall is that responsible behavior (for example, "work") results in benefit (for example, "pay"). If you can see things in that light, you may accept that there is nothing inappropriate in rewarding children as part of teaching them to be responsible.

We have two kids. One gets most things done easily and the other
always dawdles and fails. How can we be fair if we reward the
second for things the other does anyway?

Many families have one child who learns responsibility easily and another who requires extra effort. This challenges parents to meet the needs of each without being unfair to either. It can be even more complicated when parents feel they must treat each child exactly the same, regardless of their differences.

A woman with identical eleven-year-old twin daughters came to see me. She struggled to treat them equally all the time and felt as if she was walking on a razor edge so that any tiny false step could be disastrous. The twins were so focused on "fairness" that the mother could barely operate. As one example, she was expected to wake the

114

kids but hated to do so. If she woke Nellie first and she woke Ellie even a second later, she was told that she didn't love Ellie as much. Of course the same would work the other way around if she started with Ellie, nor could she win by waking them together or alternating which she woke first.

This mother could not imagine giving up her struggle to be entirely equal with the two of them. And she was amazed that she could be inadvertently teaching her children to feel fragile and vulnerable by accepting that each was justified in feeling wounded when she didn't come first in every way.

I share this anecdote to emphasize how, at extremes, attempting to treat two kids exactly the same can have detrimental effects. These twins put much energy into assuring that they were treated with preference. They had little energy left with which to learn that taking responsibility for their own behavior could give them benefits, including control over their own reactions and emotions.

As you design and operate your program, keep clear in your mind that your job is to start where each child is and to help each to increase the level of responsible behavior from there. When you write your program, include target behaviors that fit each child. For example, if one child makes the bed regularly already, don't include that in the program; whereas if the other doesn't, you might well include it.

Of course the child who already makes the bed may complain. It is altogether reasonable for the child to feel that way, and you can count yourself fortunate that your child communicates that well with you. How you respond is the key, and it is pretty straightforward. You might, for example, say something like:

"Well, Marty, I'm pleased to know you are interested in how you and Missie are both doing. I can see it seems unfair that she gets credit for making her bed and you don't. I'd wonder if I were you, too, so let me explain. Our job as parents is to help each of you kids learn to take responsibility for your behavior. That includes things like making your beds. We are really pleased that you learned to do this a long time ago so that you don't need our help. But as you know, Missie has a hard time getting her bed made even though she can do it when she tries. So, we put this in her program to help her get used to doing it on her own. We'll keep working with her until that happens. That is the same reason we put getting your math assignment turned in on time in your program, to help you with something that has been hard for you even though we know you can do it when you try."

Children approached with this clear, thoughtful, and truthful explanation recognize how reasonable it is and tend to complain much less. Whenever they do, just explain again. Defending yourself is not a constructive response, and if you are pushed, I suggest you rely on the guidelines for tuning out persistent arguing discussed in Chapter Thirteen.

We have three kids, and it is difficult to be sure that each can earn exactly the same reward. How can we handle this?

The answer to the above question goes a long way toward addressing this one. To be specific, I strongly suggest that you give up trying to provide each child exactly the same reward. Each child is an individual and is best dealt with accordingly. Explain that you are working to meet the needs of each. The rest of your response will be delivered by how you act.

On the reward side, most kids have their own interests and thus do better with reward choices that fit them. Beyond that, if your kids pay attention to the number of credits each can earn, I suggest that you intentionally revise one or all of the credit structures so the numbers add up to quite different amounts. For example, you could plan on one child being able to earn 50 or so credits on a perfect day while another can earn 100 or so. Of course that also means adjusting how many credits each would have to earn for specific rewards. It is important to be reasonably balanced from your own point of view as to how much effort each must make to get about the same level of reward, but that is something you can keep to yourself. If the child who earns fewer credits complains, you can simply point out that fewer credits are required to trade for rewards, also.

The idea here is to assure that each child has another opportunity to earn desired rewards by investing a reasonable amount of effort. How the child is doing relative to siblings should be of secondary importance for kids who are succeeding.

Our twelve-year-old daughter is doing very well on the program, but lately she seems a little less enthusiastic than she was. She has earned about two-thousand credits but doesn't want to trade any in because she doesn't want her total to go down, and we wonder if this could have anything to do with her losing interest.

This is an interesting development that I have seen only a few times. Some kids watch the total number of credits they earn as a kind of score that reflects their success, and they do not want to see their scores go down. So, for whatever reason, for these kids it is the accumulated score that they care about – perhaps in the same way that billionaires continue to strive for more money than they can ever spend. This is an admirable reaction in that it reflects her interest in her own continuing success, but it carries with it one risk that you are seeing in the gradual lessening of her interest.

Early in the program, gains from one day and even from one week to the next were quite prominent so that acquiring ever more credits was a noticeable achievement. For example, when she went from 100 to 200 credits, it was a big thing, and even from 1000 to 1100 may have seemed an accomplishment. However, by the time she reached a couple thousand, adding another 100 probably had lost its sizzle. At the same time, since she is reluctant to let the number go down, she has not yet experienced the material reinforcement side of the program. Eventually, it is likely that she will feel no incentive at all for continuing her good progress.

Fortunately, there is a pretty simple way you can deal with this issue. You can arrange a kind of "double-entry" bookkeeping. That is, you can simply keep two balances: one the grand total of all the credits she has ever earned and the other the balance after deducting credits for whatever rewards she chooses. That way, she can continue to observe and enjoy her large total, and still use her credits as intended in the program design. Since she has so many credits, I'd suggest you let her know how you will keep track and then encourage her to trade in credits soon so that she has direct experience of the reward side of things.

Our problem is that we do lots of things together as a family, so it is hard to come up with rewards which are special enough to interest the kids. Do we have to stop our family activities in order to make this program work?

Yours is a problem most kids would like their parents to have. In some families it is hard to come up with things special enough to provide incentive for kids to exert effort. However, in my experience this is very rare and typically occurs only in families with a child who is so challenging that the parents may have to take more drastic measures to assure compliance.

For most families the issue is more easily managed. First, using this program does not mean parents can no longer be generous and loving with their children. Your challenge is to identify incentives that are interesting enough to drive them to complete their responsibilities. There are a variety of ways to make reward choices special to kids, and with some creative thinking, you are likely to be able to hit on things your kids would like.

As described in previous answers, you may find choices that involve time with you will be appealing. So, for example, if you typically take the family out for ice cream on weekends, you could include as a reward choice "treating the family to ice cream." Some kids will scoff, realizing that they may get the same reward for no effort. Remember, if you have it on the list and it isn't chosen, there is no problem. Others, though, as previously mentioned, actually willingly trade credits for such a reward, apparently finding satisfaction in doing the treating through their own efforts. Another example might be to include as a reward choice "planning a special family outing on the weekend," where the privilege of choosing what to do is the rewarding aspect. Again, the idea here is to be creative in planning reward choices. You also can ask the kids for their own ideas.

Now, what about those rare families to whom I alluded, those with a child whose behavior is in need of drastic change and who seems unresponsive to available rewards? This could in part be because the parents provide so many extras in the course of their daily lives. In such a situation, the parents should reconsider how many extras they normally provide. That would mean reviewing their priorities, weighing the importance of the changes that are needed against the importance of continuing to do so much for the child.

In some instances the outcome could be cutting back on the free extras so that the child has to earn credits to do the same things. Make sure that the child understands that in our world benefits, including choices and privileges, are directly coupled with responsible behavior. In some families such adjustments may not improve things enough for a reasonable level of cooperation. In that case, it may be necessary to seek a family evaluation with a professional who can more directly determine what underlies the child's resistance and provide guidance for moving beyond it.

Chapter Fifteen

"But Doctor, what do we do when . . . one of our kids mostly does as he is told while the other is always dawdling and fails, so we feel like we are putting all our energy into dealing with the one in trouble?"

Page 114

STEP 3. BUILDING YOUR PROGRAM INTO YOUR FAMILY LIFE

Once the program is laid as discussed, it is time to work out the way the program will operate in your family. If this is done poorly, the program can demand an inordinate amount of family time and attention. If done well, it can be minimally intrusive and yet contribute to a warm and loving atmosphere and a special time together each day. There are two parts of making the program work smoothly, the behavior chart and the daily review.

The Behavior Chart

This first aspect involves developing a method of monitoring your expectations as well as the progress of each child in meeting those expectations. The program uses a simple but carefully designed behavior chart for this purpose (some aspects of which you have already seen in examples above) which will serve several important functions:

- **First**, the chart details your expectations for your **child**. To assure it is readily available throughout the day, I suggest posting the chart in a prominent place in your home. This will make it is easy for all of you to consult it, particularly the child who may need to check on what is to be done and by what time a number of times during the day,

  Many families post charts on their refrigerators within easy view. This removes one excuse for those kids who fail to follow through. If you prefer more privacy, however, you can keep the chart at hand in a drawer or in a small folder.

- **Second**, the chart gives **you** a way to keep track of developments in the program. The chart records most components of the program on one simple page for your review at any time.

- **Third**, the chart records the child's performance and credits earned on each item each day and , as well as a line for totals, clearly shows

119

the child's progress toward meeting goals set by the parents.

- **Fourth**, the chart tracks the child's progress toward rewards of interest to the child. This helps parents prepare to provide rewards in a timely manner to assure the child does not have to wait long enough to become discouraged.

The chart can be a simple grid with space for each of the needed elements. A full-sized blank sample chart appears in Appendix 2 for copying as you choose. The shortened version here shows the general idea. Note that there is one column for listing the behavioral items, one column for the amount of credits assigned for each success, and one column each for the days of the week. Rows include one for the column headings, one for each of the behavior items, one for the daily total number of credits earned, one to record any credits traded for rewards, and one for a running balance of remaining credits (with carry over from the previous week going into the "Credits" column). While these are the basic elements of a chart, it is important to stress that it is the functionality of the chart that is most important, not how fancy it is.

HOME BEHAVIORAL PROGRAM

_____ is successful when: for the week of _____ to _____ 20____

Behavioral Item	Cred.	Mon.	Tue.	Wed.	Thu.	Fri.	Sat.	Sun.
1.								
2.								
10.								
DAILY TOTAL								
CREDITS USED								
RUNNING BALANCE								

A father, an engineer, brought to a class his child's chart on a large plastic board with professional lettering and lining. He explained proudly that he used a grease pen to record on the board in a special hanging place in the family room where everyone could see it. Unfortunately there were two problems with his chart.

One problem was that at the end of each week it would be necessary to erase the board, leaving no permanent record of the child's specific successes. This could be dealt with by also recording the same things on a paper chart, but adding additional tasks to make the program work may discourage follow-through on the program.

The second problem is that all programs need fairly frequent changes, both to fine tune them in the early stages and to accommodate progress later on. Making such changes would be difficult with glued on lettering, possibly tempting the parents to stay with details not in the best interests of either the child or themselves.

A sample chart for our mythical nine-year-old Johnny appears below. I will discuss the details of the structure of the chart here, and the day-by-day application of it below as part of discussion of the daily review.

You'll note that some of the boxes are shaded (though corner to corner X's would work as well) to designate times when an item doesn't apply. For instance, for Item 7, shading for days other than Monday, Wednesday, and Friday show that Johnny is expected to take the trash out only on those three days. This clarification may appear to be a little thing, but it serves a couple of important functions. First, it makes it clear to the child what is expected when. If Johnny checks his chart Thursday morning he will see he needn't worry about the trash that afternoon. In addition, anyone looking at the chart can see how things are going.

Parents who came in for review of several weeks of charts were discouraged because of all the x's indicating what the child had not done. However, item-by-item review showed that in many boxes an x had been used to denote that it "didn't count that day." After diagonal lines were drawn in those boxes, what remained were just a few of the original x's. It was then clear that the child had succeeded far more than not, and both the parents and the boy were encouraged enough to continue what became a very successful program. You don't need discouragement like that, and shading or otherwise denoting items when they do not count can help keep things clear.

Note that success on items 5 and 6 is measured in 30-minute intervals. Small hash marks are shown in each day's box, one for each success, to help keep track of how many times Johnny stayed friendly or played outside. Then the hash marks were counted and entered as the number of credits earned for the day. Additional details about the chart appear in the discussion of the daily review below.

HOME BEHAVIORAL PROGRAM

Johnny is successful when: for the week of _October 6th_ to _October 12th_, 2007

Behavioral item	Cred	Mon	Tue	Wed	Thu	Fri	Sat	Sun
1. he is up, dressed, and done with breakfast by 7:30.	10	10	10	10	X	10		
2. he is home from the bus by 2:45.	10	10	10	X	10	10		
3. he has his school clothes changed by 3:00.	5	X	5	5	5	X		
4. – he cooperates with his teacher – he is friendly on the playground – his math in on time, 75% correct.	5 5 20	5 5 X	X X X	X 5 25	5 X 20	5 5 20		
5. he stays friendly with Billy (per 30 minute interval).	5	// 10	// 10	/// 15	// 10	//// 20	///// 35	//// 30
6. he plays outside with other kids (per 30 minute interval).	5	// 10	// 10	/// 15	// 10	//// 20	///// 35	///// 40

Top portion of a sample behavior chart for a nine-year-old boy

HOME BEHAVIORAL PROGRAM – Continued

7. he has the trash out of every room in the house by 5:30.	5			5		5	5
8. he eats the dinner prepared for him within 20 minutes.	15	15	15	X	15	X	15
9. he is in bed and quiet by: –8:30	10	5	10	X	X	10	15
–9:00	5	5	X	5	X	5	X
10.							
DAILY TOTAL		75	55	75	70	90	95
CREDITS USED					500*		
RUNNING BALANCE	410	485	540	615	185	275	380

* 500 Credits used for a family outing for ice cream

Bottom portion of a sample behavior chart for a nine-year-old boy

HOME BEHAVIORAL PROGRAM

Sally_____ is successful when: _____ for the week of __June 10th__ to __June 16th__, 2007

Behavioral item	Tok	Mon	Tue	Wed	Thu	Fri	Sat	Sun
1. she is completely dressed by the time the timer rings (15 minutes).	1	1	X	1	1	1	X	1
2. she plays quietly in the family room while the baby sleeps (per 30-minute interval).	1	2	2	3	2	3	1	3
3. she stays at the table and eats all the food from her plate by the time the timer rings (20 minutes) breakfast / lunch / dinner	1	2	1	1	2	2	2	3
4. she has all the toys put away in the family room by the time the timer rings (15 minutes).	1	X	1	1	X	X	1	
5. she cheerfully does an extra task assigned by Mommy or Daddy (each).	2	2	X	4	2		6	8
DAILY TOTAL		7	4	10	7	6	10	15
TOKENS USED			30*				50#	
RUNNING TOTAL	52	59	33	43	50	56	16	31

* Used 30 tokens for a toy   # Used 50 tokens for a trip for ice cream

Sample behavior chart for a five-year-old girl

Charts for younger kids look very similar to those for older kids. A sample for a five-year-old girl is presented here for convenience as you read about the next step. You will note that there are fewer items for younger kids and the number of tokens that can be earned each day is also less. Otherwise, the elements are all the same as for older children, as discussed above.

124

The Daily Review

The second part of making your program powerful and yet minimally demanding on family time involves establishing a daily review period from the very outset. The review is designed to tie all the elements of the program together and is key to making the program work. The review typically takes less than five minutes for one child, less than ten for two or three. The actual time varies widely from family to family since some enjoy the process enough to prolong it. These are the key elements:

- First, set up a regular time each day for the review. The time of day the review occurs doesn't matter much. What does matter is that it happens every day at a time when all members of the family can attend. Many families meet either right before or right after dinner when they are already together. Other people, because of their schedules, don't find that convenient and prefer to meet in the morning before leaving the house. To repeat: the time doesn't matter as long as it is a routine for the family, and your child can be confident that the review will occur as planned.

- Second, for families with two parenting figures, it is important for both to attend and to share responsibility for managing the review meeting. This takes full advantage of the joint strengths of the parents. It also means that your child can get used to things being done by either parent. Then when one cannot be there, the other can go on with the routines and the family need not miss the review. It is important to stress, though, that families with only one parent can manage a fully powerful program although clearly more responsibility falls to the single parent, something these parents do not need me to tell them.

- Third, when you all assembled, you should use the chart and systematically guide the process through consideration of each item that applies for that day, in order to determine the successes.

A Sample Scenario

With those thoughts in mind, let's turn to how a daily review meeting actually works by reference to a sample scenario. It uses a chart showing one week of experience with nine-year-old Johnny. My intention is to highlight the important elements of the review. You can adapt this to your own way of operating and of communicating, The process might go something like this:

- The parent who happens to have the chart for the day starts the process by asking whether the child completed the first task on the list; for example:

"Was Johnny up, dressed, and done with breakfast by 7:30 this morning?"

This question is answered by whomever knows, perhaps the parent who just read the question. Do not accept your child's answer to the question unless you can verify it. This is not because children aren't trustworthy. Rather, it is to keep the focus on the identified behavior and on your role in measuring its success. It also avoids tempting kids to fudge since even the possibility can divert energy and attention from achieving responsible behavior.

After the answer is clear, if Johnny was successful, the parent should comment on the success by saying something like:

"Oh, yeah, I remember. You got done so fast you had time to watch some cartoons. You seemed so happy this morning that it made my day get started really well. And look, Johnny, we've just started, and already you have earned ten credits. Way to go!"

This simple comment effectively ties together for the child (1) the expected behavior, (2) the social reinforcement, and (3) the credits that stand for the material reinforcement.

Sometimes things come up outside the actual structure of the program that may support your efforts. In the above example, notice the comment about Johnny having time to watch cartoons. There was nothing in the defined success behavior about this, but it represents a reward. By being efficient, he earned this bonus. That little reinforcement just happened the way the world works sometimes for responsible people. That is a good lesson for a child to learn, and it doesn't require a big lecture to teach it. A simple comment such as the one about the cartoons making Johnny happy may be enough for him to make the connection. This could well increase his interest in further successes.

- If another parenting figure is there, that person can add praise and further comment on the credits; for example:

"Wow, Johnny, good work! I wish I could have been here. My day got off to a kind of bum start. And boy, if you keep it up, you'll have enough credits to get that new baseball glove in no time at all."

The second parent's comments add to the benefits from the first. And reference to the actual reward Johnny is working toward ties in the material reinforcement as well.

- But what if the child did not successfully complete the task as assigned? As before, the parent who knows still answers the beginning question aloud. The parent with the chart writes an "x" on the chart in the correct spot, and. . . **then just goes on to the next item**. This won't come naturally to a lot of parents. Good parents that we all are, we have some great lectures saved up for situations such as this:

> *"Gee, Johnny, if only you would get started on time and try a little harder and were more like your cousin and wouldn't goof off so much and showed a little initiative and cared about your family and didn't play so many of those stupid video games, then maybe you'd do something right once in your life and wouldn't be on your way to a living in abject poverty and misery like your Uncle Herman – because you forgot to take the trash out on time. . ."*

I trust this harangue is exaggerated enough to suggest my view of this approach. It is an oddity of the human condition that when we praise, it tends to be short and to the point while our criticisms tend to go on and on and on.

Therefore, avoid lecturing at this point since doing so would just give your child a good deal of attention and a strong sense of control directly associated with failing to complete the assigned task properly. Remember, for your program to work, you have to make it more rewarding for the child to do what you expect than for the child to do the opposite.

The idea here is for the successful child to feel your strong, warm reaction and to think about the credits earned. In contrast, the unsuccessful child should experience no benefit and a brief, unenthusiastic response.

This sample interchange concerning Johnny's first item shows the manner of the daily review process.

You should go through all items on the list in the same fashion, praising successes and mentioning but not dwelling on the rest of the items. If, perhaps, you have a flair for the dramatic, you can leave a little pause so that the difference between praise and no reaction can sink in, but please stifle the urge to point the difference out since doing so again provides attention for failing to complete the task.

- Once you have gone over each item on the child's list of behaviors, it is time to add up the credits for the day. At the beginning, it will be important to comment on what the child can do with the number of credits earned. For example, if the child earned 80 credits on the first day, Johnny's parent might say something like:

"Great, Johnny, you already have 80 credits. If you have another good day like this, you could choose dessert the next night, or you could save them a couple more days and choose 25 cents."

The intention of all this is to help the child understand the association between earned credits and choices from the list of material reinforcement. Within a few days, the child may well know all this better than the parent, and by then, the parent may need only to comment on the child's progress toward the reward known to be of interest.

The idea here is to assure that the child grasps the direct connection among:

- The **target behaviors** selected and defined by the parents,

- The **child's effort** in completing the expected tasks,

- The **social reinforcement** from the parents' praise and encouragement,

- The **credits earned** for each successfully completed task, and

- The **anticipated material reinforcement** represented by the chosen reward.

Do not assume your child is eager for a particular reward just based on past comments. From time to time check for current interest. For example, you might ask something like:

"Fernando, now you have 320 credits. Are you still working toward the baseball glove you've been talking about, or do you have something else in mind now?"

If the child continues to show enthusiasm for the baseball glove, you can talk about what fun it will be when he has earned it. If the child expresses interest in some other reward, then you can show enthusiasm about it and maybe even reinforce the advantages of having choices:

"So, Sammy, you decided to work toward a trip to the park to play catch. That will be fun. Isn't it great that you have so many choices, and that all your good work can pay off in so many different ways?"

Some Additional Considerations

Earlier I stressed putting an "x" in the space on the chart when a child does not succeed. It may seem more natural to enter a "0" instead since you will be entering numbers for all the successes. While this may seem like a small point, it can be important because sometimes kids are tempted to put a number in front of the "0" and thereby perhaps gain credits they didn't earn. I have seen charts with a "10" for an item where only 5 points were offered, and the parents were astonished that they didn't notice, but on closer look they could see the "1" had been added in childish handwriting. It is best to avoid offering children temptations to fudge to meet their needs.

Sometimes in families with more than one child, children attempt to drag their sibling rivalry into the program. This may show up during the daily review when one child tries to undermine another's success by snide or challenging comments. One way to deal with this is for the parents to meet with each child separately. This prevents one child from putting down the successes of another while the parents are reinforcing those successes. This can be an effective way to avoid the problems that might otherwise arise. However, you may actually be able to increase more supportive sibling relationships while doing your daily reviews with two or more kids at the same time. Suppose, as you review one chart, another child makes an unsupportive comment. You can choose to disregard the negative content and respond only to the child's attention and interest. For example, you might say something like this:

> *"Kevin, it is so nice to see that you are interested in how well Rachel is doing on her program. I hope she will want to hear how you are doing, too, when we get to your chart."*

Generally sibling conflicts are based on a belief that parents don't have enough love to go around. In keeping with laws of supply and demand, if someone believes the supply of some vital commodity is insufficient, that person will do whatever is necessary to have as much of the supply as possible. A child who believes love and caring are limited can be expected to struggle mightily to gain parental attention and nurturing. In the process the child will attempt to undermine any siblings who are seeking the same love. Keeping this in mind may help if you notice rivalry between or among your kids. Then you can make it clear that each child is loved and valued. One benefit of the home program is that it provides a concrete way to show that each child can do well without detracting from another's successes.

Variations Related to the Child's Age

All of the notions discussed so far apply best to children from ages six or so up to early adolescence. That **middle group** can read and thus can follow the chart, but they still require a good deal of parental guidance and support. The **younger group** requires more effort because the children must rely on parents for frequent guidance. The **older group** is becoming more independent and self-sufficient and so requires a different style of response from parents. For both the younger and older groups, there are special considerations not true for the middle group. These considerations impact the daily review process in addition to those details already discussed.

For the Younger Group

There are several developmental factors that must be accommodated for children up to reading age or so. First, younger kids can't always remember what is expected of them nor what are the benefits of complying. As a result, they can't reliably associate a behavior and its consequence, especially if there is much delay between the two. This means that rewards must be provided very soon after the child performs successfully. This also means rewards must be provided more frequently. Of course you already know this from lots of experiences with your child, but it is important to keep in mind.

It is also important to recognize that all of the principles of the program apply to children of all ages, and to adults, too, for that matter. But since a younger child cannot read the chart, cannot remember all the details, and cannot tell time to meet deadlines, parents must instruct the child frequently. This includes telling the child what is to be done when. After the pattern is established, the instructions may be shortened considerably as long as the child clearly understands.

These reminders are essential but carry some risk. When too frequent, reminders can blend into nagging. Nagging generally is about motivating the child, a direct competitor for the incentives built into the program. Nagging is likely to undermine directly the very foundation of the program. Specifically, nagging can inadvertently provide attention and a sense of control that allows the child to meet those important needs directly by failing to take responsibility. Of course most children would enjoy being rewarded for taking responsibility far more than they would enjoy the negative interactions that accompany failure. However, for a child with little success in doing what is expected, meeting needs in such a negative fashion may be very natural, and the child is unlikely to risk trying for a less certain reward.

The point is to avoid excessive reminders to the child and to stay away from urging the child on, however tempting it might be to do just that in hopes that the child will succeed.

> **Remember that a child who does only what is demanded by repeated parental urging is not taking personal responsibility for anything.**

Some parents have learned to recognize feeling "kind of yucky" when nagging their children. By recognizing that feeling, they were able to learn to check their tendency to fall back into the practice. By realizing how easy it is to keep going back to an old and familiar – if counter-productive – style, you may be able to change any similar habit.

Another issue for younger kids comes from their undeveloped capacity to relate the number of tokens that they have earned to the reward list. When our older son was small, we were confronted with this challenge. We recognized that he understood well the concept of simple board games. Based on that, we devised a token game board with a trail of spaces connected by directional arrows and with a picture for each reward choice. See Appendix 3 for a sample game board. Our son quickly learned that he could place his earned poker chips, one on each space, and easily see whether he had enough to trade in for a specific prize. In due time, our second son developed the same understanding. In addition, each quickly recognized that he could remove the tokens required to earn a reward of interest. Then when he put his remaining tokens on the board, he could see how many more he would need for another reward, a kind of meaningful early experience with subtraction that may have been good preparation for arithmetic later on.

For the Older Group

Remember that all of the principles that I have discussed apply fully to all age groups. That means they also determine how to work with kids from early adolescence on. As kids reach pre-teen and early teen years, it is useful to think about their advancing capacity to assume more responsibility even if they rarely spontaneously show any behaviors suggesting that.

In fact, virtually all such kids carry all sorts of responsibilities, many of them weighty and unrecognized. These responsibilities include crucial decisions relating to members of the opposite sex, responding to offers of drugs, and dealing with their futures. We may think of adolescence as carefree; reality is quite different.

It is particularly important that kids in this age range assume responsibility for their behavior. This includes knowing what they are expected to do and when tey are expected to do it. They then should act, free of parental reminders. Kids who rely on parents for reminders may meet some of their needs for attention from being fussed at, just as younger kids sometimes do. In addition, older kids may find some security by keeping parents responsible. This allows them to avoid taking responsibility themselves, and maybe in the process, they can keep from thinking about the scary future. Of course, they would deny this and likely are not even aware of it, but they may continue to fail because of well-intentioned parental reminders.

To avoid this, be sure the child keeps track of the chart and complies with it. You both know that the child can read, can remember, and can tell time, all that is required to get the assigned tasks done as specified. Of course for kids who have shown little responsible behavior, you may have to start very small with your expectations. But it is a big step to get a child, who for years has done little or no homework independently, to complete one math problem. It is the beginning of assuming total responsibility for completing homework – automatically. This first step is much better than for you to continue the self-defeating practice of taking all of the responsibility. After all, you ultimately cannot deliver on getting the child actually to complete assigned homework. Further, even if you could force a child to do so, such a pattern would be poor preparation for assuming full responsibility for success and failure completely independently of you.

In support of maturation, even early in the program and increasingly over time, it is wise for the parent to focus as much as possible on **areas of responsibility** with kids in this age bracket. For example, assigning the child the responsibility to clean up the kitchen after dinner may be quite feasible for some kids, rather than having to specify on the chart each individual task. However, if the child does not show the capacity to manage that much independently, then breaking it into parts is the way to get on track. On the reward side, areas of privilege might be more broadly defined for kids showing the capacity for larger areas of responsibility. For example, a trustworthy teen might be able to earn a reward of getting home an hour after school is out if there are appropriately safe and wholesome activities available and other circumstances are fitting.

As part of the transition toward approaching adulthood, many teenagers show progress in taking responsibility for themselves. For them it is appropriate to consider developing a written contract, a modification of the basic program chart discussed earlier. An example is presented on the next page for handy reference. The process of developing the

132

contract might include direct negotiation with the teen, allowing open expression of preferences and discussing the reasons to accept or decline them. Of course the parents retain control over what ends up in the program, but it is appropriate for teens to have an increasing level of say in their own lives. Surely parents don't want to send them off to college with no experience in looking out for what is in their own best interests. Once the contract is developed, the teen signs what amounts to a pledge to complete the designated tasks, something kids tend to take very seriously; of course the parents also sign and must be as serious about what they have agreed to do.

Fundamental to our overall approach is moving each child from:

- Birth, when nothing is expected and privileges are few, to

- Middle years, where specific tasks are expected and rewards are provided in careful measure, to

- Later teen years, when much responsibility is expected (safely maneuvering a three thousand pound vehicle down a crowded highway, for example) and considerable freedom of movement and choice are allowed, and to

- Adulthood, where the level of one's privilege is directly proportionate with the level of responsibility taken.

133

Considered in this light, the challenge we have set for ourselves for kids of all ages is nothing less than preparation for successfully participating fully in the adult world.

Some Illustrative Examples

The home program introduces unexpected changes in family interactions. Children often become uneasy when they first encounter such changes because things don't work the way they are used to. They may react in a variety of ways, typically including some testing of the new arrangements. In addition, parents also may be uncertain about their own revised roles. The resulting pattern can produce a variety of challenges, some of them rather unusual. To help you deal with unanticipated situations, I have included another set of illustrative examples, along with my thoughts about them, mostly focused on the day-by-day operations of the program.

Because of our work schedules, we do not have the same times together each day of the week so there is no time we can set up for a daily review. What can we do?

The daily review is an essential aspect of the program since it ties together your expectations, the child's responsible behavior, your praise, the credits the child is earning, and the ways the credits can benefit the child. I have stressed the importance of building into your family life a regularly scheduled time for the daily review, based on experience that families who don't do that are likely to let those special times slide and, as a result, their programs weaken, sometimes irretrievably.

The fact that your schedule is so variable that you cannot follow this recommendation exactly does not have to mean that you cannot have daily reviews; it may mean that you will have to plan carefully to be sure you have one **sometime** each day. This will demand more discipline from you, as likely do many aspects of your complicated lives, but certainly it can be done.

There will be one complication due to reviewing your charts at different times each day. Some days you may find you are actually covering as many as 36 hours worth of behaviors while on other days you may cover as few as 12 hours. For instance, suppose you were to hold your review at breakfast on Monday, say at 7:00 a.m., and then on Tuesday you were to meet after dinner, say at 7:00 p.m. In that case on Tuesday you would need to review the 24-hours between Monday's review and breakfast Tuesday, plus the 12 hours from breakfast until your 7:00 p.m. meeting. That would mean covering two days' worth of some behaviors. This could be confusing, and you could forget some details. Be particularly diligent charting when things are completed and not rely on memory. Also you might add a word or two to remind you of anything particularly important about your child's successes.

The longer delays in getting recognition at your daily reviews could also reduce your child's enthusiasm for doing well. You can lessen the importance of this somewhat by making sure you socially reinforce the child especially warmly at the time each task is completed, or as soon thereafter as you can.

Your program is meant to help you and your child and so should be made to work in your real-world circumstances. The key, then, is to remain true to the underlying principles that give the program its power while adapting the details and your operating procedures to best meet your family's needs.

We have things working pretty well, but every once in a while our lives get very confusing, and things come up so Brandon can't meet the criteria for an item. How can we manage when that happens so that he still has a chance?

What you describe is pretty common because everyone seems to be so busy. I have stressed the importance of maintaining the elements of the program as carefully as possible, but I recognize that the best laid plans can get lost in unexpected demands. So, while it is important to strive for consistency, it is useful to remind yourself that the program does not depend upon you suddenly turning into saints who never get off track. How you deal with situations such as this will determine how well it preserves the integrity of the overall program.

One potential pivotal error can arise in this and similar situations and result in a negative influence on your overall program. In response to that reality, here is a strong rule to follow as you think through your concerns:

Do not change your agreement in response to complaints from your child after the fact.

For instance, as you are driving Brandon home from the dentist, he realizes that it is too late for him to get his homework done on time. He starts fussing, telling you how unfair it is that he didn't get to earn his credits. You recognize that he has a point and feel bad for him, and thus you agree that he can have extra time to do his homework.

This sounds like a very reasonable response, but a problem lurks in the background. By allowing your son's fussing to change your mind – or at least allowing him to think so – you are actually reinforcing fussing when things don't go his way. In such a situation it is better simply to acknowledge that it is unfortunate that things did not turn out as he would like. Then remind him that neither of you noticed ahead of time how the day would go, adding that sometimes *"that's just the way it is."* You might also suggest that in the future he let you know ahead of time of coming conflicts in the schedule so that you can work it out.

Fortunately, whenever either of you recognizes an **approaching** problem of this sort, a little planning ahead can fix things without risk of reinforcing fussing. Whenever you anticipate that things during the day will not work as usual, you can make temporary adjustments in your expectations ahead of time. For example, if one of you remembers during breakfast that your son has a dental appointment after school and can't be home in time to finish his homework by 5:00 p.m., you can acknowledge the problem then, and add something like,

> *"Because of your appointment this afternoon, we need to change things a bit. Just for today, you will be successful when you have your homework completed by 7:00 p.m."*

With that consideration and plenty of time to organize himself around this modification, Brandon has every chance to succeed. By consistently operating this way, you will teach him that he can expect fairness and consideration but that it requires advanced planning. Many children get good at looking ahead, and they ask for needed changes in time to avoid disappointments, good preparation for adult functioning.

You can make the program work for you, including necessary modifications to fit changes in the family routine. For more about this, note Section Four, which deals with other reasons and ways to adjust the program to meet changing needs.

Well, we started the program and things are going pretty well in some areas, but now our son thinks he should get credits for everything that he does. What do we do now?

I was doing some heavy trimming in our yard, leaving piles of cuttings in my wake, when our four-year-old son decided to help by picking up after me. It was common for him to want to help, but this time he stuck with the task as long as I did. He worked so hard filling trash cans that I had to hustle to remove and replace filled bags while also trimming more. As we were putting away tools hours later, I informed Mike that I was going to give him two tokens because he did such a great job helping. These amounted to a "bonus," since there was no item in his chart to fit this work into. He responded with delight, dashing in to tell his mother. Clearly the reinforcement value of this was far greater than two tokens.

But that is not the point of the story. A week or so later when I was out to do some yard work, Mike was quick to come help. He asked immediately, *"Daddy, do I get extra tokens for helping this time too?"* Of course this was a very reasonable thing for him to ask, and, in fact, had he not, we might wonder why not. After all, the question was based on his experience the last time. He needed to know whether the world would always work that way. My answer was this: *"No, Mike. I gave you the two tokens because I was so pleased with how hard you worked to help last time. I wanted to say thank you that way. But trimming the yard and picking up stuff is what we have to do to keep our place looking nice. We do it because we love our home and our family."* Mike thought about that for a moment and that was the last I heard about it until he explained the same thing to his mother later that day. Clearly he was satisfied with the explanation even if though he may not have liked it.

I share this story to illustrate what I think is a sensible and fair way to deal with your son when he quite reasonably asks to be rewarded for whatever task he completes. It is important, though, to be sure that he fully understands how the program works. Your challenge is to make it clear that each of you has certain responsibilities to the family. Explain that part of your job as parent is to help each learn to do what is expected.

If your child continues to demand rewards for every deed after you have clarified things, review your efforts so far to be sure you have laid the groundwork well. Have you clearly conveyed your expectations and how the reward side of the system works? Have you explained, preferably not more than a couple different ways, what you will reinforce and what you won't, as well as your reasoning? If so, all that remains is to repeat that you have explained the best way you know how, acknowledge that it is too bad that the child didn't understand, and then calmly add, *"But that is just the way it is."* You then should disengage from the child since at that point it is the child's problem to come to grips with the reality of accepting something undesirable. You cannot do that for him, but you can avoid continuing a pattern which uses up energy he could better spend by behaving responsibly. If you find you are having difficulty disengaging, you might benefit from rereading Chapter Six about control struggles, which gives more detail about how you can tune out.

We think we may be able to make a program work, but we know our

daughter will fight it and still screw up from time to time. We are thinking it will be a good idea to fine her some credits when she doesn't do what she is supposed to. What do you think about that idea?

Fining children credits for failures is an approach that has been suggested by some writers. There are several reasons I think this is not a good idea. For one, it perpetuates the notion that discipline is really about making it bad for kids to screw up. This carries with it all the risks associated with punishment described in Chapters Five, Six, and Seven. For another, some kids are likely to make a good many errors on their way to learning to take responsibility for themselves. For such kids, taking away credits for each error could mean that they rarely, if ever, achieve enough credits to trade for a material reward. Anyone who has had to continue making payments on a car that has long since ceased to run understands what it is like to be in such a hole. Rarely or never achieving a reward would mean that, however nice the program might look, the child really wouldn't be on a reward system. The power of the approach is in coupling material and social reinforcement with responsible behavior, and if that association never gets a chance to occur, there is no program. I strongly urge you to avoid resorting to "fines" for inappropriate behavior.

Chapter Sixteen

"But Doctor, what do we do when . . . our child expects a treat
whenever he does something right, but we want him to want to do
the right thing, not just for a reward?" Page 217

MAINTAINING YOUR INFLUENCE WHILE YOUR CHILD IS AWAY FROM YOU

So far we have focused on a program for your home. However, many parents report concerns about their children's behavior while away from their influence. Fortunately you can extend your influence in such situations through your home program.

To accomplish this, you need a responsible person to observe what happens when you are not there, just as you would do if you were. This person can be another adult or even a mature and trusted teenager, including child sitters.

School is where this need most commonly arises. In fact, many parents report that teachers expect them to fix school problems while they have no way to do so. Because of such concerns, I will discuss how to extend your influence to that setting. However, the same approach is useful in any number of other settings, such as soccer practice, Girl Scout meetings, or overnight at the grandparents' home.

Here are steps to set up the school extension of your program:

Step One: Meeting with the Child's Teacher

Gaining the teacher's support

Arrange a time to meet with your child's teacher. During the meeting, tell the teacher you have been working on some things at home using an approach that focuses on the positive. You can describe your program in more detail if you like or if the teacher expresses interest. After that ground work, share the concerns about your child's school behavior and performance which make you want to include school items in your program. Then ask for the teacher's assistance in setting up a system to provide you with reports on your child's successes in school.

It is important how you go about seeking the teacher's help. If you approach this by *telling* her (or "him" as the case may be) what she must do, she may agree, but she may do so reluctantly. After all, the teacher knows better than you can know exactly what your child may need help with at school and deserves to be included as a full partner in your efforts.

With somewhat varying levels of enthusiasm, most teachers will readily agree to participate.

Only a couple of times in my years of working with families did parents report that teachers refused to participate in the program. Nearly all of those, after I had clarified the approach, agreed to do their parts. Only one refused even though the child involved was described as in constant trouble both academically and behaviorally. Despite these strains in the classroom, no amount of information or encouragement would budge this teacher from her conviction that the child *"just should do what she is supposed to do!"* She considered it immoral to reward a child for doing what is expected in school. Nor would she accept the idea that adults might use rewards to guide children to cooperate. Fortunately other teachers have been very helpful in maintaining successful programs of this sort.

Establishing the format

Once the teacher has agreed in principle, the next task is to discuss her observations of your child's performance at school since she is best situated to know your child's specific needs. You then can compare concerns and settle on those specific behaviors that you and she agree are important to modify. You will note that this process is the same as you have already carried out at home. Your goal is to define a list of success behaviors by using the format of *"(Child's name) is successful when . . ."* just as you did at home. Remember to focus on:

- Identifying realistically reachable goals,
- Putting those in positive terms, and
- Assuring that the criteria of success are so clear that you, the teacher, and the child will all know exactly what is required for success.

Meeting these characteristics can be challenging in a busy classroom where the teacher may prefer to tell the child to *"be good"* for part or all of the day. This is of concern because *"good"* is so vague as to give your child almost no guide for improved behavior. Further, expectations that cover too much of the school day may be unrealistic as well.

Your challenge is to assure respectfully that the items are realistically reachable, positive, and clearly worded.

Defining the content

At school there generally are three categories of behaviors to consider though some may not apply to your own child:

- Perhaps the central area of concern at school is **academic performance**, where a typical item might be something like:

  "Morgan is successful when she has her math assignment turned in on time and at least 80 percent correct."

  Of course, such things as the amount of work and the level of correctness expected must be realistic, based on your child's own past successes. If Morgan typically got very few answers correct, it would be inadvisable to start with 80 percent correct as the standard of success. It might be more realistic to specify 25 percent correct then work to higher levels as the successes begin to mount.

- Even children with no academic problems may have considerable difficulty with **peer relationships**. Here a sample item might be:

  "William is successful when he willingly takes turns while playing with the other children during recess."

  It should be noted that such an item would be useful only if there is appropriate supervision on the playground so that accurate reports on William's behavior can be provided to the parents. The reporting process is discussed just below.

- The final area of potential concern has to do with **respect for authority**; for example:

  "Mary is successful when she cooperates with the teacher during reading circle."

Perhaps the biggest risk in developing a program extension for the school is that their enthusiasm for change can encourage teachers to want to take on too many tasks at once. It is important to remember that your child is one of perhaps 25 or 30 with whom the teacher has to deal throughout the school day. In order for her to attend accurately to and report on your child's behavior for the program, it is essential that you limit the number of items on the chart at school. The teacher, of course, can speak for herself in this regard, but I would suggest that you lean toward fewer rather than more. Handling a few items well is better than trying to do more than the teacher's time allows.

Step Two: Developing a School Behavior Chart

Once you have agreed on a set of items for the program, the next step involves developing a simple chart for the teacher to use – again, exactly the same thing you did at home. The chart need not be fancy, but it should be very useable. A sample school chart appears here:

Name _____ for the week of _____					
...is successful when:	Mon	Tue	Wed	Thu	Fri

Sample behavioral chart for school use

A small, sturdy index card works well for this. Note that the chart is like the home chart except it includes only Monday through Friday and has space for fewer items. The wording is identical. As you can see, you'll need a new chart each week; therefore you might want to draw one up without the items, copy it, and then fill in copies as you need them.

Some enthusiastic teachers offer to make the charts. I encourage you gently to decline this nice offer and make the chart yourself. It is simple to do, and you can be certain it gets done right away so that you don't lose any momentum in implementing the program. On the other hand, a busy teacher might let the task slide in the face of other demands, and starting the program could be put off. It would be pretty uncomfortable to have to ask a busy teacher when she'll have it done, especially for the fourth or fifth time. It is far easier and more certain to do the job yourself.

Step Three: Establishing Operating Procedures for the School Extension

The final step in organizing the school extension of the program is to work out the operating procedures between the teacher and you. Part of this task is to assure that both the teacher and your child understand all of the relevant details.

First, explain to the child that it is the child's responsibility to take the card to school each day and to place it wherever the teacher requests, typically in some special place on the teacher's desk.

Second, the teacher's responsibility is to record the child's successes for each item on the chart by writing her initials in the appropriate place on the card.

> Some teachers, excited by the program, opt to use gold stars or other stickers, but I suggest you discourage this. It takes only one spilled box of stars during a busy day to make the program seem unduly time-consuming. Further, stars are easily found, therefore tempting kids to add ones they never earned. On the other hand, they also fall off, meaning kids may get home with fewer than they earned, a discouraging prospect for a program focused on success.

Teachers virtually always have a pencil or pen at hand and can quickly write in initials. Initials are better than check marks since kids eager to earn a reward can too easily add them to their cards. We cannot build responsible behavior while tempting kids to be irresponsible. Therefore, to assure no confusion, ask the teacher simply to initial each success for the day.

Note that, just as is true for the home portion of the program, it is important that the teacher not focus on any item that the child does not complete successfully since attention to a failure can *increase* the likelihood that it will occur again. The idea is to leave blank any item not deemed successful and to avoid any comment about it.

One more note: Some teachers find the card a convenient way to let parents know of all other concerns about the child's behavior during the day, probably particularly for kids who are struggling a lot. Discourage this gently since any such note on the card taints the process. For example, if the card said something like, *"Today Emile did not pay attention during reading period,"* the parents would be presented with a dilemma. The child would have seen the note, and if the parent were to ignore it, it would appear that it didn't matter to them. On the other hand, were the parent to comment on the failing it might undermine the positive reinforcement of whatever successes were recorded on the card. Better to ask the teacher to communicate to you in some other fashion about concerns not addressed on the card.

Third, at the end of the school day, the child is responsible to pick up the card from the teacher in whatever manner she prefers during what is typically a busy time of day. However, if it can be arranged, there are advantages to having the child take the card directly from the teacher's own hand. That way there is a good chance that the child will receive an extra offering of social reinforcement when the teacher passes on the card indicating successes for the day.

It will be noted that I have stressed the card going home **each day**. There is good reason for this.

A ten-year-old girl, whose behavior had been very troubling initially, showed great and consistent progress at home but a confusing pattern at school. Review of school cards for five weeks, when lined up for comparison, showed:

- Near perfect success for all items on Mondays,
- Somewhat less success on Tuesdays,
- Little or no success on Wednesdays,
- Somewhat more success on Thursdays, much like Tuesdays, and
- Near perfect successes on Fridays, much like Mondays.

Attempts to make sense of this odd outcome led us to all sorts of conjectures, including wondering what sort of unsettling things were scheduled for Wednesdays at the school. Then it was revealed that the parents had chosen to have the card come home only once a week. Discussion with the girl indicated that after receiving some reward on the weekend, she was enthusiastic about the program on Mondays with carry over to Tuesdays. By Wednesdays, though, lacking any reminders of her successes at school, she'd forgotten about the rewards. Then on Thursdays she began to think about possible rewards on the weekend. By Friday those thoughts were strong and influenced her behavior accordingly. Learning this, the parents and teacher agreed to change to a daily turn-around for the card, and from then on the child did very well all through the week.

As this example illustrates so well, it is vital that the card comes home from school each day so that the child is provided appropriate feedback for successes on a timely basis. As a part of this, it assures that the teacher notes and records successes each day, rather than perhaps putting off recording successes in the face of the many other demands on her time. This timely recording means accurate information so that the child is reinforced for each success and so that there is little likelihood of inadvertently rewarding failures.

One other point: many parents think this plan is doomed from the outset since they are certain their child will never bring the card home. After all, the kid loses the lunch you sent, forgets homework, occasionally comes home with only one shoe, and never brings home school papers. But remember that most papers kids are asked to take home are either boring things such as PTA notices, or worse, notes starting *"Dear Mr. and Mrs. Johnson, today Justin broke classroom rules by. . ."* Clearly Justin would rather such a note not make it home.

Despite these concerns, almost always kids on this sort of program do, in fact, take their cards home. Indeed, it appears that most kids view the card as "money in the bank," more valuable than many other possessions. In some cases, this includes actual money so that even kids who have a history of regularly losing their lunch money tend to get their cards home. The likely reason is that the card represents a direct link to **both** the material reward associated with the program (which is, at best, what money represents) **and** the more valued parental social reinforcement, something even money can't buy.

"Okay," you may say, *"that might be right for other people's kids, but you've never met our guy. He'll never follow through."* If you remain unconvinced and concerned that the child won't bring the card home, you have at hand a simple tool to help. Add an item to your home program that says something like:

> *"Samuel is successful when he brings his school card home and gives it to Mom before our daily review meeting."*

The worst that can happen by adding this item is that you may end up providing reinforcement the child really didn't need, not a big thing at all.

Fourth, once the card has arrived, the parents use it during the daily review as a substitute for their own observations. That means that whoever is reading off the chart for the day reads the school items along with those from home, and both parents, after consulting the card for answers, comment positively about the successes. Whatever credits are assigned to each successful item are written into the home chart, and the review continues as usual. At appropriate times you might also comment about the teacher's positive feelings about the child's performance based on the chart to add to the child's good feelings about success at school.

Fifth, remember that the principles underlying this approach apply to teachers as well as the rest of us. With that in mind, you can make it a point to reinforce the teacher for working with you on the school portion of your program. A call after the first day or two and a nice note by the end of the first week would be a good idea. After a couple weeks, a note to the teacher's principal, with a copy to the teacher, commenting on your gratitude might be especially appreciated and therefore effective. And while you are at it, make sure that you recognize your own success in making this work and take time to feel good about it.

When a child hits a child, we call it aggression.
When a child hits an adult, we call it hostility.
When an adult hits an adult, we call it assault.
When an adult hits a child, we call it discipline.

~Haim Ginott

REDUCING INAPPROPRIATE BEHAVIOR

If a child is to keep his inborn sense of wonder, he needs the companionship of at least one adult who can share it, rediscovering with him the joy, excitement and mystery of the world we live in.

~Rachel Carson

Chapter Seventeen

"But Doctor, what do I do when . . . I can't tell my kids 'no' when they want to do something I think they shouldn't, and then we end up fighting about it later after they do it anyway?" Page 221

OVERVIEW AND ORIENTATION
TO A VITAL TOOL

Whenever I have been asked "But what do you do when . . ..?", I have always been left uncomfortable because I never have compelling answers for these sincere requests for help. As I have emphasized repeatedly in these pages, such concerns require more than simple advice to do a specific thing. That is the reason I have stressed here the development of an overall approach to teaching children to assume responsibility for their own behavior.

In keeping with this, so far I have discussed the importance of focusing your energies and attention on your children's appropriate behavior while essentially eliminating your attention to inappropriate behavior. The idea is to build into the child the capacity to behave responsibly so that the child continues to self-reinforce appropriate behavior.

It would be naive to suppose that, once in place, this approach would produce kids who always do the right thing. Even the most compliant children are prone to occasional lapses if only as part of their exploration of what is expected of them or of their ongoing efforts to meet their needs as the needs arise. Our strategy here starts by building into the reward program items that will deal with such lapses.

However, as we all have experienced, there are times when behaviors occur that simply cannot be ignored, nor can we wait for the impact of the reward approach to eliminate the unacceptable behavior. Given this reality, parents need a constructive way to respond when their kids do things that they feel must be stopped right then.

It is crucial that parents respond to unacceptable behavior in a way that fits with the overall program. That means assuring that the response is consistent with the fundamental principles of reinforcing appropriate behaviors while withholding attention from inappropriate ones. If each time that a child breaks an expectation or a rule the parent gets into a tizzy, the child will quickly learn how to get such a response, and the unacceptable behavior will likely increase. Therefore, what we need is a way for parents to react that is completely compatible with the overall principle of positive reinforcement and that is effective in stemming the undesirable behavior. This section discusses a tool that provides just such a way for parents to respond.

One more preliminary thought: the title of this section may directly attract the attention of parents with children whose behavior is especially distressing. In all fairness, I must make it clear that as powerful as the tools provided here can be, they are likely to be considerably less so for anyone attempting to utilize them in the absence of the rest of the approach. Said differently, this section will be fully valuable in reducing inappropriate behavior in children only when coupled with consistent positive reinforcement for appropriate behavior and with the withholding of parental response to inappropriate behavior. The first three sections of this book provide the basis for the overall approach.

Chapter Eighteen

"But Doctor, what do I do when . . . my child responds well to limits set by her father and teacher but whines and fusses when I do the same?"
Page 164

FULLY UNDERSTANDING
THE "TIME-OUT" PROCEDURE

Time-out is the most effective tool available to reduce children's inappropriate behavior. It has been around for quite some time and has been used effectively in a variety of settings by parents, teachers, and many others. Unfortunately, it also has been widely misused, turning it into just another form of punishment with all those unfortunate implications.

> Several decades ago the popular press reported on a facility for mentally retarded individuals which was investigated for its practices. It seems that the staff acquired some very large cardboard crates from which flaps had been cut to form a door. They then put patients with poorly controlled behaviors inside, sometimes for many hours at a stretch, justifying this abuse as "time-out."

Such reports tainted the whole concept, but the approach prevailed in many settings with guidelines to prevent abuses. Still, it is common to hear parents – and some teachers – threaten children with remarks like, *"If you don't stop that and behave, you're going to time-out!"* Such threats by their nature throw the whole notion into a punitive context.

The term *time-out* is short for "time out from positive reinforcement." As this implies, it is used to reduce the benefits to children of their inappropriate behavior, a restatement of half of our overall strategy.

As a result of its mixed history and perhaps your own experience, you may find yourself feeling time-out is old stuff and dismiss it out of hand. This would be unfortunate because it would mean you rejected the tool best suited to support your efforts to teach responsible behavior to your children. When fully understood and applied constructively, it is truly powerful and effective and can serve you well, even under very provocative circumstances. I hope you will take the time to read this entire section thoroughly. It discusses in detail this essential component of the overall program for teaching children to behave responsibly. You will find this quite different from the usual presentation of time-out.

The Purpose

The time-out procedure is designed to reduce inappropriate behavior. It provides a means of stopping behaviors that you wish to eliminate when you cannot wait for the other tools in the system to have that impact. Once such behaviors are stopped, the change allows the positive reinforcement program to establish the incompatible, appropriate behavior. That is, the inappropriate behaviors must stop to allow more acceptable ones to occur, behaviors that then can be reinforced and gradually become internalized by the child.

The Procedure

How the time-out procedure is used determines its effectiveness. As already mentioned, it can readily be turned into punishment. But it can also be established as a solid tool for containing children's inappropriate responses. There are several components or steps to applying the technique well, each of which is considered here in some detail.

The "Test"

How does a parent know when to use the technique? The answer is very simple. When a child is doing something you consider inappropriate, **tell the child to stop**.

Notice that I did not say "ask" the child to stop. Most of us, trained to be polite, feel it is more appropriate to ask, rather than demand. In fact, parents often request that kids *"please"* stop, and even add the all-too-common *". . .okay?"* at the end of the sentence. Each of these indicates to the child that there is a choice. While there are many times when it is appropriate to give children choices, the times when parents have determined a behavior is inappropriate are not among them.

A mother brought her seven-year-old daughter to see me because of "out-of-control" behavior. As the mother described her concerns, the girl wandered about the office, delving into all sorts of things. Several times the mother said things like, *"Please don't do that,"* or *"Stop getting into the doctor's things, Debbie, okay?"* At some point the girl started banging on the floor-to-ceiling windows behind my desk, especially alarming her mother who increased her pleading with the girl to *"please don't hit the window"* and *"please stop."*

After observing this interaction for a time, I said quietly to the mother, *"Tell her to sit down in her chair."* The mother seemed perplexed and started to again plead with the girl. I interrupted and repeated, *"Tell her to sit down in her chair."* This time she said to the girl, *"Debbie, sit down in your chair."* Debbie looked at her mother for a moment, then immediately sat down. The mother looked quite relieved, then perplexed, and, almost in tears, asked, *"Why did she do that?"* My response: *"Because you told her to."* Of course she and I discussed the difference between *"ask"* and *"tell"* to be sure she had the distinctions clear, but that simple notion seemed immensely helpful to her as evidenced by her report a couple weeks later of how much better things were at home.

I should add that the other difference was that the mother told her daughter what to do, not just what not to do, therefore providing the child with a specific action to take rather than just discontinuing what she was doing.

If your child stops when told to stop, you don't need the time-out technique. If your child does not stop, you may, depending upon the circumstances and your style, tell the child a second time to stop. However, here is a very useful **rule of thumb:**

> *<u>Never</u> tell your child to "stop" more than twice*
> *before turning to use of time-out.*

While shopping in a small clothing store, a young mother with a small child in a stroller looked through the rows of circular clothing racks. As she did so, her youngster made repeated attempts to climb out of the stroller, the attempt met each time that the mother noticed by comments of the sort, *"Don't do that, okay?,"* *"Please sit down!",* or *"I told you to sit down, okay?".* She took no other action. Eventually the child slipped out of the stroller, got behind it, and pushed it around. After a time she tripped as the stroller scooted ahead, pushing it into a clothing rack. The mother suddenly noticed, and, perhaps out of embarrassment, rushed to the child and spanked her harshly across the bottom while proclaiming loudly, *"I told you not to get out!"* It was clear that the child had no way to know when her mother meant what she said and to understand why she was spanked.

This little vignette illustrates one problem with more than once or, at most, twice, telling a child to stop; it is unlikely that a parent will be consistent in following-through. It is just as unlikely that a child will keep track of the number of "warnings" given even if the parent always "means it" when arriving at number five or ten or whatever. It is far better to make it clear from the outset that what Mom or Dad says must be taken seriously when it is first said. Kids simply can't learn much from rules that are enforced inconsistently.

To summarize the "test," then: if the child stops when instructed to do so, the technique is not needed. If the child does not stop, the test for determining when time-out is appropriate has been passed, and it is time to proceed.

The Set up

First, it is vital in applying the time-out technique to intervene early before your own patience and internal controls are taxed too heavily. This is consistent with telling the child to "stop" no more than once or twice. In both situations, it is unlikely that you'll be effective if you wait until you are upset and you find yourself angrily screaming, *"I told you to calm down!"*

Second, it is important that you go to wherever the child is to use the time-out technique. If you sit in your chair in the family room and yell at the kids at the other end of the house, they may not hear you – or they may assume you don't know if they heard you – and you will get little result. Likely you will then yell louder, introducing an element of anger, which can begin feeding the power struggle discussed earlier. Meanwhile, you may have no way to know if the child (or children) is complying with your directive. To be effective, go to the child, go through the technique carefully, and then follow through as needed.

A Prototype of the Technique

To illustrate the constructive use of the time-out technique, consider the following **prototype statement** to a child:

> *"Ethan (or Ethan and Abigail), I told you to calm down. I see that it is hard for you to stop right now. It's not good to be out of control like that, so I'm going to help you. The way I'm going to help is to have you go to the quiet chair. Stay there until you feel calm inside. When you feel calm, come back and check with me so I too can know you are calm."*

You may note that the term "time-out" is not used in this prototype statement. For one thing, by itself the term means very little. In addition, if you have used the term in the past, there is a good chance that it has taken on negative connotations for the child, connotations that could thoroughly taint the process. Of course if you have used the process successfully in the past, you have no reason to change what you are doing; there is no reason to "fix" what isn't "broken."

154

This statement is offered as a model, but to some extent, you can adapt the wording to fit your own style. However, I'd suggest that you stay close to this wording as you introduce the approach in your family since any very great departure can weaken the impact.

There are a number of additional considerations that determine the effectiveness of the technique.

The Place for Time-out

Identify a place in your home for the child to go to calm down.

> In our home, a chair in our little-used living room became the "quiet chair," and it was used whenever one of the boys needed time for calming. We found the term "quiet" itself to carry with it a soothing tone. (Try saying it aloud, and listen to how it sounds to you.)

> We noticed several times that when the boys had a bunch of friends running around the house, sometimes things could get rather intense. When this happened, occasionally one or the other of our sons would peel off from the group and sit in the quiet chair for a few minutes as if to regroup. While we don't know for certain what it meant to our sons, we were pleased that they seemed to see and use taking time out as a way to regain their own composure.

There is one proviso regarding the time-out place: if you have in the past angrily sent your child to the bedroom or other spot with instructions to calm down, the child may now associate that place with punishment. If so, that location may not support good control, and I suggest you find an alternative location.

By the way, many experts stress placing the child in a bleak and unrewarding place, such as the corner that is the focus of so many cartoons. Many families don't have many choices in their homes, however, and most have found that they could use the child's bedroom successfully. In fact, it appears that there may be no reason that the time-out area has to be all that bleak or forbidding. My guess is that that notion is left over from using time-out as a milder form of punishment where the intention was to assure that the child experienced enough discomfort to "get the message." But when we understand time-out is a tool to help the child regain internal control away from other stimulation, then we can see that the real issue is not that the child suffers. Rather, it is to assure that the child has the break from activities that allows recovery of composure. And if we intervene early enough in the process, we can perhaps avoid any need of our own to have the child feel as badly as we do.

The Time in Time-out

Many child specialists recommend that a child stay in time-out for a set time, usually about one minute per year of age up to ten minutes or so. If you have successfully used this standard, there is no reason to change anything. Otherwise, I recommend you use the approach suggested above with the length of time-out determined by the child's own needs. As noted in the prototype statement, our approach is to have the child "stay until you feel calm inside;" thus how long time-out lasts depends entirely upon how quickly the child becomes calm.

Some children may need little time; for them, insisting that they stay longer just makes them feel mistreated. Others may need much longer to regain their composure; having them return to other activities too soon may just make it likely that they will "lose it" soon after. Better that the child's own needs determine the time away from preferred activities.

Another reason not to recommend the timer approach is that kids tend not to be very good at tracking time. For example, a five-year-old may fuss and storm for four minutes and forty-five seconds, then unsuccessfully attempt to regain calm in the small remaining time. This means the child would still be upset when five minutes are up, and the usual recommendation then is to reset the timer for five more minutes. Typically this leads to a renewed storm, based on the feeling that it is so unfair, and that storm could last long enough to ensure missing the next deadline as well. Some families report such a pattern going on for cycle after cycle until everyone is exhausted, frustrated, and unhappy, and the child has learned little about being able to regain calm. By allowing the child to calm alone and then check with you, you can bypass all of this.

Time-out with More than One Child

If two or more children are involved, it is important that they be separated, preferably beyond ear-shot to stop their squabbling. Kids like parents to take sides. Avoid becoming police officer, judge, or jury. Instead, simply declare that since the kids are unable to be together, they each must go to the specified quiet place, and each must stay until achieving internal calm.

The Elements of Success with this Technique

Some parents may still see what I have said so far as just "the same old thing" they have tried without much success. However there are significant differences between the typical way that so many parents and teachers have used time-out and what I recommend as your approach. To clarify and illustrate that point, below is a comparison of the two approaches in the form of a table, contrasting the "usual" approach with our more carefully applied version of time-out:

"The usual" approach vs	"Time-out"
Parents prod child, then react when angry	Parents act early while they are still calm
Parents' message: *"You are bad!"*	Parents' message: *"Your behavior is inappropriate."*
Implicit message: *"I'm angry at you!"*	Explicit message: *"I'm going to help you"*
Implicit message: *"You're a brat!"*	Implicit message: *"You can regain control."*
Angry instruction: *"Get in your room . . .."*	Calm instruction: *"Go to the quiet place."*
Continuing: *". . .until I tell you to come out."* (Or *". . .for an hour"*) (allowing time for you to feel angry)	Continuing: *". . .then check with me so I can know you are calm, too."* (and can reinforce your better control)
Result: Often grouchiness and nagging, lowered self-esteem for both parent and child, therefore a continuation of poor parent-child relationship, a set up for likely replay of the pattern next time	Result: Resolved problem, increased sense of competence and control for both parent and child, reaffirmed parent-child relationship, increased likelihood of cooperation in the future

Comparing "the usual" approach to "time-out"

In a typical "usual" response, parents wait until they become upset and then angrily send their kid to a bedroom, indicating by their tone and sometimes by their words, that the kid is bad, a brat, and so on. They then tell the child to get to the bedroom, followed by one of two alternative pronouncements. One represents a determinate sentence, typically for a very long time, such as, *"And stay there until you are 18 and ready to leave for college."* The other is indeterminate, e.g., *"And stay there until I tell you to come out."* Neither of these gives the child incentive to regain control. In fact, both provide the child reasons to sit and fume.

Long punishments, while meant to lead to contrition, more often allow both time and reasons for the child to think about how unfair the parents were and ways to get back at them. The non-specific arrangement, on the other hand, allows the same dark thoughts but is further complicated by the child's having to wonder how long the exile will last. And sometimes parents, enjoying the peace and quiet in the home, actually forget the child is in time-out. I have known parents to realize hours later that their child is still being punished, causing the parents to start feeling guilty, often leading them to apologize to the child. While that might be appropriate in some sense, it carries a very big risk. The risk is that of "making nice" to a child in the context of inappropriate behavior, perhaps even in the process giving the child reason to have a similar fuss the next day in hopes that Mom or Dad will end up being warm and apologetic again.

There is yet another way such an approach can lead to complications. Some parents insist that the child stay in the room until ready to apologize. Here is an outraged kid, seething inside, being told to apologize. This presents a dilemma. At first the child may well just determine not to apologize due to continued anger and a wish not to give the parents satisfaction. But a good while later the child may start getting hungry or otherwise wanting to get out of there and may say grumpily, *"I'm sorry."* Typically, a parent would not accept that, insisting that the child "mean it." The child may respond with a better facsimile of *"I'm sorry."* The question, though, is whether the child is truly sorry. Often the answer will be that the child isn't sorry at all but knows saying so is the only way to get out of the situation. What the child may well conclude is that, *"Mom or Dad wants me to say I'm sorry even though I'm not. I guess it's a good idea to lie to them in order to get out of jail."* So the kid says it. What can we expect to be the impact of this on the child the next time a decision about whether to be truthful or not truthful arises? The unfortunate message is that, depending upon the circumstances it might be okay to lie, because *"Mom or Dad asked me to."* Now, Mom or Dad never intended to ask that, but it still may well come out that way.

There can be even greater complications for kids who are less certain about their own feelings. The child who is feeling angry inside but who trusts the parents who are demanding an apology may think, *"Gee, Mom is pretty smart and knows a lot. Maybe this is what feeling sorry really feels like."* So the child in all honesty apologizes even though the feelings experienced are anger and frustration. At some point the child may truly confuse the two feelings. That may help create lots of business for psychotherapists, but they have too much business already. I encourage a more straightforward way of dealing with this: avoid insisting the child say something not really felt.

The overall point here is that too often parents fall into a pattern of tolerating their children's misbehavior until they become annoyed and then react angrily. This reaction tends to give the child attention and a sense of control – that is, reinforces the very things the parents don't like. Whether done using the term "time-out" or not, interventions with a child done in this manner are highly unlikely to produce constructive results.

Managing the child coming back from the quiet place

To avoid these destructive interchanges, have your child remain in the quiet place until calm inside and then check with you when calm. At this point your child may display one of three distinct types of demeanor:

- The child is still actually poorly controlled. Clever parents will notice this and should respond, every time, by sending the child back to the quiet place with a message like:

  "I can see you are still not calm enough to be back with us. Go back to the quiet place and stay until you feel calm inside and then come back and check with me."

  Note the reference to "every time" since it is crucial that you follow through each time the child's behavior demands it.

  The demeanor of the child in the second and third alternatives will look very much the same, and the difference will become evident only after you check things out, part of the reason for instructing the child to check with you.

- The child has made some effort at regaining control and comes to you looking calm. However, the level of control remains tenuous. Since you won't immediately know the difference, you initially will have to respond as if the child has achieved calm with some comment like:

"It's really great to have you back with the family. You seem to feel so much better now that you are calm."

This reinforces both the calmer behavior and the feelings behind it, helping the child to recognize and understand the good feelings associated with regaining internal control.

However, if not enough time was allowed to regain a completely calm demeanor, the child who initially appeared to be calm may return to the previous misbehavior. Whenever this happens, whether seconds or minutes later, simply do the same thing you would do if the child came back not yet in control. Return the child to the quiet place. Here, though, the comment should include recognition that both of you had reason to think the child was doing better, such as:

"I could see you were trying, but now I can tell you are still having some trouble staying calm inside. Go back to the quiet place and stay until you feel really calm inside, then come back again and check with me."

You must follow through as many times as necessary to assure that it is understood: the child can and must become calm before resuming other activities.

- The child has fully regained calm and has enough control to remain calm and will not require a return to the quiet place. For a child truly calm inside, confirmed when the child checked with you, you have a perfect opportunity to reinforce the child for the achievement with a comment such as shown above. At that point the process is over!

As you can see, in contrast to the "usual" approach, in this time-out approach, you intervene early while you are calm and you put the focus not on the child but on the behavior. You emphasize that you see the child as somebody who is capable of regaining control. You send the child to the quiet place with instructions to stay – not a long time or until you decide it is over – but until the child feels calm inside, making it clearly best for a quick return to control.

As noted in the comparison chart, the overall result of the usual angry interchange tends to be a setup for a repeat hassle the next day. It tends to leave both parent and child still tense, annoyed, or angry, feeling put upon and reactive enough to be triggered easily back to the same feelings again.

With our time-out approach, in contrast, after the child has come back to touch base and received reinforcement for being calm, there tends to be little residual except for a growing confidence for both parent and child in the capacity to regain control when things get overly intense.

A staff nurse came to my office to ask how to deal with her three-year-old boy and his frequent tantrums. Her practice when he was having a tantrum was to *"finally . . . tell him to go to his room,"* typically having to take him there, herself. Asked what happened then, she replied with a sigh, *"He just follows me right back out with this big grin on his face!"* Intrigued, I asked what her goal was in sending him to his room, and she said, *"To get him to calm down!"*

Given her description, I responded, *"It sounds like you are doing a great job!"* She looked at me as though I had left my senses and asked, *"What do you mean?"* I reminded her that her goal was to help her little boy to calm down, and since he followed her right back out of the room with a grin on his face, I thought she must be doing a great job. This gave her pause, but then she said, almost to herself, *"Yeah, but I'm not ready for him to come out yet. I'm still upset."*

That revealing response suggested a very simple solution. I recommended that as soon as she saw her son begin one of his "tantrums" she send him to his room, and if he should come back calm, she should congratulate herself for doing a good job. That way she did not wait until she was so upset that she needed time away from him. She came back a few weeks later and told me she didn't know that children could behave so well, but then she acknowledged with a shy smile that it was probably more that she had changed her way of looking at things. She added, though, that she had found a lot of opportunities to praise her child for cooperating since she determined early time-out was effective.

What was important in this interchange was the mother's discovery that she had the capacity and – perhaps more importantly that her son had the capacity – to contain and control inappropriate behavior.

The time-out procedure, as described here, establishes an entirely different pattern of parent-child interactions. Central is communication to children that the parents believe their children have the innate capacity to regain and then to maintain internal controls. And that means, in part, intervening early enough so that parents are as calm as they want their kids to be. In order to assure this constructive outcome, it is critical that parents follow through in the manner described.

Follow Through, Follow Through, Follow Through

Because follow through is critical, it is important to be prepared to deal with any child who might test the limits. One aspect is to plan to use time-out the first time on a day and under circumstances that will have you at your best. Perhaps you could select a weekend when you have the time and the energy to devote to assuring a complete and positive outcome. That way, you could make this your project for the day, much as you might make cleaning the garage your project on another day.

What, exactly, does follow through really mean in the time-out situation? It means that:

The child must be returned to time-out <u>as many times as necessary</u>. At first the child may well test how far you will go, and you could even see an escalation of resistance. Difficult as that could be, it makes it all the more critical that the message be clear: You <u>will</u> follow through every time, for as many times as it takes. You <u>demonstrate</u> this by your behavior, rather than in lecture form. And take heart: it is realistic to expect each use of time-out after the first few to be easier than the one before it.

- **If a child resists going to or staying in the time-out (or quiet) place, the parent must insist** and even use some restraint if necessary. Here the goal should be to utilize no more restraint than is absolutely required but enough to make it clear that the child must remain where sent.

Particularly for a young child, I do <u>not</u> recommend shutting or locking a child away from parents because this is too frightening. However, you may be able to restrain a younger child in a bedroom if you do it in a manner that maintains communication between the child and the rest of the family. Some parents use inexpensive portable gates. Others have described securing the partly open door against a wood block or book on the floor, using a towel around the door knob so as to avoid marring the finish. The idea is to assure the child cannot leave the room, will not be hurt, and can still sense family in the rest of the house. Just be certain to tie things securely so that there is no chance for them to slip and for little fingers to be smashed in the door. Of course an arrangement that allows the child to hear the rest of the family means that you all will be able to hear shouting or crying coming from that room; therefore be prepared for some loud complaints and resolve not to respond to them.

If the child is so large and strong and so willing to resist that physically moving to the designated area would result in too big a tussle for you or for the child, you could simply decide that time-out should be right where you are. For example, if the child is sprawled on the floor, you might say, *"Okay, I guess this is a good place for quiet time."* Just make sure the child stays there until calm. Use only enough pressure to assure compliance. Be as firm as you must but no more forceful than is required to avoid further upset.

If a child is too wild or aggressive to stay in the time-out area using these guidelines without risk of personal harm or damage to property, then you would be well advised to seek direct help from a child and adolescent psychotherapist. Whenever a child is actually willing to fight with those most needed for support, guidance, and love; whenever a child is distraught enough to risk the most important human relationships; then that child is clearly in need of – and deserves – a careful assessment and whatever treatment is found to be indicated to relieve the situation. Anything less is a formula for lasting severe unhappiness for all concerned, as well as the establishment of grossly dysfunctional patterns of relating to others.

A Warning

If you are unclear about your commitment to this approach and therefore your readiness to follow through fully, I urge you **not to start with the time-out approach described here**. Beginning the technique and failing to follow through will simply teach your child that continued resistance to regaining control will pay off eventually. The child will recognize that if a little fussing doesn't pay off, then probably more fussing will. Failure to follow through, then, can be expected to make things worse.

If you recognize that you are not prepared at this point to follow through with this technique, remember that does not mean that you won't be ready to do so later on. At such time, I hope you will reread this chapter and proceed accordingly.

Some Illustrative Examples

The time-out concept and approach may be clear, but applying them can be more challenging. Here are a number of examples that I hope will help you use time-out in your own home.

The first time that we sent our son to time-out he stayed a long time. Later he told us he didn't think he could really come out when he felt he was ready – because we used to tell him to stay until we told him he could come out. Comment?

You describe an interesting development. There really isn't a problem with your son staying longer than he needs to get calm, other than you won't know when he has succeeded and therefore may be unnecessarily delaying other family activities. Chances are that once your child learns the new arrangement, things will go fine and you may not need to take any action. I'd suggest talking with him about it and stressing that he is to come to you to check so that you can know he is calm and so that you both can know things are okay again. However, if your son continues to show some confusion, you might want to consider changing the time-out area to some other part of the house, just so he can better see that things are different now. You also might benefit from changing the name from "time-out" to "quiet place" or some such to emphasize the changes. Otherwise, I think you can feel good about the fact that your son – and therefore you – are succeeding in the use of time-out.

My child responds well to time-out with her dad and even with her teacher, but whines and fusses for what seems like hours when I send her there. What can I do?

Kids often respond somewhat differently from one person or one situation to another. The best way to understand such differences is by assuming that the child has learned that she can best meet her needs by behaving as she does – in each situation. That means she has concluded that calming herself works best when with her dad and teacher, but whining or fussing works best with you. I am sure that you did not set out to teach her that whining will get her what she wants, but she learned it anyway. As discouraging as that must be, you can be pleased by the success so far because your child has shown that she has the internal resources required to regain suitable control when guided and motivated to do so.

Now you must learn how to guide her to regain the same control when she is with you. Review the preceding detailed discussion of the elements of time-out, concentrating on how to avoid responding to whining and fussing. Once you have all that clear in your mind, observe and talk with your child's father to learn what is different in his handling of time-out. When you know the adjustments you need to make, talk with your daughter. Tell her that you are pleased that she is doing so well with her dad and her teacher and that you are sorry that things haven't yet gone as well with you but that you intend to change things so that they will. Then tell her you are going to handle things differently from now on, alluding to using her dad's approach if you are comfortable with that idea. The rest is a matter of following through on what you know is required for you to be effective. Again, she has demonstrated she can respond well; therefore success is at hand.

You say it's a good idea to have the child come out of time-out when he feels calm, but we think he should apologize when he comes out. How can we work that in?

It is easy to see why you might want your child to apologize for behavior that you find unacceptable and frustrating. However, there are risks that go along with demanding that a child apologize for breaking family rules to regain some privilege. The biggest risk is that the child will understand the necessity of apologizing and may recognize that complying does not require being honest with you. Put more bluntly, the child can readily learn that the way out of time-out is to lie. No parent wants to teach a child to lie, but that could be the effect. Even worse, some kids may be unsure enough about their feelings to conclude that their resentment is really what feeling sorry means and may develop a distorted view of their true feelings.

Further, the idea of an apology casts the whole situation as one of blame and accusation. This fails to recognize that children sometimes are not at their best, much like us adults, and are in need of adult guidance to recover and do better. With this view, the use of time-out can be understood as a way to support the child's better self. Expecting a child to apologize in this context would be asking for the child to be sorry for – what? – being a child? Clearly children should come to understand that some behaviors are unacceptable. However, there is little to gain and much to lose by making them feel bad about themselves for sometimes failing to live up to what they are learning. Apologies, then, might best be reserved for when a child genuinely feels sad or sorry for a specific behavior and can be encouraged by a parent as a way to resolve such feelings.

Whenever we send both sons to time-out because they are fighting, the young one comes out calm a lot sooner than the older one, and that makes the older one mad – then he fusses and whines about how unfair it is, so time-out doesn't work for us. What can we do?

It sounds as if your younger son has learned how to regain calm, while your older son is still seeing time-out as a punishment rather than as help for him to calm down. I'd suggest you try a couple of things to change this pattern.

One is to consider what modifications you might make to change the experience for your older son. Reviewing the discussion on time-out in this chapter should help.

You might also think about whether you are using time-out now in a similar fashion to the way you might have punished your older son in the past. For example, if you used to send him angrily to his room, are you now using his room for time-out? If so, he may have strong associations between the room and punishment that used to make him angry. It might be helpful to establish a different place for him to go, and you might do well to use a different term such as the "quiet place."

After you have reviewed your procedures, have a talk with the older boy when he is calm. Explain to him that you are sorry things have not gone as well as either of you would like. Then describe to him the changes you will make so that he can get a fresh start the next time regaining calm is hard for him. It can be useful to restate the overall idea of time-out, namely to assist him in regaining calm, the same as for your younger child. Point out that how rapidly each of them calms is not up to you but is up to each of them – and that he will probably be more successful if he concentrates on recovering his composure sooner rather than later. Take care here *not* to make comparisons between the boys since this could feed his resentment and weaken the impact of your talk.

These adjustments will assure that you have established the conditions for his success in responding to time-out. The next time the need for time-out arises, go through the steps carefully, using whatever modifications you hit upon to change the tone. And, when each son comes to let you know he is calm, reinforce him for that and let him continue with other activities. Be sure, however, that whichever child becomes calm first does not in some way goad the other.

These considerations will assure that you have done what you can to improve your son's capacity to respond constructively in time-out. The rest is up to him. However, it is also important that you avoid participating if he whines or fusses. It is highly unlikely to help if you undertake to convince your older son of the rightness of allowing the younger child to move out of time-out before the older one is also ready, however reasonable your argument would be. Instead your task at this point is to allow the storm to run its course so that the child has the experience of seeing that all the fussing gains him nothing while regaining calm can end the problem. Thus, whenever he fusses, wait it out, and when he finally calms, reinforce him for being calm. With these changes, your chances of helping the older boy become as responsive to time-out as his sibling are excellent.

Our child seemed to have lots of tantrums before we started time-out and is doing a lot better. However, when we do send him to time-out, he stays there for a long time, and when we check on him, he's reading or playing by himself. What should we do about this?

My first instinct is to suggest you congratulate yourself on a job well done. I'll try to do better than that, but it is a legitimate response since it sounds as if you have helped your child regain control, a great achievement especially for a child prone to frequent tantrums. About all that might be improved would be for the child to come to you to tell you that he is calm, and maybe he somehow missed that part of the instruction. If you think that could be, I'd suggest you gently tell him again, perhaps stressing that you would really appreciate his coming to you at the end of time-out so that you, too, know how well he is doing.

However, there is a chance that the child is aware of your expectation but doesn't choose to come to you. That could happen if he is not, in fact, completely at ease inside himself. To the extent that this is true, it would be appropriate to respect the child's need for the longer time and simply let him make use of it. A child with a history of tantrums may have been caught up in power struggles and may harbor residual anger that he is gradually working out during these times, a constructive development if true. Since you can't know about that for sure, however, I would suggest that you allow the child to work out whatever he needs to by giving him the time he needs.

If your child, on the other hand, tends to stay in time-out for impossibly long periods which inconvenience other family members, you likely will need to set some kind of limit on how long you let the process go on. Without knowing your child, it is impossible to suggest an exact time-frame, but perhaps you could decide to allow the child to stay alone where he is for a half-hour after he appears to be calm, as best you can judge that. That would allow considerable time for completing his internal calming but still would give you a time when you could expect him to participate in other family activities. If you elect to use such a guideline, try the idea once to see how it works. If you see signs that the child is edgy or loses his cool unduly rapidly, then maybe you should allow a longer time alone in time-out. Whatever way you go, you deserve to feel good that you and your child have already made so much progress.

When my kids are bickering and I send them to time-out, they each start blaming the other and telling me it's unfair to be sent when the other is at fault. What do I do?

This is a very common complaint of parents with more than one child. What you are describing is almost certainly just an extension of the way the kids relate in other circumstances, probably including those that lead you to send them to time-out. Further, clearly the kids are treating being sent to time-out as a punishment, and this negative flavor undermines the effectiveness of the technique.

The key to your response is making it clear to the kids that when you send them to time-out, your intention is to assist them in calming when they seem unable to relate appropriately to each other on their own. Then you can add that you are not interested in who started or did what but rather in doing your part when it is hard for them to work things out themselves. Kids often have trouble really believing this message, particularly in families where parents have typically engaged in debates about who is at fault. To break the old pattern, stay away from that issue and restate that each of them is responsible to regain calm. Over time each child will come to recognize the advantages in regaining calm sooner rather than later, rather than arguing. Be prepared for one kid to get the message more quickly than the other, a problem addressed in a previous example. Of course, it is also important that you separate the kids while they are in time-out and that you have them out of ear-shot of each other if your home allows.

Since we have been sending our son to time-out instead of yelling at him, he has started saying insulting things, and that simply isn't acceptable. What do I do about this?

This unsettling behavior represents a direct test of your overall program since anything you do in response to this provocation carries the risk of reinforcing the very behavior of which you disapprove. Remind yourself that however hateful sounding the child's comments are, he is still the son whom you love, and he loves you – though at the moment he almost surely isn't feeling it. Equally certainly, anything you say to him when he is insulting you will give him a sense of satisfaction and thereby make him more likely to do it more. This sounds like a power struggle; therefore a review of the discussion about control struggles in Chapter Six might be useful.

Beyond that, make sure that you are calm when you send your son to time-out so that you are in no way modeling his negative reactions. Once he is in the quiet place, "turn yourself on robot," in the process withdrawing your emotions from the child for the moment. You can think about where you wish you were, fantasize about your ideal vacation, or whatever, so that you aren't attending to the child's comments. If you do not respond, the child almost certainly will run down and eventually will stop, allowing him to calm more completely. Once that happens, you will have the opportunity to reinforce him for being calm.

I urge you, though, to stifle your likely inclination to lay a huge lecture on him at that point. By giving in to that urge, you would alert the child to how reactive you really are to his tirades. That is the opposite of what you want him to learn, which is that regaining his composure more quickly will meet his needs best. Be prepared for this pattern to repeat itself a number of times since it likely has been heavily learned, but over time you may well find both the intensity of the reactions and how long they last will diminish noticeably. At that point you'll be able to congratulate yourself for lovingly assisting your child to responsible behavior in the face of substantial provocation.

Chapter Nineteen

"But Doctor, what do we do when . . . we send Troy to his room to calm down and he doesn't want to apologize when he comes out?"

Page 164

APPLYING THE "TIME-OUT" TECHNIQUE OUTSIDE YOUR HOME

So far I have discussed use of the time-out technique in the home as a means of reducing inappropriate behavior, both to stop it at the time it occurs and to provide opportunity to reinforce the resulting better control by the child.

While parents often report that the tool is very effective in helping children comply with parental expectations at home, they point out the difficulty of using it away from home. Why the difference? Most of us parents are a bit more wishy-washy when kids test our limits where others may see how we respond. Kids are good at recognizing when we are especially likely to "give in" to them. As a result, even kids who do very well at home may whine for a special toy or candy at the mall or complain in the car. Shopping at the supermarket, eating dinner in a nice restaurant, or driving on a busy freeway at rush hour are classic situations of this type, and each is discussed here.

You are much more likely to succeed with time-out away from home after you have achieved consistent compliance with it at home. As a result, I suggest you wait to use it elsewhere until you are confident of the response at home. Then both you and your child will understand how it works and know what to expect.

To assure the best outcome possible, set the stage as constructively as possible. How to do that depends on the situation; therefore I will discuss effective steps for each of three types of settings. It will go most smoothly if you think of your effort as your special project for the day; therefore whatever else you might accomplish along the way will matter less. And it is a good idea to start with both you and your child rested and in a good mood.

Here are some situation-specific guidelines for applying time-out away from home. I hope they will help you think about how to use the technique in other such situations as well.

While Shopping

Parents often complain about their children's challenging behaviors while they are shopping. For many, this comes up most often while shopping in a supermarket, my focus below.

Basic Preparation

Planning ahead will set the stage for a constructive outing. For your first shopping trip when you might use time-out, plan to buy only a few unessential things. If you attempt this task during a trip to bring home groceries needed to feed the family for the next week, it will be difficult to be as patient and effective as you need to be. Also, avoid perishables since you could have to leave your shopping cart for a good time – or even leave it entirely. In the interest of not wasting food, be selective in what you add to your cart. You don't need the extra stress of worrying about ice cream melting and dripping onto the floor while you tend to your child.

Accentuate the Positive

You will note that I delayed discussion of time-out until after talking about the reward side of the program. The reason is that time-out is most powerful as a support when children also have reason to behave appropriately. Because of that, you should incorporate your trip into your overall home program. To accomplish this:

- Think through the task of changing behavior during shopping trips by identifying what you consider appropriate and **realistically reachable** behaviors for your child.

- Remember to focus on those behaviors that you consider appropriate and which are directly **incompatible with the things that concerned you** on your last trip with your child.

- **Write a few specific items**, once you are clear how you want your child to behave while shopping, either as part of your regular home program or as special "bonus" items.

- Remember the format: *"Stacy is successful when . . ."* You might include such things as *" . . .she sits calmly in the shopping cart for five minutes (or . . .for one aisle)."*

- Base the target length of time that your child must remain calm on past experiences to assure that the child will succeed more than a third of the time. For some children, it may be necessary to set a very short standard, even just a minute or so. Some kids may even require praise for sitting still in the cart ten steps into the store. If so you might say *"It sure is nice shopping with you when you stay so calm."* A useful motto here might be, "Catch them being good."

Carry out Your Plan

When you begin the shopping process, your tasks are to:

- Reinforce the child when the first and each additional standard is reached. Your first response should emphasize the social reinforcement; that is, praise your child with a simple comment like:

  "Melba, it is really nice shopping with you today. You've been calm for five minutes and already you've earned a token you can use for some special prize if you want to."

  With small children, you actually may want to hand the child whatever token you use to represent credits and even to arrange it so that the child has a pocket or small purse in which to store the token. With older children you may just make a mark on a card kept in your pocket, but for full impact be sure to show the child that you have done so.

  Remember, the idea is to reinforce (praise) your child socially for being cooperative as soon and as regularly as necessary to promote continued appropriate behavior. This could mean praise before you get to the first aisle if your child is used to misbehaving right away.

- Continue through the store as you typically might; collect the items on your list, and continue to reinforce your child as your program calls for.

Some parents using these steps for the first time during shopping are surprised that their children cooperate throughout shopping and that they have no reason to use time-out, a tribute to the power of positive attention to such behavior.

Check for the Need for Time-out

At some point your child may revert to old behaviors requiring the use of time-out. For those instances, here is the routine:

- At whatever point your child loses control, **as you define it**, tell the child to stop. This should not be a request but rather a clear demand from you to the child, such as:

"Marcel, keep your hands on the shopping cart rail."

- If the child stops as told, continue shopping as before.

- After a few seconds for a young child, to a minute or so for an older one, praise the child's calm demeanor, such as:

    "Wow, Marcel, it's fun to shop with you when you are so cooperative."

Refrain from comparing the child at that moment to the point when you said "stop," such as *"Marcel, it's great that you stopped grabbing things off the shelf."* The risk here is that you teach the child that *stopping* inappropriate behavior is how to get praise. And how does a child **stop** a behavior? Of course, the child has to **start** it first. Therefore by commenting on what was happening before, you may well teach the child to do the very thing you want to stop.

When Time-out is Required

So far so good. But of course many children will not stop when told to do so, or they will revert to the same stuff a few seconds later. If your child does not respond to your instruction to stop when told to, it is time to use the time-out procedure:

- Without further comment, push your shopping cart to the side of the aisle and take the child out of the store. Do so in as business-like a manner as possible so that your child gets no satisfaction from your actions. In most cases you will likely find going to the car is most practical though if you spy an isolated area nearby it might work as well.

- Put the child in the car or nearby in a safe place. If you use the car, be sure to have the keys in your own possession so that the child cannot be locked in with you locked out.

Express the time-out message clearly, something like:

    "Jose, I told you to calm down in the store. I see that you can't right now. It's not good to be out of control like that; therefore so I'm going to help you. Sit there quietly and stay there until you feel calm inside. When you do, tell me so that I'll know you are calm, too."

- After making this statement, interact as little as possible until the child indicates calm is regained.

- If the child challenges you by trying to get up, use as much restraint as is required to assure compliance. Do not use more force than required, though, to keep the focus on the child's regaining control, not on a control struggle between you two. This is another good time to "turn yourself on robot" so that you are able to do all you need to without emotions. (See Chapter Thirteen for more information on this.)

- Once the child declares calm and you are convinced, return to the store and continue your shopping. With luck, you may find your cart so that you can pick up where you left off.

- Continue to reinforce the child each time your program standards are met. Refrain from mentioning earlier misbehavior since a lecture at that point will only serve to reinforce what you **don't** want the child to do.

- If your child reverts to inappropriate behavior, again say *"Stop,"* and if there is no compliance, again use the time-out procedure as described above. Do this <u>as many times as necessary</u> to complete your planned shopping.

Once you have completed your shopping with your child cooperating, you are in a great position. You can comment on the way home about how nice it was to be together in the store. You can comment on the credits the child earned in the store. You can mention how pleased that others, such as the absent parent and the grandparents will be to learn what a good time you had. And you can reinforce all of this during your daily review. Further, before the next trip you can review how well things went during the last trip to the store. These are the ingredients of responsible behavior.

Some Potential Complications

Despite typical success with this approach, things don't always go so well; therefore, a couple more comments are in order:

- Most parents report good success with this approach, but occasionally one will describe a child who challenges far beyond the parent's patience. If this happens and if after ten or fifteen minutes you find yourself getting upset with no signs that the child will regain control, take the child home without further comment. Avoid showing anger since this will reinforce the child's sense of control. When you get home, restate the time-out message and send the child to your typical time-out location. Note that this is not suggested as a good outcome but rather is intended to minimize the negative impact on the child's future behavior.

- I have repeatedly stressed here the importance of follow-through but recognize that a variety of things can challenge even the most dedicated parents' resolve. For example, there is a good chance that a parent who is leading a screaming child from a store will encounter some well-meaning but uninformed passers-by who will frown and even comment critically about what the parent is doing.

In the face of such potentially embarrassing circumstances, keep your own goals clear. As unpleasant as your interaction with your child may appear to others, you are providing a loving and necessary life lesson by teaching better control in public. You need apologize to no one for such an effort

At a Sit-down Restaurant

Another setting that parents often find difficult is a sit-down restaurant with delays to be seated, be served, and eat in contrast to more child-friendly fast food places. All the principles discussed so far apply here just as they do during shopping. However there are some specific things that are good to think about to assure you are prepared.

Basic Preparation

The first time you take an often-challenging child out to dinner, plan ahead to assure a positive outcome from your efforts:

- Make sure that you are well rested and therefore likely to be as patient as required.

- Plan your first meal out using this approach when you will not be disappointed if things don't go smoothly or if the dinner is disrupted for a time. For instance, dinner out for your tenth anniversary where you want everything to be just perfect would not be a good time to start using time-out.

- It is probably best to take only the child or the child and siblings to minimize distraction from your goal. If you do include others, be sure that they will respect your efforts and your approach. Grandparents, who might suggest, *"Oh, he's only a baby, so don't be so harsh,"* will not be helpful. Therefore ask everyone not to comment when you deal with your child.

- Choose your meal so that if you have to leave the table to use time-out, your food won't be spoiled. That means avoiding things that must be either piping hot or very cold to enjoy and choosing instead something that can sit while you are away from the table. For example, investing in an expensive lobster dinner is probably not a good idea.

Accentuate the Positive

Recall the basics of our overall approach, namely eliminating benefits of inappropriate behavior and making it good for kids to behave appropriately. To apply these notions to dining out, follow these steps:

- Before you leave home, identify the success behaviors that are most likely to help your child get through the meal, remembering to focus on those that you value and that are directly incompatible with the behaviors you are concerned might occur. Also make certain that each item defines a behavior that is realistically reachable by your child and that the wording is clear. For example:

  "Kelly is successful when she talks in a calm voice for ten minutes during dinner."

- Prepare a simple card with the target behaviors and with a place to record successes. Be sure you have it with you and show it to your child when you arrive in the restaurant.

- Because sitting quietly in a restaurant can be boring for a child, bring a few activities for your child to use at the table. A pad of paper and a few crayons or a small hand-held game can entertain a child for a good deal of time. Make a point from time to time to comment on the child's play.

Anything that will make you more upset if your child doesn't cooperate will undermine your effectiveness. Think of this as an opportunity to teach your child an important lesson for life so that your focus is on that outcome rather than on the meal itself or on the occasion or the company with you. You must be ready to respond as required by the child's behavior unconstrained by the reactions of others or by your own hopes for the evening.

Carry Out Your Plan

With this constructive groundwork, you are ready to venture into the restaurant to begin teaching your child how to deal with a situation requiring restraint and cooperation:

- Soon after arriving, comment about how nice it is to be there with your child.

- Make waiting easier by providing appropriate activities.

- Track your child's success in meeting your target behaviors. Comment on each success, mark it on your card, and mention the credits earned. Put a token directly into the hand of a younger child. Continue in this fashion.

Check for the Need for Time-out

- If the child behaves in a way that concerns you, quietly but firmly tell the child to stop. (Remember, **don't ask; tell**.)

- If the child complies, after a few seconds for a young child or a couple minutes for an older one, praise current appropriate behavior, avoiding comparison with the just-stopped inappropriate behavior. Comparing could reinforce **stopping**, a situation which can only happen if the child **starts** the behavior. Continue through the meal as before.

When Time-out is Required

So far there has been no need for time-out. But, if your child misbehaves by your standards and does not stop when told to do so, it is time to use the procedure. Doing so is essentially the same as described at length in the section focused on shopping, but there are a few specific considerations:

- Take the child calmly from the restaurant, probably to your car (being sure to keep control of the keys yourself) and state the time-out message:

  "Kahil, I told you to calm down in the restaurant. I see that you can't right now. It's not good to be out of control like that; therefore I'm going to help you. Sit quietly in the car and stay there until you feel calm inside. When you do, tell me so that I'll know you are calm, too."

- Once the child has calmed, likely rather quickly since most kids really like to be inside, go back to your table and resume the meal. If the child stays calm, after a few seconds for a young one, a minute or two for an older one, comment on how nice it is to be in the restaurant together.

  As with all uses of time-out, **it is crucial that you follow through as many times as required** and that you remain as calm as possible while doing it. Remind yourself that if you begin losing your patience, you are doing the loving thing of teaching appropriate reactions in a place your child will go many times over the years. Note also that there are a good many other situations kids must learn to tolerate, however tedious they may be, and that this is preparation for many of them. And, remember that you may have to steel yourself against the disapproving reactions of others in the restaurant who don't know your child or your challenges but who may feel they would handle it all better.

- Once things have settled down, return to rewarding any instances of success according to your target behaviors.

Note that you may be annoyed and may not feel like giving positive remarks to the child. That is a perfectly natural reaction. However, this is the time that the most discipline is required of the adult. The approach requires showing your child that cooperating will gain social and material reinforcement. It also requires showing that you will continue your approach for as long as it takes for the behavior to become internalized, that is, self-reinforcing. Make a point of rewarding yourself for meeting these challenges despite your frustration; we all operate on the same principle of positive reinforcement as your child does.

Remember to follow-through, repeating the time-out procedure as often as required until the child has resumed internal controls. This follow-through allows the child to experience the capacity for doing so and to enjoy positive reactions from others in response to the better control.

In the Car

By now I have talked about use of time-out on a shopping trip and in a sit-down restaurant. These discussions can be applied as prototypes in a number of other situations in which your child may find it difficult to cooperate with adult expectations.

Another circumstance is different enough from the other two that it warrants its own discussion. It arises when your child is in the car. Riding for any great distance can be tiresome to kids, and confinement in a seat belt can be very distressing to an active youngster. In addition, kids seem to recognize that parents are usually focused on the road rather than on the kids, certainly while driving but even while riding as a passenger. Together those circumstances can make traveling a very tedious business for all concerned – and sometimes dangerous as well.

Fortunately, with preparation and timely use of time-out, children typically learn to behave appropriately in a car, even on lengthy trips. In fact, parents often report that their kids are more responsive to time-out in this environment than when they are home, some possible reasons for which I'll discuss below.

Basic Preparation

All of the principles and concepts discussed so far concerning the home program and the time-out procedure apply here. The following represent specific aspects to consider the first time you use this approach with your child in the car:

- Make sure that you are well rested and therefore likely to be as patient as required.

- Plan this first trip to focus on teaching your child to maintain control in the car. This means going somewhere not very important. If you have a crucial appointment, it will be difficult to meet your child's challenges calmly and patiently. Similarly, don't attempt this for the first time on your way to some place your child dislikes, such as the dentist, since that could make everything more difficult.

- Bring a few small activities that the child can use while buckled in the car seat. Older children can be encouraged to bring things for themselves. As in the restaurant example, a stiff pad of paper and a few crayons or a small hand held puzzle can entertain a child for a good deal of time, especially if you make a point to comment positively on what the child is doing, such as:

  "Sally, I can hardly wait to see what you are drawing. I hope you'll show me when we stop at the mall."

- Do not take with you anyone whom you can expect to defend your child's behavior since this will reinforce poor behavior and defeat your efforts.

- Plan your route so that if you have to stop the car, you can do so relatively quickly and safely. The shoulder of a busy freeway does not qualify. Heading for a destination that allows driving on fairly uncrowded streets can help.

Accentuate the Positive

As in all settings, be sure you clearly state your expectations and praise your child's cooperation so that time-out is less likely to be needed.

- Before you leave home, identify how you want your child to behave

178

in the car, focusing on specific and realistically reachable target behaviors that are directly incompatible with past misbehavior in the car. For example

"Tyrell is successful when he sits calmly in his car seat with his seat belt fastened for five minutes while Mom is driving."

The amount of time specified should be determined by your best estimate of what is realistically reachable for your child, taking into consideration the length of your trip.

- Prepare and take with you a card with the target behaviors listed and with a place to record successes. If you are driving and can't immediately record success, be sure to remember them. If available, a passenger can record for you. Praise your child for each success by commenting on it, for example:

    "Tyrell, it's nice to go to Grandma's with you when you are so calm. Already you've earned ten credits!"

Carry Out Your Plan

With this preparation, you are ready to go, but because driving is such an important activity, extra care is essential to succeed.

Those considerations are spelled out here:

- **Do not start the car** until the child is buckled in. Plan to use time-out at the outset if the child whines or resists. Similarly, if the child gets out of the seat while you are moving, find a safe place to stop immediately; turn off the engine, secure the keys, and do not move the car until the child is properly restrained by the seat belt. See below for how to proceed.

- Once you are all buckled in and on your way, remember to comment on how nice it is to be driving with your child.

- Each time the child meets your standards for success, express your appreciation and mention the credits earned toward some reward. Proceed on your way.

Check for the Need for Time-out

- If your child should begin to misbehave according to the standards you have set for the car, say *"Stop"* (Do not ask, tell!).

- If your child stops very shortly after, comment on the appropriate behavior and on how nice it is to be together.

When Time-out is Required

- If your child either does not stop or immediately resumes the misbehavior, find the next safe place and without comment park the car. Turn off the engine and take the key so that, should you get out of the car for any reason, there is no risk of the child locking the doors with you outside.

- Express the time-out message:

  "Tyrell, I told you to calm down while we were driving. It is dangerous to drive when there is extra noise and disruption in the car. I see that you can't calm yourself right now; therefore I'm going to help you. We are going to stay here with the car stopped while you quiet yourself. Stay in your seat (Or "Get back in your seat and stay there") until you feel calm inside. When you do, tell me so that I'll know you are calm, too. Then we can start up again."

  Some parents prefer to step out of the car and open the door on the passenger's side, both to be away from the child and to be ready to get in next to the child if misbehavior escalates. If you do that, be alert, and if possible, lock the door on the street side to assure the child is safe. Do not interact with the child, either pleasantly or angrily; it can be tempting to show some annoyance at such a time, but that is more likely to reinforce the inappropriate behavior than to reinforce the behavior you want from the child.

- Note that if there are two children in the car and if both are involved in the ruckus, either directly or indirectly, give them both the time-out message. Remove one child from the car with you and have that child stay close at hand. Avoid interacting with the child outside the car since doing so could evoke cries of favoritism and further the disruption. Do not provide any reinforcement to either child during time out. Try practicing "turning yourself on robot."

- Once the child has calmed and is safely buckled in, start up the car and proceed as before. After a short time of calm, comment to the child about how good it is to be calm and about how much you enjoy traveling together. Do not comment further on the disruptive behavior, even for comparison.

- If the child loses control again, as you define it, immediately stop the car as before and go through all the same steps. To the extent possible, keep yourself calm and focus on the goal of teaching your child an important behavior change.

As with all uses of time-out, remember that **follow through is critical**. Accordingly, consider carefully whether you will be able to follow through long enough to assure your child is cooperating in the car. If you aren't sure you can make it work, I urge you not to start since using the procedure without completing the process will teach the child that if a little fussing doesn't work, then maybe a lot will.

Children seem to hate sitting still in a stopped car even if they don't particularly like the destination. As a result, stopping the car and turning off the engine alone have a significant impact on how ready kids are to calm themselves. If you avoid giving them further reason to challenge you, you can expect fairly rapid changes. This is why time-out in the car seems to be more quickly and thoroughly effective than it is in some other settings for those who are consistent with their follow-through.

An Illustrative Example

In my experience, parents who have used time-out successfully in their homes have found comparable success in applying the approach away from home by using these guidelines. As a result, I have not included the sorts of illustrative examples that appear in other sections. However, because keeping a child in a car seat is so very important, I have included this additional discussion dealing with the issue.

You stressed several times that our child should ride in his car seat, but he really likes to lay in the space behind the back seat of our van with his toys. What's wrong with that?

I am glad you noticed that this is something that I consider very important. Of course, most states now require kids to be buckled in age-appropriate car seats, but I was stressing this long before the laws were passed. During my years of consulting on hospital pediatric wards, I had several deeply saddening experiences of working with families whose children had been badly injured and, in a couple cases, killed in auto collisions. In each case, the child was not buckled into a car seat or was not using a seat belt. All those who survived were left with years, or a lifetime, of misery and limited capabilities.

It did not matter where in the car the kids started. If they were not restrained, they were battered by their own movements as they struck other objects. On two occasions the children had been standing in the front seat when the collision occurred. One of these involved a bump of the car ahead soft enough to barely dent the bumpers on both cars;

however, both kids smashed into the windshield and both ended up with severe brain damage. Both, after healing on the outside, looked like the beautiful little children they had been, but neither was responsive to the outside world in any meaningful way.

The parents involved in these cases reported tearfully that their children had refused or objected to staying in their car seats. All were equally sure nothing serious would happen to their kids. Yet they were living a parent's ultimate nightmare. I needn't tell other parents how these parents felt as they beheld the damage to their precious children. These children paid enormous prices for the "freedom" to sit as they pleased in the car. My hope is that no other child ever suffers the same fate and that no other parent lives the lifetime of regret and pain that goes with it.

The program presented here includes tools necessary to assure your child's compliance and therefore safety. While sitting buckled in a car seat may be a bit inconvenient, it is easy to provide a comfortable, safe seat and easy access to toys.

For our family's many lengthy trips, we filled a sturdy box with a selection of safe toys and games. The box cover worked very nicely as a table for things they could play together. This arrangement provided enough entertainment to keep the boys occupied during many otherwise tedious hours of driving. Reinforcing them for their cooperation completed the system that allowed for enjoyable travel. Since those years, we have noticed many more toys designed for travel, as well as tables that can be hung on the back of the front seat and situated in front of the child seat to make things even more handy.

The key here is for parents to take seriously their role in protecting their kids so that travel can stay a healthy, happy, conflict-free experience.

Section Four

MONITORING PROGRESS

Our greatest natural resource is the minds of our children.

~Walt Disney

Chapter Twenty

"But Doctor, what do we do when . . . we send our kid to his room for misbehavior and later when we check on him he is reading a book or playing a game and doesn't seem to mind the punishment?"
Page 166

OVERVIEW AND ORIENTATION

By now you have read my notions about:

- How children learn to take responsibility for their own behavior,

- How your actions – intentional or otherwise – contribute to that process,

- How you can structure a simple program for your own home, utilizing your expanded understanding,

- How you can design your program to extend your influence over your children even when you are not with them,

- How you can prepare to reduce inappropriate behavior, and

- How you can incorporate all of this into your family life with a minimum of disruption and a maximum of benefit.

I hope that you have decided to institute a program to meet the needs of your family and that you will find the process uplifting and supportive of constructive and loving family interactions.

If you have begun a home program, you likely have seen progress on some target behaviors while other behaviors may have been slower to respond, requiring some of the fine-tuning already described. Fine tuning may have involved assuring the items were realistically reachable by reducing the specific expectations set for them. Or fine tuning might have involved assuring a proper balance between the task required and the benefit provided to the child by increasing the amount of reward – "credits" – the child could earn toward a material reward.

Chances are, though, that, after a few days or a week or two, you were able to refine things to a workable level, and you and your family have been able to settle into a comfortable routine. As the program moves along, you likely will find that some target behaviors are consistently occurring as expected and that your child is regularly successfully completing at least an item or two. Good for your child and good for you for setting things up to support this change! Better still, you may find that your daily reviews have added a warm and pleasant few minutes to each day. If not, it might be a good idea to review the portion of Chapter Fifteen dealing with the daily review to assure that you are getting the most out of this special time.

It is ironic that such successes carry with them a very real risk, which tends to show itself at this very point in the process. As discussed earlier, some parents begin taking for granted the child's improved compliance and begin to slack off on the program. While this seems natural, it can undermine and even destroy your good work. Until the child has internalized the appropriate behavior – that is, has begun self-reinforcement of behavior – there is a great likelihood of reverting to the old behavior if the assigned rewards are discontinued. In my experience, doing so is among the most common reasons for failure of positive reinforcement programs.

This inherent risk presents a significant challenge. How do you know when your child has been reinforced enough so that the behavior is now mastered? The answer is not so obvious since the child's behavior is likely to look pretty much the same while reinforcement is still needed and after it is not. That is the very reason that parents are inclined to discontinue reinforcement prematurely; the child appears to be doing things just fine even in early stages of internalizing the behavior.

In order to avoid falling into this problem, what follows is designed to walk you through the process of reviewing your progress and thereby determining whether your child has achieved mastery or whether there is continuing need for reinforcement. Note that for most children and for most behaviors, this stage is unlikely to occur for at least a few weeks – and for some children and some behaviors, it could be a good deal longer.

Chapter Twenty-one

"But Doctor, what do we do when . . . we try to make the program work as you described but then things come up that throw us off track?"

Page 135

REVIEWING YOUR PROGRESS

First, Your Impressions

Based on my observations of the inherent wisdom of parents, I urge you to start your formal appraisal of your program by considering your overall impressions. I will get to how to look at the data from your charts shortly, but it is a good idea to ignore them for a moment while you ask yourselves what you **think** and how you **feel** about how your child is doing on the program:

- Do you think that overall things are better in your home?

- Are your concerns about your child lessening enough to give you more peace of mind?

- Are things no better than when you started?

To gain perspective on how you are doing, let your mind run over each item on your child's chart, considering how things were when you started and how they are now. Ask yourself what seems to be the reason for any changes that you have noticed. It is interesting how often people discount their efforts in the program but rather attribute change to all sorts of other things. *"Maybe my son just grew out of it,"* or *"Maybe my daughter is just being nicer because Christmas is coming,"* or *"It could just be that our child got to spend the summer with Grandma."*

While any such observation could be correct, it is important to pay most attention to your own efforts to improve things so that you can learn how useful your approach can be for you. Your program seems a likely source of change since that is what you set it up to do. If you dismiss that idea too easily, you may ignore a powerful approach which you can control and which does not depend upon luck or happenstance.

Many times parents have called me long after we completed our work together because of renewed concerns about their child's behavior. Often I learned that the parents had discontinued their program after some success and that typically they had supposed other factors had caused their child's improvements. As a result, they didn't think of the program to address their current needs. Fortunately, in many cases, simply starting a new program was all that was needed to turn things around to the parents' satisfaction.

The reason to consider your impressions first is that your chart may show success, but if you don't feel things are better, there still may be a need to make changes. Or you might be so busy that you haven't noticed the progress despite real changes that show up on the chart. Either way, it is important to go on to the detailed evidence from your charting of your child's progress.

Next, a Look at Your Charts

Part of the review process is to determine whether your child is progressing as you had hoped at the outset. If the program seems to be going okay but you find the original issues remain pretty much unchanged, it is time to think about how you might modify the program to better meet your needs. More about that as I discuss reviewing the results captured in your chart.

So far I have discussed the chart as a simple tool to specify your expectations for your child and to record successes to track progress toward a material reward. Now I will discuss the benefits of a permanent record of your efforts.

For your first review, you likely will have several weeks' worth of experience and charts. You then are ready to assess how far your child has come toward mastering one or more behaviors. Arrange your charts on a table from left to right so that you can read across from week to week for each item. If you have made changes while fine tuning, some items may have changed or may even have been moved on the sheets; therefore take care in looking across the row of charts to stay with the same item.

With things ready for easy viewing, examine the charts item by item across as many weeks as your charts provide. Focus on trends showing improvement, lack of movement, or decline.

Below is a sample from our mythical Johnny's charts for just one item across six weeks. The results for the six consecutive weeks have been lined up here in six rows just for convenience of presentation and ease of discussion. For purposes of this illustration, here, unlike on the chart above, we had Johnny responsible to take the trash out every day of the week. Before you read further, please spend a moment looking over these results and getting a feel for how to understand them. What do you notice about how Johnny is doing, based upon the above record for this one item over four weeks? Once you have your own thoughts in mind, read on for my comments.

A look at **Week 1** shows that Johnny got the trash out on time on Monday and Wednesday. Whether that is good or not so good depends on how often Johnny had done the task before the program was started. If he never did it, two out of seven seems promising. On the other hand, if he typically did it two or three times a week, this doesn't show any progress – yet.

Item	Week	Mon.	Tue.	Wed.	Thu.	Fri.	Sat.	Sun.
"Johnny is	Week 1	10	x	10	x	x	x	x
successful	Week 2	x	x	10	x	x	x	x
when he has	Week 3	x	10	x	10	10	x	10
the trash out	Week 4	x	10	10	x	10	x	10
by 5:00 p.m."	Week 5	10	x	x	10	10	x	x
	Week 6	10	10	10	10	10	x	10

Sample of Johnny's progress on one item over a period of six weeks

Week 2 shows Johnny succeeding only on Wednesday, a decline from the previous week and surely not what his parents had hoped for. It would be easy to be discouraged about this, but it is important to remember that this is a new program and that both Johnny and his parents are getting used to the new system. Johnny may not yet have come to appreciate fully the way things will work and thus isn't so invested in earning credits yet. Or maybe the parents haven't yet gotten into a smooth routine of withholding negative reactions that might work against the reward program. Or maybe they haven't followed through each day with the daily review, the component that ties all the elements together. Whatever the cause, there is no reason for alarm so early in the new program.

A look at **Week 3** provides more reason for optimism. That week Johnny succeeded on Tuesday, Thursday, Friday, and Sunday, four of seven, a nice doubling of successes from the beginning week. That surely is what Johnny's parents were looking for but may or may not be an ongoing trend.

Week 4 reveals that Johnny succeeded on four of seven days: Tuesday, Wednesday, Friday, and Sunday. What do we make of that? It doesn't show any improvement over the previous week, but that week showed a doubling of the first week, and maybe holding his own for a week is good enough. Investors watching the stock market are pleased with no change after a day of dramatic increases since it is more likely for what went up to go down. So, I think we can say, "So far so good."

During **Week 5** Johnny got the trash out on time on Monday, Thursday, and Friday, three of seven. This represents a bit of a decline from the previous two weeks but still is above the starting week, and only one fewer than Weeks 3 and 4. The overall trend continues to appear promising.

The **last week** on Johnny's chart shows that he met expectation every day but Saturday, a whopping six of seven days. It will take a few more weeks to be sure if this trend will hold up, but so far Johnny appears to be on track and there is plenty of reason for optimism.

But is there anything else we can learn from looking at Johnny's chart over this six-week period? Likely you will notice, as did at least one parent in every class of whom I asked the same question, that Johnny never succeeded on Saturday even in the last week when he got the trash out on time every other day of the week. What can be made of that observation? I imagine there could be several explanations, but only the parents by observing and talking with Johnny could find the answer.

Perhaps Johnny had a baseball game each of those Saturdays, and perhaps the games ran long enough that when he came home all sweaty and still pumped with adrenaline, it was difficult for him to focus on his chores. Or maybe he actually got home too late to be able to get done by 5:00 p.m. Or perhaps he often went away with friends or even a non-custodial parent many Saturdays so that his routine didn't allow him to get the trash out on time.

With some thought and discussion, the parents are likely to be able to identify whatever factors are at play. Once they have done so, they can elect to modify the program in some way to support Johnny in succeeding on Saturdays also. For our above example, the chart might be amended to say something like:

"Johnny is successful when he has the trash out by 5:00 p.m., except on Saturdays, when he has until 7:00 p.m."

The idea here is to recognize legitimate barriers to success and act accordingly. Remember that this whole approach is intended to meet your needs in helping your child assume appropriate levels of responsibility. Anytime the structure of the program interferes with that end, things are out of whack. The structure is to support your efforts to get to your goals and therefore is subject to change as you require. Please keep this in mind as I continue the discussion of managing the program over time.

In summary, from the sample chart, we have watched Johnny move from two to six days of success per week, over a six-week period. That impressive change shows that Johnny is responding constructively to the approach. Most importantly, we know that if his parents continue to reinforce Johnny's behavior, it is virtually inevitable that he will reach the 100 percent probability of continuing to meet expectations. That is, he will be responsible for this behavior. Or, in other words still, he will have begun internally reinforcing this behavior for himself.

Whatever way you put it, this boy will have mastered the behavior and will no longer depend upon his parents for direction or for rewards, the goal of all their efforts and something of which they can be pleased.

Return to the Basics

Let us go on to consider in a somewhat more structured way how you can get the most out of reviewing your child's chart a few weeks into the program and then periodically thereafter. If you followed my suggestion, you will already have considered your overall impressions of how things are going. Now I will focus on how you can guide your efforts by considering in detail the results showing on your charts so far.

As you look over each of the items in your child's program (as illustrated above), note any items that seem not to be responding as well as expected – or not as well as other items. Anywhere progress seems unduly slow, do a review of how things are set up consistent with the principles laid out from the beginning. That is, for each item that seems stuck, make sure that it meets the three basic characteristics of well-worded target behaviors. Here are some easy steps to guide you:

• Check each under-performing item to be sure each is **realistically reachable**, considering what you know about your child. Items showing little or no progress often are too demanding for the child. You might think that the child "just should be able to do it," but the child's actual behavior will guide you better than thinking what the child "should" do.

You may have observed your child actually completing the task. While this may seem to prove the item is realistically reachable, sheer ability is only part of the issue. It is also important to consider the child's feelings and past reactions in similar situations when setting standards for each item.

When you recognize that an item that isn't showing improvement may not be realistic for your child, consider breaking the item into parts, then reassign credits and remember to provide praise for completion of the newly defined smaller items as they occur. As an example, an item may state that:

"Maria is successful when she is up, dressed, and down for breakfast by 7:30 a.m."

For some kids who get most of the steps right without help, this item may be a very useful, prompting them to focus just a bit more and to get everything done on time. But it may be too much for a child who seems to struggle to get up and who eventually appears at the table wearing one sock and the opposite shoe. In such a situation, it might be more constructive to break the item into two or more parts. An alternative might be:

"Maria is successful when:
1. she is up by 7:10 a.m.
2. she is completely dressed and down for breakfast by 7:30 a.m."

Chances are that at the beginning Maria will not get both items done successfully but that she may be able to do one and, through reinforcement, build on that success to do it more, gradually completing the other as well. Surely the chances of overall success are improved by such a change.

- When you are sure that each item is realistically reachable, look closely to assure each is worded in **positive terms**, that is, focusing on what you **do** want your child to, do not on what your child should not do. On the surface, this seems like a simple thing to tell at a glance by making sure that the words *"no"* or *"not"* or *"doesn't"* does not appear in any item. And for sure if you find any, reword the item by asking yourself what behavior you **would** like to see in your child that is also **directly incompatible** with the one you'd like to stop. You may want to review the portion of Chapter Thirteen focused on writing behavior items.

But even if none of these clearly negative words appears in items that are stuck, look more closely at the wording. Watch for the insidious insertion of the word *"without,"* as in a phrase like *"without sassing"* or *"without whining"* or *"without reminders."* Such phrases, by their nature, introduce a negative tone because they draw attention to the very behaviors you are trying to eliminate, and we know that attention itself can be very reinforcing.

You can include the same ideas in the item with positive phrases. As examples, *"without sassing"* might become *"in a respectful way,"* *"without whining"* might become *"in your ten-year-old voice,"* and *"without reminders"* might become *"on your own."* Also note that while words such as *"respectful"* may seem pretty fancy for some kids, the way kids learn the meaning of words typically is through experiencing how they are used. An example: a child behaves respectfully, even if by accident, and a parent comments at that moment with something like, *"Sally, it is so nice when you are so respectful to us."* That is, you teach the meaning as you go along and your child will rapidly come to understand those traits that you prize even if she never actually says the word.

Note that even substituting the word *"if"* for "when" in the phrase *"Troy is successful . . ."* can introduce a negative component. *"If"* suggests doubt that the child will succeed, whereas *"when"* shows a clear expectation that the child will succeed, if not now, then later, and when we have constructed the program correctly, the child **will** succeed.

> I am a bit chagrined to acknowledge that only after years of working with these programs did I recognize the above truth. Since then, I have stressed using the more positive *"when,"* and I strongly urge you to do so.

By going over the first two steps, you will have made sure that all items are realistically reachable for your child and that items are positively focused on what you expect your child to do.

- What remains is to look at each item of concern one more time to assess whether the **criteria of success are as clear as possible**. Remember that phrases such as *"is good at"* or *"what the child is supposed to do"* provide little clarity for a child. At the same time, they offer a child working to gain some sense of control an opportunity to challenge the parents by doing the minimum implied by the vague statement.

> Many parents have assured me confidently that *"Our daughter knows exactly what she is supposed to do,"* only to discover that what was so clear to them was not at all clear to the child. In fact, very often it turned out that the two parents often didn't have the same understanding of their expectations, something they

193

recognized only while trying to define them for their program. This vagueness also allows a child to exploit parental inconsistencies. Clearly stating expectations in this program is one aspect that makes it so effective.

Note that it can be especially challenging to define clear expectations in a school extension of your program. Teachers, busy with a large class, may wish to keep things general for their own convenience, leaving the child with all the uncertainties already discussed.

If you have any doubts about how clear any of your statements are, ask your child to explain the standard of success. If the child can't explain it clearly, please don't just tell the child verbally what you want understood, but rather make sure the written standard includes the new wording. And if you have items that don't lend themselves completely to defined standards (e.g., *"gets along with"*), be sure that you handle things consistently and in a manner that avoids tug-of-wars with your child. If that is happening with you, I suggest you reread the part of Chapter Thirteen providing guidelines for such circumstances.

These three steps are designed to help you consider carefully any items in your program that are not moving well. Once you have identified needed modifications, you can rework the relevant items to assure that they are realistically reachable, positive, and clear. That will allow you to continue working day by day, week by week to support your child in assuming evergreater levels of responsible behavior.

Chapter Twenty-two

"But Doctor, what do we do when . . . we get busy so we can't do all the things you said are important for the program?" Page 134

MODIFYING YOUR PROGRAM OVER TIME

Overtime a variety of circumstances will require you to make modifications in your program. Most of these can be anticipated and will not present major problems. What follows is intended to prepare you to deal successfully with them as they arise.

Responding to Ongoing Success

Sooner or later, as you work with the program your child will improve enough on a specific behavior to make you wonder whether you need to continue reinforcement. This improvement is what you have worked so hard for and is worth a moment's pause to congratulate yourself. However, there is some risk in dealing with this development. Done carelessly, you can teach kids that they must fail from time to time in to keep the goodies coming. Done carefully, you can convey how great it feels to be master of one's own behavior, a splendid gift from you to your child. So, what is required to assure the better outcome?

What to Look For

First review your child's successes on a specific item from start to the present, as discussed above. This review will show you how adequately the child is completing the task. It will not, however, tell you how much the child still relies on your reinforcement, or, conversely, how adequately the child has taken personal responsibility for the task.

Lacking such certainty, look for **several weeks of <u>near</u> perfect performance** on the item; waiting for perfect performance would likely prevent any chance of moving on.

> Ask yourself, for example, whether you ever forget, ignore, or neglect some important task you know you should do. Most of us slip up from time to time, not because we are irresponsible but because we are human. Kids deserve the same acceptance for occasional lapses.

Unfortunately, there doesn't seem to be any certain way to define "several" weeks. Some kids may reach mastery on some behaviors after

195

only a couple of weeks while on other behaviors after much longer times. What matters is not the speed but the certainty since you are building a life-time of responsible behavior. Here is a rule of thumb to guide your next move:

> **Six weeks of near-perfect performance on an item is sufficient to warrant considering a check for internalization of the behavior represented.**

Such success does not guarantee that the child has internalized the behavior, but we find out in a way that allows easy recovery if we are wrong. We do this by "fading" out the reinforcement.

Guidelines for "Fading" Reinforcement

Once you think that your child may be ready for less reinforcement – that is, has had near-perfect performance for several weeks – move on to the next step. Begin the process of **fading your reinforcement out of the child's life in a step-by-step manner.** While you are doing this, you'll also be assessing how ready your child is for this step.

Your task while fading an item out of your program includes:

- Preparing your child for a change in the frequency or in the amount of reinforcement provided for successful completion of the behavior.

- Assuring that your child recognizes and feels good about achieving mastery of the behavior.

- Assuring that your child does not have reason to conclude that it might be better to screw up from time to time in order to continue reinforcement for misbehavior, a potentially appealing idea to a child working hard for enough credits for a coveted material reward.

You can best prepare your child during a daily review when you all are relaxed, you have time to go over the whole situation carefully, and you can watch your child's reactions.

After completing the usual review, identify the item you think your child may have mastered and comment on it specifically. Point out on your chart all of the successes over the past several weeks. Then begin the fading process with a comment like:

"Jeffrey, look! Your charts show that you have done great at getting

196

the trash out on time for the past six weeks. It looks as if you may not need our help so much anymore!"

Note that an alert child, hearing this the first time, may run up the radar and start scanning for any threat of a loss of benefits. But you can calm such worries by going on:

"We are really proud of your progress. Because you seem to have mastered this job, we are going to change the program a bit. Starting next Monday, instead of ten credits each time you finish the job correctly, you will earn five."

At this the child's radar will be in a spin, and you may hear, *"Hey, that's not fair."* Whatever the reaction, a quick request that the child hear you out should suffice while you go on with:

"We know that being able to earn credits for the baseball glove (or whatever) you want is important to you. Therefore, we are also going to make another change. We have noticed that it is still hard for you to get your math assignment done on time each day, and we want to help you get more used to doing that. We will add the five credits you don't seem to need anymore to get the trash out, to the ten credits you can already earn to get your math done on time. We hope this will help with that task also."

Typically this helps kids calm enough to show some interest and at least to listen. Once it is clear the changes will not interfere with chances to earn a prized reward, the child is likely to be more accepting. That, then, allows you to complete this central and hugely important message:

"Jeffrey, we are really proud of how well you have mastered this job of getting the trash out on you own. Your dad and I have noticed that you also seem kind of proud of yourself for getting this done so quickly each day and both of us are really happy about that, too!"

Mastery is all-important in a child's life, particularly among kids who seem not to show a lot of it. But remember when your child was two or so and you tried to help with various tasks, you likely were rebuked a few times with a haughty *"I can do it myself!"* That is the refrain of a child eagerly pursuing a sense of mastery, something most of us continue to do in a variety of realms for our entire lives.

Watch a boy playing a video game for a while. You likely will see times when he is frustrated, even cussing at the video screen while still working intensely to progress. Too much of that and you may see him toss the controller aside and quit for a time. But it is likely that he'll go back again and again, until finally "winning" the game. He may brag and strut briefly and then start all over again. He may go through many of the same reactions, though this time he may show less frustration as things go better. He may complete the game a number of times getting better each time, before finally tossing it aside, once he feels competent and ready to move on to new challenges.

By this point you have told the child how things will change beginning the next day. And you have calmed any concerns about losing benefits. Next you must follow the new plan faithfully and respond to the child's successes just as you did before, although it is a good idea to increase the amount of your social reinforcement for the first few times:

> "Great, Jeffrey, you are doing great at getting the trash out! It is so good to see you doing things so much on your own."

When Things Don't Go So Well

Sometimes your best guess will be wrong and your child will not yet be ready for less reinforcement. If so, you might notice fewer completed tasks, which could mean the child is checking things out. Remain calm and continue your strategy of praising successes and not reacting to failures, even with a comment like *"But you had been doing so well!"*

Even if your child does not complete the task for a few days in a row, you need not panic. But if it continues after that, it is time to move back to the previous arrangement. Doing so should not be seen as a big thing but rather as recognizing what you couldn't know for sure until you tried the change: that the child wasn't yet ready. At the next daily review, again at the end of the normal process, very calmly say to the child something like:

> "Well, Jeffrey, it looks as if we acted too soon when we reduced the number of credits you were earning for getting the trash out on time. We see it is still harder for you than we thought. We are going to put those five credits back so that now you can earn ten credits just like you did before. We are sorry we made it harder for you, but we know you can get back on track and do as well as you did before."

Because in our illustration with Jeffrey, we actually moved the five credits taken from getting the trash out to the item on getting his math assignment done and in on time, we have a small dilemma. This is especially true if the child has shown any improvement in getting the math done. Do we really want to take away those credits and thereby perhaps discourage increased effort and success there? Probably not, but what to do then? Well, the easy answer is simply to add five more credits into the system, leaving the moved credits where they were placed. The only real effect is inflating the system just a bit, meaning the child may get to his reward a bit sooner. Most parents seem not to care much about doing so if they are seeing good results. I suggest this choice, but you could just reduce the math credits to the prior level.

Final Steps to Your Child's Mastery

So far I have discussed how you can begin fading the number of credits a child earns for completing an item that seems to be going well. What remains is to talk about completing that process. If the child continues to do well after the reduction in credits, you have evidence that you were right in your estimate that not so much of your help is needed. After a few more weeks at that level of credits, you can again go through the fading process during a daily review with the child. As before, fade the credits by reducing the number by a reasonable amount, typically half. Explain what you intend to do, and express your pride in the successes that allow for the changes.

For items that start with few credits, only a step or two of fading may reach a level where cutting the number further leaves too little to be meaningful. In that case you may move to remove the item entirely. Reaching this point should be seen as a **big** deal. Make sure that your child recognizes that achievement. At your daily review you can emphasize the mastery and can point out how pleased you are. You also can add a special "certificate of mastery" to acknowledge the child's success. The simple sample shown here was constructed on a computer.

Certificate of Mastery

This is to certify that

Jeffrey Sontag

has successfully mastered

and

has assumed responsibility for

Removing Trash from our Home on Time

Recorded this 14th Day of July, 2007

Signed _____*Mom and Dad*_____

Sample certificate to enhance reinforcement

Regarding younger children using tokens for credits: chances are the item you want to fade out received only one token in the first place and it isn't so obvious how to cut them in half. You may be able to think of other ways to handle this, but some parents have typically provided the child with one token for two successes as the first step in fading out the tokens. With these kids, give extra praise during the fading process to make up for any sense of loss from less tokens. Otherwise, the process is pretty much the same as for older kids.

Discontinuing the Program

My wife and I found this approach such a central part of family life that it is difficult to imagine completely stopping the program. However, some parents choose to do so, some with negative outcomes. Below are some guidelines to minimize negative outcomes if you pursue this option.

Keep in mind that the program represents a contract between parent and child. It establishes the clear and constructive relationship between responsible behavior, on the one hand, and reward and benefit, on the other. Discontinuing the program must be done in a manner which honors that relationship and which furthers its goals. Thus, the process must be thoughtful and must allow time for appropriately fading out the structured material reinforcement for the identified behaviors. Ideally it will mean working through each targeted item to completion while simply not adding any newer ones.

A good starting place in the process is to review the original goals and agreements to assure that there is no broken faith with the child. Discuss with the child what you intend to do as well as the reasons as best you can explain them. Part of the message should be that as the child completes each item, the program will have fewer items. Kids are likely to become concerned since that will mean less opportunity to earn credits toward desired rewards. You can lessen such concerns by increasing the number of credits earned for each behavior still on the chart in order to maintain the same total possible.

Use the fading steps described above for each item in the chart. As you near the last items, make sure the child will have a chance to earn enough credits for the selected reward so that there are no leftover bogus credits at the end. Remember the importance of supportive social reinforcement throughout this process. Keep in mind that all of these principles will continue to operate in your child and in your home even after you no longer use a structured program. That is, work to assure that you continue to utilize the principle of positive reinforcement even if you provide your support in an unstructured format. Avoid slipping back to the all-too-easy pattern of paying more attention to inappropriate behaviors than to those you consider appropriate.

These steps, I hope, will lessen any negative impact of discontinuing your home program. I hope, though, that you give some thought to continuing the program for the long run as a constructive and flexible tool for guiding your child to responsible adulthood.

Chapter Twenty-three

"But Doctor, what do we do when . . . our daughter who was doing pretty well on the program seemed to lose interest and doesn't want to use any of the many credits she has earned?" Page 116

FITTING YOUR PROGRAM
TO SPECIAL OCCASIONS

So far I have focused on building your home program into your family routine and making things systematic so that all of you are clear about how the system will work and can follow through accordingly. I anticipated making modifications to fit special circumstances, as I did for Johnny, who never got the trash out on time on any Saturday over a six-week period. Now I will focus on other family circumstances that may require modification of the program. I hope that you will recognize that the program can be flexible enough to respond to a variety of changing situations. Perhaps the only real limitation in this regard is your own capacity to assure that your child understands the changes and to keep track of the changes you make.

Special Days

Changed family routines due to special occasions sometimes require program changes. Perhaps the most common and simplest occasions to deal with are special days or short periods, such as holidays. For such days, the program can easily be adjusted to fit whatever changes in routine are involved. The key here is to make the changes **ahead of time** to avoid later trying to make adjustments in the face of disappointed children unable to follow their programs. It is important not to reinforce fussing inadvertently.

On the way to visit grandparents for Thanksgiving, the kids in the back seat begin fussing with each other, the conflict growing as the miles pass. The parents get annoyed and tell them both to stay quiet. This momentarily calm things, but the din picks up again along with some whining about the long trip and one child encroaching on the space of the other. Eventually the parent reacts angrily, the kids pout, and the trip, which was meant to be such fun, turns bleak and dark. A parent using this program may be tempted to insert a "fix" by asserting that if the kids behave themselves, they can earn a certain number of credits. However, by that point with irritation in the air, it is

201

likely that the real impact would be to reinforce the earlier conflict, at least as much as the intended calm, and perhaps taint the program as well.

By planning ahead, you can avoid such hassles and set the stage from the beginning for a pleasant and joyful family outing, in this case an appropriate beginning to Thanksgiving. The idea is to be aware of departures from the routine and to anticipate what may be challenges to the kids and to you during the atypical routine. That way you can build a resolution into the program on a temporary basis. For example, during the family review a day or two before the planned trip the parents might say:

"Kids, tomorrow is Thanksgiving. You don't have school. That means that the stuff on your program about school doesn't apply. However, we are going to drive to Grandma's for dinner, and we know it can be boring and tiring to stay calm in the car all that way. To help you with that, just for tomorrow and for Sunday when we come back, we are going to have a special part in the program. For each of you for every half hour you stay calm and pleasant in the car, you will get five credits. We know you can earn lots of credits. We are going to have such a good time!"

This requires the parents to praise the kids for each half hour of success and to bring along a card for recording each success. It also requires improvising a time and place for the daily review while away from home. And, if the parents so choose, they might modify other aspects of the home program for the days while at Grandma's, depending on whether they anticipate any other challenges for the child's behavior.

Special Seasons

A variation on this sort of change arises during longer changes in the routine, most commonly with the arrival of school breaks. I will focus on that period, although the discussion could apply also to any similar and substantial breaks in routines.

If You Decide to Take a Recess from the Program

Parts of your program likely will not apply when school is out. Some parents may choose simply to take a recess from the program. This approach will present no problem as long as they reinstate it when school resumes. However, there are several important considerations for this sort of change to avoid new problems. Your child likely has gotten used to and comfortable with the routine of the program and also is surely focused on a specific reward. If you just suddenly stop the program, the child will feel as if earned credits are really bogus, much as we might if our money suddenly was declared unspendable. Of course you and I know that the program will resume in a few months. However, no child, facing a summer of freedom from school, wants to anticipate the arrival of fall and the end of vacation to enjoy benefits of already completed efforts.

To avoid such an outcome you can anticipate changes in your routine and prepare suitable modifications. Tell your child what to expect and when to expect it. Also track closely what reward the child is working toward to assure that the goal can be reached by the time you suspend the program. Since it is unlikely that the reward will be earned exactly when you want to stop for vacation, plan ways your child can get to the reward even if it isn't reached by then. For example, you could continue an item or two with enough credits to allow earning the reward. Or you could add a few items specific to vacation just to reach the goal. For instance, if there are a few chores that you might want done one time only, you could offer credits for their completion. You can be generous in this regard to assure your child feels good about the program and does not feel cheated by its suspension. This will also help when you are ready to resume it in the fall.

As the vacation winds down and resumption of the program nears, plan the steps necessary to restart your program. Think through the target behaviors to include on the chart and the rewards to offer, the latter considering what the child prefers to have included. Reviewing the basics of the program will provide a good guide to this process. For any items that you will keep from the earlier program, be prepared for your child to start back a few steps from the previous level. It could take a while to reach the prior levels of performance. While you may be impatient, it is important to maintain the same supportive attitude as before and allow the child time to readjust. Teachers recognize this and thus spend the first few days of school helping kids settle in and reviewing things kids learned in the spring. And most of us know managers who say they have to do the same thing when their employees return from vacation.

If You Decide to Adapt the Program to Vacation Needs

I have discussed how to suspend the program for vacation periods. You may, instead, prefer to continue the program through such times with suitable modifications to support your overall goal of teaching responsible behavior. To do so, consider your daily routine and add items to fit your expectations during vacation periods. Just write realistic, positive, and clear items to cover the behaviors of interest and then assign credits accordingly.

You may decide to reduce expectations, just as you may expect less of yourself at those times. Even then you can maintain focus on the larger picture, supporting the child's maturation as a responsible person.

We lived far from family as our sons were growing up and in order to visit them we took a good many long car trips, several of 5,000 miles or more. While such trips can be exciting and fun, they also can be taxing to the patience of all involved. Even the best planning sometimes left long stretches of driving through unexciting terrain. In anticipation, we brought along suitable activities and games for the kids. We also scheduled abundant stops and time to stretch and play along the way.

Because we used a behavioral program, though, we were able to further assure harmony and calm along the way. We also worked to support confidence in our sons' mastery of new and different situations. For each trip we identified age-appropriate sets of target behaviors and rewards and developed special charts just for the trip. Among the items we included, adapted for each son's age, were:

"Danny (seven years old) is successful when he draws a picture of something special he sees during the day's driving."

"Mike (nine years old) is successful when he writes a half-page description of something special he sees during the day."

The boys were awarded credits for completion of these activities so they benefited directly from doing something that also helped us all have a pleasant trip. An added advantage was that they paid more attention to things they saw and thus got more out of our trips.

Consistent with our goal of teaching responsible behavior, we also included a few items identifying age-appropriate chores so that they each contributed to family life. From very early ages, they could respond successfully to an item like:

"Danny is successful when he carries his toy case into the motel room."

Whether you continue the program during vacation periods, though, remains your choice. There is not a right or wrong answer to the decision, but there are opportunities to further your goals if you so elect.

Note that while I focused here on the universal of school vacation, the same concepts apply equally well to any other extended period during which circumstances might suggest a modification in your program.

Chapter Twenty-four

"But Doctor, what do we do when . . . our son responds to our instructions to go to time out by telling us how unfair we are and saying insulting things to us?"

Page 168

"TROUBLESHOOTING" YOUR PROGRAM

Even the most successful program may at times show some problems. Fortunately some sleuthing and changes are likely to get you back on track. What follows focuses on families who have had some success, followed by signs of decline.

As with most problems, those that arise in a home program are more easily resolved if you take action sooner rather than later. One bonus of the daily review is that you will constantly be aware of how your child is doing, and thus you will be likely to notice any significant set-back early on. Taking calm action then will pay long-term benefits.

The First Place to Look

Fortunately, the most common problems in programs showing initial success but declining effectiveness turn out also to be the easiest to identify and resolve. They most often involve the reinforcement side of the program in the form of snags that can creep into the program for a variety of reasons.

To determine whether this could be the case for you, check to see whether your child has lost interest in the rewards available on your list. The child could lose interest either because of having already earned the things of most interest or because of changing interests. Fortunately, it is usually simple to sort this out and just as simple to correct.

As you complete one of your daily reviews, ask the child something like:

"Well, Carlos, what reward are you working toward now?" or
"Carlos, are you still working on that family trip to throw frisbees at the park?"

A child eager for a specific reward is likely to describe the reward enthusiastically, explaining in detail how much fun it will be and maybe even exactly how many days and hours until that will occur.

On the other hand, if the child appears rather vague or unenthusiastic when asked about the reward, chances are interest has waned. To clarify, ask a question like this:

> "Gosh, Carlos, you don't seem very interested in any rewards on our list right now. Is there something you'd like us to consider adding to your reward list?"

A child who has simply lost interest in choices on the list may respond by producing a long list of all the things hoped for on the last birthday but not received. If that happens, you probably have identified the key issue. Your next step is to:

- Consider choices your child suggests;

- Select those that fit your family's values, resources, and time; and

- Settle on the number of credits required for each new item.

With that done, just monitor the situation for a few days to see if the modification accomplishes what you had hoped. If so, enjoy.

However, some kids aren't so eager to suggest new reward choices even if they have lost interest in those on their list. Therefore don't assume the problem is elsewhere just because you get a disinterested response when you ask about adding items. Instead try to determine whether there might be new reward choices that will increase your child's interest and motivation to do well on the program. You can address this further with a comment such as:

> "Looks like you can't think of anything special to add right now. Why don't you think about it a bit, and when we meet for our daily review Sunday, we'll discuss it again."

This may be enough to start the wheels turning and encourage the child to think of things to work toward. In a few days you can ask whether the child is considering anything interesting to suggest.

Meanwhile, as the one who knows your child best, you can think about things you know are of interest to your child and plant some seeds or even just directly suggest a specific idea. You are most likely to succeed in this effort if you watch the things the child shows ongoing interest in during the course of routine days. Once you have hit on some ideas, you can explore them with the child in a comment such as:

> "Carlos, we've noticed how much you like to watch the Padres play on

television. Would you like to have a trip to a game with Dad as a choice on your reward list?"

Once the child shows interest in one or more additional choices, the task boils down to working those into the program and proceeding from there as discussed just above.

Another Place to Look

But what if your efforts to increase your child's interest in rewards fails to improve your progress? This outcome suggests the problem is somewhere deeper in the basics of the program.

The place to look in this case can be uncomfortable for parents to confront. Decreasing or inconsistent follow through on the basics of the program by parents is the second most likely source of decline. Just as children sometimes fail to follow through, so sometimes do their parents for all sorts of reasons. My intention here is not to chide you, but rather to provide a guide for review those basics which, if they are allowed to slide, may undermine the program's ongoing effectiveness and which, therefore may require some fine-tuning.

A simple way to approach the review of your program in this area is to ask yourself several questions, each designed to help you determine what may be causing problems.

- **Are you remembering to ignore inappropriate behaviors?**
  It is very natural to operate on the "squeaky-wheel principle" so that things going well are taken for granted and ignored, and attention and action are reserved for things that go wrong. Children dealt with in that way quickly learn the value of "squeaking" to meet their needs. Add the stresses of everyday life and a touch of impatience, and things can pretty rapidly deteriorate. If you have allowed yourself to return to old practices of reacting to your child's inappropriate behavior, you can expect the program to lose effectiveness. A child who finds it easier to meet important needs by misbehaving will misbehave more. To correct this pattern, work consistently to withhold your attention to inappropriate behavior.

- **Are you remembering to reinforce your child "on the spot" for successful behaviors?**

  You need not send up skyrockets every time your child does something well. In fact over time it is appropriate to respond less and less frequently. However, it is still a good idea from time to time to praise your child's successes on the spot. For example, when you see your child returning to the house with a just-emptied trash can, you might say:

"Thank you, Juan. It is so good to see you take responsibility for getting the trash out on time. Your good work sure makes things neater and more pleasant for the whole family."

You might toss in a warm hug to further enhance the impact. And, by the way, allowing your child to overhear parents praising the child to each other can be powerful.

- **Are you continuing to meet daily to review the entire program and to show the child your continuing commitment to improving your child's behavior?**

It is easy for busy parents to let routines slip. Allowing that to happen with the daily review, however, can directly undermine your entire home program. You may find it difficult to meet as planned every single day, and an occasional unavoidable omission need not destroy the program. On the other hand, if finding you can get away with it once encourages you to put it off more and more, you may well find the program begins to lose its potency.

Your child may conclude that hard work and success aren't really as important as you first indicated and even that maybe the child isn't so important either. Many children will have learned long before that one way to be important to parents is to misbehave. They may resort to that old behavior if their constructive actions turn out not to meet their needs. Solidly building the daily review into your family's daily routine is the way to avoid this deterioration. The result could be among the most pleasant minutes of the day for your family.

- **Are you making sure the child is able to trade in earned credits as agreed?**

Busy parents have to balance a whole lot of demands for their time and attention. Faced with more to do than time will allow, they must choose which things are less critical and can be put off. At a tense time, providing earned rewards to a child might seen less critical, particularly for a child doing well overall. But to a child working hard for a desired reward, delay may seem like a serious breach of contract.

I anticipated such problems in my discussion of how to build your program. There I urged identifying any needed delays in delivering rewards and defining those delays in the reward. For example, a fishing trip would be "within a month" of the child's earning the credits and choosing that reward. Such clauses in the reward list allow parents to consider demands on their time and alert kids to conditions that they must accept to claim a reward. Kids will naturally experience any delays beyond those in the contract as unfair. Think how you, as an adult, would feel if your boss were to say on pay day, "We've been too busy this week to print your paycheck." And imagine asking when to expect it and being told "We'll see. . ." If you realize you have been delaying rewards too long, resolve to make the necessary changes and follow through.

- **Are <u>you</u> getting reinforced for your own efforts to teach your child responsible behavior?**

The principle of positive reinforcement, the basis for this entire approach, applies to all of us. That means you are much more likely to complete your responsibilities for your child's program if you are reinforced as well..

I hope your child's successes are in themselves rewarding to you. However, over time you may take gains for granted and miss the good feelings you deserve. Regular comparisons of your current status with your status when you started may be helpful. You can also find ways to reward yourself for successes with the program. For instance, if you have a parenting partner, you could plan some special time together, or one of you may provide some special treat for the other. I'll leave it to your own creativity to consider what particularly special things you can offer each other for your rewards.

Asking yourself the five questions just reviewed likely will identify aspects of a sagging program that can be tweaked to revitalize it. If the answer to any of these questions is "no," you need to rethink your efforts and refocus on how to make the program work. This is a powerful and efficient tool when used appropriately, but, as is true with most things in life that pay dividends, your program requires continuing attention to the elements that make it that way.

We worry about what a child
will become tomorrow, yet
we forget that he is someone today.

~Stacia Tauscher

Section Five

SOME CONCLUDING REMARKS

*Children are one third of our population
and all of our future.*

~Select Panel for the Promotion of Child Health, 1981

Chapter Twenty-five

"But Doctor, what do we do when . . . we tried to develop a program like you suggested but our daughter has no interest in any rewards?"

Page 109

SOME CONCLUDING COMMENTS

This book attempts to convey my experience in supporting parents who are working to help their children become responsible for their own behavior. Decades of research provide the underlying principles. Many useful books for parents have been based on the same principles. However, feedback from those using these books has been mixed. Many parents found the ideas appealing but said that they were left hanging as they attempted to apply what they had learned in their own homes.

To address such limitations, I worked across two decades with parents to identify what is helpful and what is not. The result was clarification of how parents can best apply the principles in their own homes. Further experience with parents identified refinements that were required to assure acceptance and usefulness across families.

This book was undertaken to capture the best of that experience, of what works and the pitfalls of what does not so that readers can learn to adapt the approach to their individual circumstances. To the extent that I have succeeded, the many parents with whom I have worked deserve your thanks.

You have my best wishes for success in developing the positive parenting style most likely to get you to your goals and for great joy as you watch your child blossom into a responsible, capable, confident individual who finds equal joy in mastering life's challenges.

I leave you, in our final chapter, with a few more illustrative examples of situations parents found challenging.

It behooves a father to be blameless
if he expects his child to be.

~Homer

We are apt to forget that children
watch examples better than
they listen to preaching.

~Roy L. Smith

Don't worry that children never
listen to you; worry that they
are always watching you.

~Robert Fulghum

Chapter Twenty-six

"But Doctor, what do we do when . . . our son hassles his little brother and sister so much that we have to do something but don't want to interfere with the program?" Page 220

ACTUAL FAMILIES, ACTUAL CHALLENGES

As I developed this book and presented various aspects, I attempted to provide illustrations of how each related to real people's lives. Various sections were followed by examples of concerns that related to the content presented in hopes that the examples might help you in developing and using your own home program. A number of other questions don't fit neatly elsewhere but may be instructive and are included here. Some address very specific situations, but it is my hope that every parent may find some benefit from considering these concerns of parents and the thought processes involved in the responses.

You say it is a good idea to reward children for appropriate behavior. Isn't that just a fancy way to say you should bribe your kids?

Many parents asked this question before I began sharing the survey showing that parents typically report using some form of punishment and find little success in changing their children's behavior. Still, it warrants comment because the question implies that there is something inappropriate about rewarding kids "for doing what they are supposed to do anyway."

So what is bribery, anyway? According to the Online Merriam Webster Dictionary, bribery is defined as:

"Something given or promised in order to improperly influence a person's conduct or decision," for example "That judge refused a huge *bribe* to dismiss the charges against the wealthy defendant."

A somewhat older version of Webster's Collegiate Dictionary further illustrates the point:

"The act or practice of giving, offering, or taking rewards for corrupt practices; the act of paying or receiving a reward for a false judgment or testimony, or for the performance of that which is known to be illegal or unjust. It is applied both to the one who gives and to the one who receives the bribe, but especially to the giver."

Well! It is difficult to see how we could reasonably label as "improperly influencing," "corrupt," "false," "illegal," or "unjust" the practice of a loving parent rewarding a child for doing something the parent deems appropriate.

Of course, if you feel your kids "just should do the right thing," you might take some issue with the "unjust" part. In this regard, it is useful to note that most of us "get paid" for a good deal of what we do. As a psychologist, I consider myself devoted to the care of the people with whom I work, "doing the right thing." However, I am paid for my effort and my time; as are most workers. It is difficult to accept that such interchanges are somehow corrupt.

If you accept that idea, is it not just as fitting that children receive incentives to do the things that, over time, contribute to their assumption of responsible behavior? My point here is that saying a child "should" do something carries little force, while the program described here has been shown over and over to support the maturation prized by their parents.

Our daughter never does anything without first saying, "You help me!" What can we do?

Some children display what has been called "learned helplessness," perhaps the case with your child. Whether or not that label fits, your task is to help your child become self-sufficient, and any child whose first reaction is "you help me" is not feeling at all sufficient. Ironically, it appears that your daughter has developed very effective ways to get adult help. Success in getting parents to react the way a child prefers is a sign of considerable interpersonal skill. Unfortunately, that fact probably does not improve her own confidence.

Chances are that there was a period of time, perhaps at age two or so, when your child reacted to your attempts to help by announcing, "I can do it myself!" Perhaps you were sometimes impatient enough that you did things the child could have done, or you otherwise conveyed the message that she was incapable. Whatever the cause, your daughter now needs you to teach her that she is quite capable of doing what you expect of her so that you will not help her with everything. Remember that children learn to feel capable by observing themselves successfully complete tasks. You can rely on that fact in building your program to support your child's maturation.

Be sure as you set up your expectations to clearly and carefully define items that you know your child can complete. Strive for items she can complete a third or more of the time. Each item could include a phrase such as, "on his (or her) own," as in:

"Teddy is successful when, on his own, he has all his toys in the family room picked up by 7:00 p.m."

Once you are confident that your expectations are realistic, the next step is to assure that the incentives you have established are adequate and well focused. Based on her pleas for help, it is likely that for some reason your daughter feels a need to stay close to you. If that is true, include on the reward list a number of special activities with you. Make sure your child can rapidly earn enough credits to trade for meaningful rewards, particularly early in the program. Having access to some relatively easy successes will assure she can independently succeed on assigned tasks and earn enough credits to trade for time with you, meeting that need after acting alone. Working this out will take some of your time, but once you guide your child out of this helpless stance, you may well find that you have actually freed up more of your own time than you required by the program.

Remember that your role is in defining the target behaviors and in providing the reinforcement. You must avoid directly helping with any task, or you will defeat your immediate and long-term goals. What you can do instead is talk about the way the program will work in your home, emphasizing the great rewards that the child can achieve. With these factors all in place and working for your family, you can anticipate that your child will be on the way to mastery of life's challenges rather than to continued helplessness.

We can reinforce our child for getting his chores done, but we want him to want to do the right thing, not just do them because he gets something for it. How can the program help with that?

Many parents share your wish to teach their kids to do the right thing for its own sake, not just for a payoff of some sort. That is also my wish to help you help your son learn to take full responsibility for his own behavior. However, success with that long-range goal depends upon providing your child direct experience with the benefits of being responsible. Based on natural developmental factors, you can best provide that experience by coupling material and social reinforcement with your son's efforts, continuing long enough that he internalizes the connection and no longer requires external reward. The structure of the home program is carefully designed to move a child through the necessary steps to achieve that goal.

As you operate your program, you will assist your son in moving through three distinct levels of appreciation of the process:

- On the most obvious level, the child feels good about rewards for completing an expected behavior.

- The level above that can be observed when the child seeks approval for doing the task extra early or extra well with a comments such as:

    "Look, Mom, I got the trash out right when I got home from school, and it only took me two minutes so I can go with the guys to ball practice!"

    This more advanced response shows the child's recognition that, when the task is done, other benefits accrue. This provides an opportunity for the alert parent to acknowledge – that is, to reinforce – that fact in a comment such as:

    "Noah, that's great! It makes me so proud when I see your work is done and that you have time to play with your friends."

    The mother might add to this benefit to the child by telling the father about it at dinner within Noah's hearing.

- A still more sophisticated level of development appears in a relatively subtle addition of pride at taking responsibility for getting the job done well. The child may not even verbalize this change, but you may observe it in behavior. For example, you may notice a child taking the trash out when the can is full even before required by the program chart. At this level, the child has moved on from focus on a reward and even on from feeling good about getting the job done to the new and higher-level experience of feeling good about being a responsible person. A parent seeing signs of this enormous accomplishment has a wonderful opportunity to support the child reaching the goal you mentioned: doing things because they are the right things to do. This could take the form of a comment such as:

    "It is so great to see how proud you are of always getting your chores done on time! You have become a very responsible guy, and we really are glad for you"

Attending to these other levels of maturation works directly toward your goal of teaching your child to do the right thing for its own sake, also the goal for this program. That is what makes an effective individual, family, community, and society.

I am a single mother, and I am trying hard to make the program work, but sometimes I just get fed up and yell at the kids when they get too wild. Then I feel like I've blown it. How can I overcome this problem?

As you know better than I, many aspects of family life are more burdensome to a single parent than to those with the luxury of two parents to share the many tasks involved. It is not surprising that you should occasionally become overwhelmed and find it difficult to maintain your composure in the face of too much to do and in the face of challenging kids. It is true that I have stressed the importance of consistency and follow-through in dealing with children. I realize how inflexible that may seem, but it truly is important. However, it is also important to put this all in perspective. The critical underlying concept appears below.

To the extent that you can consistently avoid responding to inappropriate behavior and consistently provide benefit for appropriate behavior, to that extent your child will demonstrate increasingly responsible behavior.

The importance of this statement is that it recognizes that none of us is always at our best yet makes it clear that **to the extent that** we manage adequately, **to that same extent** we can expect continuing gains toward our goals. The relevant implication for your concern is that while you may get off track at times, **to the extent that** you get back on track, **to that extent** the program will be resumed and the benefits restored.

This guideline allows parents what we must allow our children: to be human and therefore sometimes to fall below our best.

Therefore, my first suggestion to you is that you accept that you cannot – and need not – be perfect but that you can nonetheless continue to provide constructive guidance for your children. It is probably appropriate to express your honest feelings to your kids, though doing so in anger carries a risk of reinforcing the very behaviors you dislike. If you choose to express your dismay, be sure your comments are about the behaviors you dislike and not about the children themselves.

Perhaps the most constructive way of dealing with the kids is to catch them before their behavior escalates to a "too wild" stage. When you notice the process starting or when you realize things are getting out of hand, even if it has just started, tell the kids to stop, clearly and firmly (but don't **ask** them to stop). If they do, a few minutes later make sure you go to them and comment on how nice it is that they are calm (without lecturing about how bad they were before). If they do not stop, use the time-out approach described in detail in Section Three.

You are to be commended for trying to make things better for your kids and for you in the face of difficult circumstances!

We haven't started a chart, but we are trying hard to do what you said and give attention when our child is cooperative. The problem is that he always seems to be hassling his little brother and sister, and we have to do something! What can we do about that?

From your description it sounds as though you are working hard to make things better with rather little return from your efforts. However, each time that you feel compelled to react to your son's hassling of his brother and sister, unintentionally you are providing attention – and possibly a sense of control – for the very behavior you would like to stop. There is a very good chance that your son is meeting his needs for attention and control by continuing those things that have worked for him in the past, and you could be supporting him in that practice despite yourselves. It would be very difficult for you to reward him enough in your informal approach to teach him that he could better meet his needs by cooperating with you.

It is difficult for any parent to withhold response to inappropriate behavior consistently. It is also difficult to provide benefit to children for their appropriate behavior consistently. It is for this reason that the structured approach described in Section Two was developed. My suggestion is that you take the time to institute such a program designed to address your concerns for your family. While it will take you an hour or two to get a program laid out, once it is operational, you likely will find that you spend a good deal **less** time and effort on maintaining it than you do now – and almost certainly with a good deal more success. The gain you likely will experience is a reflection of all the time that you now spend in attempting to deal with things in an unstructured way.

One other thought: your program will be much more effective if you use the time-out procedure described in Section Three to deal with any "hassling" that continues once you begin.

We are having problems agreeing on a program. My wife says I expect too much from the kids, and I think she's too soft. How can we get past this problem?

It is common for parents to have different expectations for their children and you are clearly not alone. In fact, parents in this situation often actually grow further and further apart over time with each consciously or unconsciously attempting to compensate for what they see as the errors in the other's style. Typically, as in your case, the mother is "too soft," causing the father to become more demanding. In response, the mother tries to soften the impact of the father's stance. And the father, in his own turn, tends to expect still more, a pattern that can feed on itself even to the point of actually destroying the family.

To avoid such an outcome, find a calm and unhurried time to discuss where each of you stands on parenting. Often parents haven't actually discussed what they want for their kids and as a result they don't have a good basis for how they deal with the kids to meet their goals. Parents who see themselves as far apart on child rearing frequently discover that they actually have pretty much the same goals for their kids. Virtually all parents, in one way or the other, say they want to raise responsible, hard-working, caring, and even-tempered children. The issue, then, comes down to the best way to reach those goals.

For most couples, the approach discussed in this book is different from what either of them has done before. That fact presents a potential benefit, if only because it represents a kind of "neutral ground" from which to start. As a result, they can work together to design a program focused on their shared larger goals, recognizing that the steps to getting there may not be so important as they otherwise seemed. How "hard" or "soft" the parents might be inclined to be in this approach is less an issue since asking too much – that is more than the child is ready to do – will simply lead to the child's not completing the task as defined but with no onerous consequences.

Thus, you can think of your program as inviting your child to do what you identify on the task list. You then reinforce successes, and you don't reinforce lack of success. That means that the "soft" parent need not be overly concerned about things being too harsh while the "hard" parent can have a test of how realistic the expectations are. Working in this fashion may well help you find a happy middle ground from which you can pool your resources and can work together to meet your overall goals for your child. The child's success in assuming responsibility for his or her own behavior will be well worth your efforts.

It is just so hard for me to tell my kids "no" when they want to do things that I think they shouldn't, and then we end up in fights. How can I get past this?

Quite a few parents these days say it is hard to put limits on their children. It is interesting how many of those parents also report the high price that they end up paying for leniency with their kids, in your case, the price being that you "end up in fights." Imagine, for a moment, offering your children a choice of one of the these two reactions whenever one of them asks for something you don't think is right for the child:

- You eventually will give in, whatever the request, but the family will almost always end up in fights, or

- You will say "no" sometimes and the family will end up at peace more of the time.

Now imagine which of these reactions your kids would pick. Even without knowing your kids, it is a pretty safe prediction that they would choose hearing "no" sometimes if it meant fewer fights if they really understood what their choices meant.

Teenagers in psychotherapy, even some in serious difficulties because of resisting parental controls, often say, "I wish my parents cared for me enough to stop me." Such a comment is powerful evidence that children need the safety and protection provided by parents who set reasonable limits. It might be useful for you to reread the portion of Chapter Six about what causes control struggles between parents and children.

Your question, of course, shows that you already realize that you should be able to say "no" and make it stick. The issue seems to be one of fully understanding just how important that is and then finding a way to make it happen. This book presents an approach that relies on parents' guiding and supporting children in taking responsibility for their own behavior. I suggest you review the basic principles and the specific steps to develop a home program to be sure you have a clear understanding of all the elements that make it work.

Then design a program for each of your kids, including behavior items related to your concerns. Be sure that you address those situations that have typically led to the conflicts that you described. By defining success behaviors that focus on what you **do** want each child to do, you may have fewer conflicts over what you don't want each child to do.

Keep clear that your most loving and helpful gift to your children is the benefit of your greater life experience, including when you establish suitable boundaries for them. Your home program designed to support your expectations will serve both them and you well and will reduce the conflicts that make you all unhappy.

We were doing pretty well for a few weeks after we started the program, but then our twelve-year-old daughter got very upset.

When she came out of time-out, she came to me in the kitchen and dropped a pile of tiny scraps of paper on the counter. She announced angrily, "there's your stupid program." The pieces were her chart. Since she destroyed the program, what do we do now?

Your daughter surely let you know how she feels, or at least how she felt when she tore up the chart. Somehow she managed to construe the program into something punitive. A reasonable guess about the reason is that it is a bit scary for her now that you are operating differently. Perhaps before she felt confident about how to meet her needs, and now she isn't so sure. Or maybe now it looks to her as though she has to exert more effort to get what she got before with less effort. Whatever is behind this reaction, what matters more is how you deal with this situation.

I note that you report that your daughter gave you the torn up **chart** and told you it was "your stupid program." You therefore concluded that she had "destroyed the **program**." Please understand that tearing up the chart can destroy the program only if you agree that the chart **is** the program. My view is that the chart is a tool – a very useful tool, to be sure – for keeping track of the program, but it is **not** the program itself. I think you can best think of the program as consisting of your expectations for your child and your manner of assuring your daughter meets them. If loss of the chart makes you change your expectations or makes you give up your commitment to dealing with her by reinforcing what you expect from her, then she will have, in fact, destroyed the program.

But that choice is yours, not hers.

With that thought in mind, how might you react to this turn of events? The first step, I would suggest, is sitting down with your daughter when she is calm, telling her you realize that she was upset when she tore up the chart and asking her to help you understand what was bothering her. Then try to listen only without trying to defend yourself or to explain away whatever she says. You may learn that the chart and program had nothing to do with the reaction, and if so, you can discuss the concern separately and determine a suitable way to respond.

And remember that some concerns may even lend themselves to inclusion within the program. Suppose, for example, that her complaint was that her younger brother was getting all your attention because he was earning so many credits on his own program. After acknowledging that must be frustrating to watch, you could offer to review her program and determine whether some of the items might be modified to allow her more successes herself.

But suppose all you learn is that your daughter finds the program unduly demanding since she was used to having things her own way prior to its start. Your task at that point would be to make it clear that the program is still in effect and that neither your expectations nor your manner of dealing with them has changed.

Since the chart was torn up, you will have to make a new one, and that presents a problem since you are unlikely to remember each of the child's successes from the beginning of the chart. I suggest that you do the best you can to reconstruct the credits earned, discussing it with your daughter if you can do so calmly. I would not suggest that you let her tell you which points she earned since that would tempt fudging but rather that you have her tell you things that can jog your own memory. For example, she might say, *"Remember, Mom, that I vacuumed the living room right after I got home from Mary's that day, and you told me how good it was that I did it before you set up for your book club."* If your child is too angry to participate, do the best you can and tell her that you are sorry that there may be some errors that you can't fix because of the circumstances.

I urge you not to turn this into a lecture since doing so is unlikely to convey anything she doesn't already realize, but it could end up giving undue attention to negatives. If she complains about credits she thinks she should have but you aren't sure about, explain why you can't include them, and to further complaining, say *"I'm sorry if you don't' understand, but I've explained it the best I can, and that's just the way it is."* From there, do not participate further in discussion since doing so would only continue a fruitless process.

If your daughter is really upset about the program, she may still tell you angrily, *"I'm just not going to do the program again, and I don't care what you say!"* It will be good to anticipate such a reaction so that you are ready with your own response. At that moment, the most you might want to say would be something like, *"I'm sorry you feel that way, but the program is the way we are doing things in our home now."* Whatever retorts or protests you hear, just disengage.

What is important from then on is that you continue to operate as I have discussed. Even a child who is determined not to cooperate is likely to complete some expectation on your target behavior list, and when she does, be sure to offer appropriate praise, neither overly effusive, nor sarcastic, nor blah. This may be difficult for you if your daughter has been sulky and unpleasant for some time, but it will pay big dividends for you to demonstrate that the program continues to work exactly as you said it would.

Please understand that in some measure your child is testing whether you really mean to reward the behaviors in the program while withholding response to inappropriate ones. Passing the test will require you to maintain your own discipline and thereby model the very things you mean to teach: responsibility for one's own behavior. In the process you will demonstrate to your daughter that she will continue to benefit whenever she meets your expectations. At some point, she is likely to become interested in the rewards on your list. When that happens, reward yourself as well since you will have faced about as tough a challenge to the program as anyone is likely to get.

One more note: since you started by saying that you were doing rather well with the program for a couple of weeks, I am assuming your target behaviors are realistically reachable, positive, and clearly stated. However, it could be useful to review each item to be sure since if things are awry in any of these ways, that situation could contribute to your daughter's being upset. Making adjustments according to your review could be part of your response to her if you find things that bear improvement.

We have carefully considered all you have said and wished it would work for us, but our son has Attention Deficit Disorder. His medication is helping him some, but he still has a hard time controlling himself, especially on weekends when his doctor said it is good for him not to take the pills. Is there any way this approach can help in our situation?

Your question is a common one from parents whose children are burdened with ADD and deserves a complete response. I would like to share with you an experience I had with a family with a similar concern. It is rather long, and the point I want to make with it probably is not what you will hope it to be; please read the story but wait for my comments at the end before drawing any conclusions.

Early in my experience with this approach, a young couple brought their son, referred by his pediatrician, to my office. The referral indicated that the boy had been treated with medication for years for hyperactivity and distractibility. The pediatrician was concerned because after increasing the dosage several times over the last couple years he was reluctant to increase it again. Still, the boy's behavior problems had escalated both at home and at school.

To be sure I didn't miss any details, I took notes as the parents enumerated their many concerns about this boy. Their son, meanwhile, roamed my office, displaying all the behaviors his parents described as constant at home and at school. He poked through the toys but played with none, pushed and pulled at books on the shelves, crawled behind the desk, fiddled with the curtains, and generally was unfocused and constantly active.

After half an hour, the parents left and I met with the boy alone. I asked him why they had come to see me. He said that he didn't know. I asked what his parents had said about that. Again he said he didn't know, and he continued to squirm and wiggle, occasionally slithering out of the chair I'd asked him to sit in while we talked. After a time, I told him I could see it was difficult for him to remember what we had talked about and that I was going to help. I drew a star on a piece of paper with a red marker and told him that for each one of his parents' concerns that he could tell me, I would draw him a star.

He said that he hadn't been listening and thus didn't know. With some urging, he finally came up with some approximation of one thing his parents had mentioned, and I quickly drew a star on the paper as he watched. Again he insisted that he couldn't tell me anything else, but with more urging, he came up with another part, this time in richer detail. As I drew his second star, I commented that we had just gotten started and already he had thought of two things. By then the boy was sitting in his chair and seemed interested, although still asserting he couldn't think of anything. But more quickly he added another of the concerns his parents had shared with me. By the time I had drawn his third star, the boy was telling me another thing he'd thought of. I won't continue with each step, but I can report that by the time we were done, he had mentioned all but one or two of the rather long list of concerns I had written on my note pad, and he had nearly a dozen stars on his paper. More impressive still, he sat in his chair looking stunned – but excited – as he considered his stars, and then he said, *"Wow! I can't believe I remembered all those things."*

As the parents returned to the office, this boy jumped up and thrust his sheet of stars at them. He told them excitedly that he had been able to tell me almost everything they had said about his problems, adding at the end, *"And I didn't think I was even listening."* The parents, interestingly, initially reacted only to what they saw as typical behavior in the form of the excited outburst as they came in. However, when the boy sat back down in his chair, they did seem to notice. I asked him then to tell them some of the things he had told me, and he rattled off several of the items in a remarkably organized and clear fashion, running his finger down the row of stars as if ticking them off as he spoke. His parents listened in apparent disbelief, then turned to me for comment. I described what happened, noting that the boy had displayed internal resources that seemed at odds with the way he had been operating at home and at school.

To make a long story manageable, we spent another half hour or so together, building on the experience in the office by designing a simple reward program. Our intention was to support this boy's success in focusing his attention and maintaining appropriate control over his behavior in key situations at home with a simple addition for school. The parents, themselves clearly as stunned as they were hopeful, asked about the medication. I urged them to keep things as they were until we could determine how their son did with the program, and then we could communicate with the pediatrician about what might be best to do.

A couple of weeks later, the family returned with the charts from their program, all three regaling me with stories about how well things had gone since I had last seen them, all clearly reflected in the data from their charts.

As this second meeting ended, I suggested that the parents talk to the pediatrician, hopeful that he would agree there was no reason to raise the dosage. I was startled to learn that the parents had chosen to discontinue the medication on their own only a couple of days after our initial visit. The boy had been medication-free for ten days, and the successes they described happened without benefit of medication.

It seemed clear to me that the most important change in this situation came about because of this boy's markedly altered view of himself. He went from seeing himself as incapable of noticing anything or containing his own squirminess to announcing that he had, and could, tell me most of what his parents had said, and that change carried over long after they left my office.

So what is the point I intended to make by sharing this story? It is not, as you might wish, that kids with attention deficit hyperactivity disorder do not need to be on medication. I share concerns of some authorities that medication may be used more quickly and more often than is in the best interests of some kids; however, clearly there are kids for whom medication provides essential support for their capacity to deal constructively with a world that otherwise is overwhelming and discouraging. Thus, it is not my intention to suggest that all children should be taken off medication and put on a home program.

Nor do I have any illusions that our simple program overcame this boy's attention and behavior control problems. I think it is likely that for some unknown reason he no longer needed medication but that along the way he had come to see himself as a "hyper" kid who couldn't be expected to control himself, and he lived accordingly. Once he discovered this was no longer true, he was able to refocus his internal resources and function much more effectively.

But what about the vast majority of kids with this condition who need help but who may or may not benefit from medication, and who may still be struggling to fit in at home and school? Every child must learn to function adequately in the world with whatever demands and expectations that entails. Because children with attention and control-struggles typically have a more difficult time managing to meet expectations, they are in special need of help in focusing their behavior. The approach described in this book is especially well suited to provide that focus. By carefully defining realistically reachable expectations put in positive terms, by providing meaningful incentives for meeting those expectations, and by consistently managing the associations among the elements of a home program, parents of such kids can support continuing maturation toward effective behavior control and – ultimately – self-responsibility.

My answer to you, then, is that the approach presented here can be very well suited to your needs. Your challenge will be carefully to design a program **to meet your son where he is**, to support his moves toward better self control, and to nurture his awareness of his progress as it occurs so that he fully appreciates his own capacities.

Everything written here is applicable in your situation. The one area I would like to emphasize for you, however, is the importance of special care in defining target behaviors – specifically to assure that each item you include is truly realistically reachable for your son. Chosen carefully, the successes for those items, however small at first, can be the foundation for continuing growth for you both.

This all sounds like it might be a good idea, but I am divorced and my kids' father won't go along with any of it, so what can I do?

This is a common concern among single parents with whom I have worked. Of course, it is better if parents can agree on exactly how to raise their children, but even in intact homes, perfect agreement is often not the case. Actually, it may be at least somewhat easier to deal with children in a home where you have complete control than in one where you and the other parent disagree strongly about discipline.

The keys in this situation are the same as in others: making it clear to the children what is expected, avoiding supplying benefit for inappropriate behavior, and meeting important needs when the children are doing what is expected.

You may be worried that your children will be confused if the expectations aren't the same in both households. But it is not essential that you and the children's father have the same expectations. Note that by three years of age many kids are in preschool where they quickly learn that things are different in school than they are at home. In school they learn that they must take turns with other kids, that they must stay quiet during nap time, that they must share, and that they must follow other adults' instructions. Most kids, after a brief period of adjustment, have no trouble going from their home, with its set of expectations, to school, with its different expectations, and back to home again. Indeed, within the school day, they learn they can be quite boisterous on the playground but must suddenly be much more controlled in the classroom. Clearly the transition from one parent's home to the other typically demands much less adaptation than do moves from home to school.

With those thoughts in mind, then, develop your program to fulfill your goals for your children and follow through accordingly. Some kids will complain that one parent is unfair (see the next example) because of differences, and if you react defensively to the complaint, your children may respond with more complaints. A better response will be to acknowledge there are differences that can be confusing to them. Then calmly reiterate that in your home you do things the way you have laid them out. Of course if there are residual strong feelings between the parents, being calm may be difficult, but it is important that you keep those feelings out of interchanges with your children, who are not responsible for the other parent.

My son returns from a weekend at his dad's house all wound up. When I try to discipline him, he tells me I am mean and says he likes it better with his dad. This makes me feel really bad so it is hard to stick to the program.

This question is partly addressed in the above comments. That is, it is entirely appropriate for you to have different expectations for your child in your home and to provide the guidance your child needs in order to meet them successfully. Since you cannot control the way things work at the other parent's house, much as you might like to, your effort is better spent on making things work in your home. I'd suggest you start by reviewing your expectations to assure they are reasonable and appropriate for your son and are in his best interest. If you decide they are not, then take time to make suitable revisions until you are satisfied. The structure of the program will guide you through the steps to define exactly what you want to focus on in teaching your child responsible behavior.

If you conclude your expectations are appropriate, then stick to them. Either way, once you have a clear set of appropriate expectations, you can be confident that working to achieve them is the most loving thing you can do as a parent – though that may or may not make you a popular parent at any given moment. With that assurance, you can be ready to deal with your child's return from his dad's house.

The transition from his dad's to your house may be a particularly trying time for your son. For example, if he has spent the weekend having fun and few responsibilities, then settling into the routine at your home may not be so easy, a bit like returning to work after vacations for us adults. Recognizing this allows you to plan ahead and prepare both of you for the transition. A day or two before your son is to leave for his dad's house find a calm time to tell him something like this:

> *"Zachary, you'll be going to your dad's Friday night for the weekend. I know you are really looking forward to it, and I hope you'll have a great time even though I'll miss you a lot while you are gone. When you come home, sometimes you are still excited about the neat things you did with your dad. That can make it hard to come back here and get ready for a regular school week. That's kind of the same way I feel each week about going back to work, but we each have to adjust to reality and get ready for what is to come. . ."*

This comment is to focus you both on the coming separation and the return to follow and to recognize the latter is not easy for either of you. Then, in keeping with our overall approach, continue:

> *". . . Since coming back and getting ready for school and your other responsibilities is kind of hard for you, I am going to help you. I always look forward to your coming home, and I want us both to be able to enjoy it. So, starting this weekend, you'll have a new item in your program.*

>> *'You are successful when you go to your room, unpack your backpack, and have your things put away within thirty minutes after getting home.'*

> *"I want us to have time for hugs and for you to tell me a bit about your weekend. But within fifteen minutes, you are to go to your room to unpack and put your things away. That will give you a few minutes of quiet time so that you can feel calmer inside and also get things organized for the coming week. When you are done, then we can have a bit more time together and maybe share a treat before bedtime."*

The specifics of this are up to you, but the idea is to set up a bit of routine in your home designed to assist in the transition, recognizing that some quiet time alone, along with getting organized a bit for the routine, can be helpful. Keeping everything focused on making things better for you and the child will also set a warm, constructive tone.

You have said that all the principles apply to adults as well. Could the same sort of program work for my wife and me?

Yes, the principles apply to adults as well as children. Some years ago in response to a similar question, I developed a sample home program for parents, which I included in handout packets for several years. Unfortunately, because of the way our contacts were structured, I never received enough feedback to learn whether parents actually adapted the idea to their own lives; therefore I have no direct basis for recommending the approach. However, I am confident that the idea is sound and that it can work for those who want to make changes in their own behavior if they follow the steps to develop and maintain a program.

The one potential snag in this assertion is that success depends upon receiving suitable reinforcement and you would have to find a way to be sure you are rewarded. Clearly, if a couple were each to use a program and agree to reinforce each other, the chances of having a viable and effective program would be greater. However, a single person who is able comfortably to do special things alone should be able to make it all work also.

The basics of building a program for yourselves are exactly the same as those for building a program for a child. You will need to develop a set of target behaviors, taking care to assure each item is realistically reachable, is put in positive terms, and is clearly stated. Then you will need to assign some sort of credits to each item and develop a list of rewards from which you can select items as you accumulate sufficient credits. And you will need to set aside a time each day to review your progress in the fashion described in this book.

In keeping with the focus of this book, you might want to include a few items in support of maintaining your children's programs, such as consistently holding your daily reviews and assuring rewards are available and provided when earned. Generally, though, the final nature of your own program, as those for your children, depends on your own creativity and effort. I wish you well.

If a child lives with criticism, he learns to condemn.
If a child lives with hostility, he learns to fight.
If a child lives with ridicule, he learns to be shy.
If a child learns to feel shame, he learns to feel guilty.
If a child lives with tolerance, he learns to be patient.
If a child lives with encouragement he learns confidence
If a child lives with praise, he learns to appreciate.
He a child lives with fairness, he learns justice.
If a child lives with security, he learns to have faith.
If a child lives with approval, he learns to like himself.
If a child lives with acceptance and friendship, he learns to
   find love in the world.

~Dorothy Law Neite
"Children Learn What They Live"

Appendices

*If you want children to keep their
feet on the ground, put some
responsibility on their shoulders.*

~Abigail Van Buren

Appendix 1

Identifying Target Behaviors Worksheet

Explanation and Instructions

The goal of this discussion is to assist you in teaching your children better control over their own actions and in teaching them a better sense of adequacy in dealing with their world. Once you have read the section dealing with the reasoning behind our approach, you will be ready to design a specific program for use in your own home based on the changes you would like to help your children make.

The first step is for you to consider exactly what you hope to accomplish. The easiest and most effective way to think about the specific behaviors that you would like to change is to focus your attention on a typical day in your home. Consider each part of the day and the tasks typically required of one specific child during each time period. Then record each behavior you think of which occurs often enough to bother or concern you or to interfere with your child's comfort in life.

On the attached sheet are listed the typical portions of the day and some of the tasks associated with each. Parents often have identified problems related to these tasks. This is meant only as a guide to your thinking. Not all parts will apply to you and your child. Feel free to add or ignore tasks.

For each issue you think of, write a brief description next to the specific task and the portion of the day during which it is most likely to occur. For example, for "After school: coming home," one parent wrote "often misses bus." Another wrote, "Forgets his lunch pail at least twice a week."

When you have finished going through the list, please check how complete you have been by asking yourself this:

"If my child changes all of the things I've written down, will there still be significant problems?"

If the answer is "yes," think about what else is of concern to you and then add the new issues to your list. Then ask yourself the same question again. When you can comfortably answer "no," you will likely have identified all the behaviors you might want to include in your program. You will deserve to feel pleased that you have done a complete job. This success will make it easier for you to think through how you might design your program as you read more of this discussion.

Keep your completed form at hand while you continue reading. This form is intended to guide your thinking about your goals and how you will go about meeting them with the home program.

Please note that I recognize that this approach emphasizes the importance of stating to your child in clear and positive terms what you want them to do, rather than drawing all attention to the behaviors you would like to reduce or eliminate. This may seem to be in conflict with the focus of this form, which asks you to identify behaviors of concern to you. The reason for this apparent discrepancy is that most people seem to find it easier to start by listing things that don't work well.

As you progress through reading the details of this approach, you will learn why it is so important to focus on success behaviors, as well as how to most effectively modify the statements to specify what you do want your child to do.

Complete one form for each child you plan to include in your program.

Identifying Target Behaviors Worksheet

Child's name _____ Date _____

PORTION OF THE DAY/TASKS	ISSUES IN CHILD'S BEHAVIOR
--Before school--	
Getting up	
Getting dressed	
Cleaning up (hair, teeth, etc.)	
Eating breakfast	
Getting off to school	
Other (specify_____)	

Identifying Target Behaviors Worksheet – Continued

PORTION OF THE DAY/TASKS	ISSUES IN CHILD'S BEHAVIOR
--At school--	
Doing assignments	
Playing on playground	
Cooperating with teacher	
Getting along with peers	
Eating lunch	
Other (specify_____)	
--After school--	
Coming home	
Changing clothes	
Doing household chores	
Taking a nap	

Identifying Target Behaviors Worksheet – Continued

PORTION OF THE DAY/TASKS	ISSUES IN CHILD'S BEHAVIOR
--After school (continued)--	
Eating dinner	
Doing homework	
Other (specify_____)	
--After dinner--	
Doing evening chores	
Getting along with family	
Taking a bath	
Putting toys away	
Going to bed	
Other (specify_____)	

239

Identifying Target Behaviors Worksheet – Continued

PORTION OF THE DAY/TASKS	ISSUES IN CHILD'S BEHAVIOR
--Anytime/miscellaneous--	
Cooperating in the car	
Playing independently	
Getting along with siblings	
Cooperating at a store	
Cooperating with parents	
Other (specify_____)	
Other (specify_____)	

Appendix 2

Sample Behavior Chart – blank

HOME BEHAVIORAL PROGRAM

_____ is successful when: _____ for the week of _____ to _____, 20____

Behavioral item	Cred	Mon	Tue	Wed	Thu	Fri	Sat	Sun
1.								
2.								
3.								
4.								
5.								
6.								
7.								
8.								
9.								
10.								
DAILY TOTAL								
CREDITS USED								
RUNNING BALANCE								

Appendix 3

Sample Prize Game Board – Pre-reading Age Child

Below is a sample game board. It is intended for use with a youngster who can't yet read or count reliably. Most little kids have played on game boards so will recognize the overall idea. Parents can draw or paste simple pictures of potential prizes on the board. Then the child can put one token on each step and then can readily see whether enough tokens have been earned to reach each prize. The child must be taught that for each prize the process starts at the first step, so, for example, it takes ten full tokens to get to the ice cream.

Index

Printed in the United States
125220LV00001B/45/P